Imad Shehadeh has provided a thorough biblical,
presentation of the nature and attributes of Go
scholarship as well as a well-reasoned presentation. ᴛᴇ ᴵˢ ᴅᴇᴇ
setting forth the God of the Bible.

Mark L. Bailey, PhD
President and Senior Professor of Bible Exposition,
Dallas Theological Seminary, Dallas, Texas, USA

Dr Imad Shehadeh is a godly theologian with a pastor-teacher-evangelist's heart. As
a beloved friend for nearly twenty-five years, it has been a joy to see the powerfully
clear truths in this book, and the soon-to-follow companion work, forged in the
heart and mind of Imad. This book has come forth through painstaking exegesis
of the text of God's Word, copious original historical research, and with constant,
prayerful waiting upon God. Through years of the fiery trials of serving on the
frontlines, Imad has come forth with humble clarity, refined confidence, and a
focused championship of the non-negotiable essentials of biblical Christianity.
The Trinity is the foundation of true biblical Christianity. The Trinity is the only
way to understand the efficacy of the just death of Jesus Christ. The Trinity is the
only way to answer the raging question of who is the One True and Living God.
No theologian of our generation has done more to advance such essential and true
theology than this work by Dr Imad Shehadeh.

Rev John Barnett, DMin
Founder of Discover the Book Ministries

Few issues separate as many people as the meaning of the unity of God. 4,342,337,000
people are divided over this question. Some Christians live as if there were three
Gods without acknowledging it. Many non-Christians believe the Trinity is
composed of Father, Son and Mary. Beginning with his doctoral dissertation, Dr
Imad Shehadeh has been studying and teaching the Trinity for over thirty years. Few
have as deep an understanding of this vital question as he possesses. Dr Shehadeh
is well aware of the scholarship and debates down through the ages and is fluent in
Arabic, English, Greek and Hebrew and he lives in the midst of the monotheistic
religions. Clearly understanding the differences and what the Bible teaches is a first
step in opening a door between the immense monotheistic religions. *God With Us
and Without Us, Volume 1: Oneness in Trinity verses Absolute Oneness* is a significant
key for all who desire to help open closed doors to the good news.

Pat Cate, PhD
Adjunct Professor of Intercultural Studies,
Dallas Theological Seminary, Dallas, Texas, USA
President Emeritus, Christar International

The appeal of this book to the believer in Oneness in Trinity is to cease from viewing the Trinity as a problem to be solved. This is a call to see the Trinity as a beauty to be continually discovered and enjoyed. The appeal of this book to adherents of Absolute Oneness is to begin the journey of trust in the perfection, equality and harmony of all God's attributes.

It is more than thirty years since I identified "The Concept of Relationship" within the godhead as a "Key to the Comparative Understanding of Christianity and Islam" (*Themelios* 11 (1986): 57–60). I am delighted that Imad Shehadeh has powerfully used this key to open an inspiring systematic understanding of the triune God of the Bible in conversation with the alternative of God as absolutely singular. The reader will be introduced to history as well as to logic, will find the argument carefully and clearly set out, and will be led towards awed worship at the sheer beauty of God.

It is a very valuable book. People interacting with "Absolute Oneness" need to rejoice in the Trinity rather than to fear trying to explain it. This will greatly help many people, and will bring much glory to Father, Son and Holy Spirit!

Ida Glaser, PhD
International Academic Coordinator,
The Centre for Muslim-Christian Studies, Oxford, UK

Dr Shehadeh has the courage to venture into the discussion of a complex doctrine. In his thorough and deep approach, he has been able to utilize western resources as well as interacting with Arabic resources that have not been translated into modern languages. I have found his discussion on avoiding common errors about the Trinity to be illuminating as he skillfully weaves together ancient and modern issues. Dr Shehadeh provides very informative arguments on the Absolute Oneness and the Oneness in Trinity. Any serious student who wishes to explore the foundational doctrine of the Holy Trinity cannot ignore this helpful resource.

Rev Riad Kassis, PhD
Director, Scholars Programme, Langham Partnership
International Director,
International Council for Evangelical Theological Education

Imad Shehadeh has written an excellent primer on perhaps the most misunderstood teaching of the Christian faith – the biblical doctrine of the Trinity. What does it mean to say that the one God is triune? How does this unique understanding of God's very nature differ from other monotheistic views? Why is it vital to grasp the difference? For Christians, Dr Shehadeh's readable and thoroughly biblical treatment will deepen and inspire them – not to mention, alert them to and guard them from all too common errors. For non-Christians, this book will usher them to the wondrous beauty and power of the triune vision of God that is the beating heart of the Christian faith.

Duane Litfin, PhD
President Emeritus,
Wheaton College, Wheaton, Illinois, USA

Comprehensive and clear. The book addresses everything I have ever heard about or thought about regarding the Trinity, and much more. The content shows evidence of thirty years of scholarly study in both Arabic and English, and the presentation shows great effort to make it all accessible and understandable even to the lay reader. I have never read a book with a clearer outline or more thorough use of Scripture.

This will be a great help to both Christians and Muslims to understand what their own religion teaches as well as what the other teaches, and I believe it will promote respectful dialogue. A wonderful and much needed resource!

Rev David Niednagel
Founding Pastor,
Christian Fellowship Church, Evansville, Indiana, USA

Beautiful, biblical, and balanced are hardly used antiphons when studying a multi-part, theological work. And yet, the beauty of the topic in itself, while privileging the biblical text, along with a conviction to serve his ministry context demands Dr Imad Shehadeh's clarifying exposition of the Mystery which decisively and definitively distinguishes the God of Bible. My worship and understanding of the Trinity is greatly enhanced by this experienced, thoughtful and studied expression.

Ramesh Richard, ThD, PhD
President, Ramesh Richard Evangelism and Church Health (RREACH)
Professor of Global Theological Engagement & Pastoral Ministries,
Dallas Theological Seminary, Dallas, Texas, USA

God With Us and Without Us

Volume 1

God With Us and Without Us

Volume 1

Oneness in Trinity versus Absolute Oneness

Imad Shehadeh

Published 2018 by Langham Global Library
An imprint of Langham Publishing
www.langhampublishing.org

Langham Publishing and its imprints are a ministry of Langham Partnership

Langham Partnership
PO Box 296, Carlisle, Cumbria CA3 9WZ, UK
www.langham.org

ISBNs:
978-1-78369-522-6 Print
978-1-78368-523-3 ePub
978-1-78368-524-0 Mobi
978-1-78368-525-7 PDF

British Library Cataloguing-in-Publication Data
A catalogue record for this book is available from the British Library

ISBN: 978-1-78368-522-6

Cover & Book Design: projectluz.com

Contents

Frequently Asked Questions

This list is intended to help the reader study this book through the application of frequently asked questions.

Absolute Oneness

Application to Life

Christ

God the Father

Oneness in Trinity

Precision in Thinking and Speaking

Reason and Logic

The Bible

The Holy Spirit

Biblical Passages Studied

Below is a list of the passages that are focused on in this book. A full Scripture index can be found at the end of this book.

Tables and Figures

Foreword

Middle-Eastern Christian leaders throughout the centuries have sought to clarify the orthodox understanding of the triune God before other world religions. The two cornerstones of historic Christian faith are the Sonship of Jesus Christ in relation to God the Father – this grounded in the resurrection of Jesus from the dead – and the resultant belief that God is Holy Trinity. All Christians insist upon the oneness of God. But in light of the extraordinary history of Jesus of Nazareth – his virgin birth, hundreds of miracles, astonishing claims, bodily rising from the dead, ascension into heaven, and promise of his return – Christians also affirm what Jesus himself declared: he was sent from God the Father into the world. "For the Father loves the Son and shows him all he does. Whoever does not honor the Son does not honor the Father, who sent him" (John 5:20, 23 NIV). As God the Father, so the Son is the one I AM (8:58).

Jesus's own witness and that of the Bible reveals a divine oneness that defies simple mathematics. As the fifth-century Athanasian Creed would later articulate: the Father is God, the Son is God, and the Holy Spirit is God, but there are not three Gods but only one God. At first appearance, such a concept is easily dismissed. But with more careful consideration, the wonder of God as abundantly personal within himself before time began unfolds in spectacular beauty.

God With Us and Without Us unveils the reasons for and the powerful truths of the doctrine of the Trinity. In the incarnate Son, Jesus Christ, we come to the fullness of God in both attributes and internal divine relationships. For example, the God of the Bible manifests perfect, unwavering justice yet also merciful, forgiving love. How can this be? No human being is holy as God is holy. We are unworthy of his mercy. Yet "God so loved the world that he gave his one and only Son, that whoever believes in him shall not perish but have eternal life" (John 3:16 NIV). We are reconciled to God, not by our own striving, but by trust in his Son. God is, as the apostle Paul declares, both the Just and the Justifier of all who have faith in Jesus (Rom 3:26). That is, God himself provides the payment that we could never satisfy. God can do so precisely because God is Trinity, together the absolutely just, the one who pays and satisfies God's own divine justice, and the Holy Spirit who convicts and convinces the unbeliever of these truths.

So it is with immense learning as well as personal experience with this living God that Dr Imad Shehadeh unfolds the Christian teaching of God as

Holy Trinity. Founder and president of the Jordan Evangelical Theological Seminary, Dr Shehadeh is a preeminent scholar and professor in many branches of theology. But it is especially the doctrine of the Trinity that has been his fascination for over thirty years. He understands and powerfully articulates that the Trinity of God the Father, the Son, and the Holy Spirit is not a peripheral teaching of Christian faith. Rather, as all the history of the Christian church has testified, the belief in Jesus Christ as the eternal Son of God and the confession that God exists as three persons in one divine essence are the very center of biblical faith.

In this volume and the forthcoming second volume, Dr Shehadeh sets forth in fresh, relevant ways why the Christian Trinity far excels in richness and personal beauty the monadic views of absolute oneness – whether from Aristotle, Arab philosophers after the Qur'an, Maimonides (Orthodox Judaism) or philosophic theism (Deism). With Dr Shehadeh's many years of teaching, such instruction guides Christians who often do not well understand the Bible and their Nicaean (Trinitarian) heritage. It also helps persuade Christians who may be conflicted because of sectarian teachings, such as those of Jehovah's Witnesses, Mormons, Oneness Pentecostals, and sub-Christian views in the Arabic and wider world. And most helpful of all, these volumes explain and defend biblical truth regarding Jesus Christ and the Trinity to those of major religious backgrounds who would argue otherwise. Christians are equipped to answer those of other religions regarding their own belief, hope, and relationship with the triune God.

The two volumes of God With Us and Without Us are filled with diagrams and illustrations that simplify complicated concepts to memorable images, a table of contents for often asked questions, an index for biblical passages, and plentiful footnotes for continued deeper research. The reading is at once solid and scholarly, yet accessible to all who enter in. The books are extremely useful for the classroom and for deeper studies whether alone or in the local church.

In the end, Dr Shehadeh asks: Is your God big enough to be God? How can God be God – that is, fully God with all that we assume him to be – outside of creation? What is God without us? Without anything but God? Before the two largest religions in the world, the concept of God – generically similar and often forced on us (in political correctness) as essentially the same – in fact, are massively distinct and finally contradictory one to the other. The practical effects of these differences have consequences in every part of our lives. Understanding the Christian Trinity provides meaning to every dimension of life, as individuals, husbands and wives, families, friends, local churches, society, and the world.

Having known Dr Shehadeh for three decades, with many others I have admired him for not only his scholarship but also his humble trust in the Lord. Dr Imad is a living example of faith, perseverance in times of difficulty, and love for our Heavenly Father, the Beloved Son, and the Blessed Holy Spirit. His life reflects what our resurrected Lord commanded: "Therefore, go and make disciples of all nations, baptizing them in the name of the Father and of the Son and of the Holy Spirit, and teaching them to obey everything I have commanded you" (Matt 28:19–20 NIV).

J. Scott Horrell, ThD
Professor of Theological Studies,
Dallas Theological Seminary

Introduction

Passion for the Trinity

The Appeal of This Book

This study is an appeal to join a journey of reflection on and discovery of the true and eternal nature of God in the midst of many untrue voices about him.

Though many books have been published and much research undertaken on the Trinity, this study shows the difference that the doctrine of the Oneness in Trinity makes in contradistinction to beliefs that deny the Trinity. Many find it difficult to understand Oneness in Trinity, which leads them to be drawn to the alternative that seems easier to understand, namely Absolute Oneness, which is sometimes called Monadic Monotheism. As a result, *many abandon or ignore the doctrine of the Trinity without realizing the implications.*

This study therefore contrasts two different concepts of God, **Oneness in Trinity** and **Absolute Oneness**. It seeks to show both the dangers and the blessings that a person may experience as a result of his or her understanding of God. Any person, of whatever religion or persuasion, may have taken on board some of the principles of Absolute Oneness, whether consciously or subconsciously. Similarly, a person may have built his or her life on the principles of Oneness in Trinity, consciously or subconsciously.

This study also presents the theological advancement of thought in the West and the East, and offers new expressions and explanations of the relationship between the persons of the Trinity through the study of pertinent biblical texts in their original languages – Hebrew, Aramaic and Greek.

This work is presented in two parts, that is, two books of eight chapters each. This, the first and introductory book, offers a study of the differences between the two systems on the oneness of God. The second and larger book, which is forthcoming, will focus on the beauty of the Trinity. A synopsis of each of the two books, as well as of each chapter in the two books, follows.

A Synopsis of the Chapters of Volume 1:
Oneness in Trinity versus Absolute Oneness

The first of the two books presents Oneness in Trinity versus Absolute Oneness. It begins by exposing some of the main obstacles of mind and heart that hinder the reception of God's revelation of himself. Explanation is then given of the differences between the concept of Oneness in Trinity, which is the Christian belief that springs from the Bible, and the concept of Absolute Oneness, which is the belief of several religions. Explanation is also given of three distinct uses of the expression "God" in the Bible. Awareness of these uses protects from unnecessary confusion and misunderstanding. Following this, the main errors about the Trinity that have been repeated through history are exposed, and guidelines for avoiding them are given. Before proceeding to examine the ramifications of Absolute Oneness, another attempt is made at answering the perennial question of whether the God proclaimed by the Qur'an is the same as the God of Oneness in Trinity proclaimed by the Bible. Then, launching from the unavoidable question in regard to the activity of the attributes of God eternally apart from the existence of creation, an example is presented in the historical struggle over Absolute Oneness between two schools of thought in the eighth century AD. This struggle was expressed by some Arab philosophers because of their rejection of the doctrine of the Trinity. It shows what God would be like if he were not triune, and the effect this has on humankind. The answer to this conflict is then presented by Oneness in Trinity at every point. Finally, though the doctrine of the Trinity came by divine revelation and not by human reason, this book ends by attempting to demonstrate the harmony of the doctrine of the Trinity with logic. The beauty of the Trinity will be the expanded study of the second book.

Chapter 1 deals with *the readiness to receive God's revelation of himself.* The first fundamental concept for the discovery of the true nature of God is for the serious thinker to examine him- or herself for any mind or heart obstacle to receiving God's revelation of himself. This self-examination involves understanding several matters: that the Bible is the highest source of truth about God; that the Trinity is presupposed in the message of the gospel and is foundational to all Christian doctrine; that the Trinity's many implications demonstrate that it is not a problem to be solved but rather a beauty to be discovered and enjoyed; and that the Trinity emancipates one from erroneous preconceived notions of God's oneness. However, this understanding cannot take place without the proper theological preparation, the proper use of reason, and the proper heart. It is in the knowledge of the true God, as revealed only in his triune nature, that there can be life transformation.

Chapter 2 *defines the various concepts of the oneness of God*. In doing so, it explains the differences between Absolute Oneness and Oneness in Trinity. The concept of Oneness in Trinity belongs to Christianity as taught in the Bible. But the concept of Absolute Oneness does not belong exclusively to one religion; it is the belief of several religions, and is the conclusion of philosophical sciences. Both concepts hold to the belief that God alone is the only necessary and sovereign creator God, with one essence or nature, without being composed of parts, and without the existence of any other or secondary god. However, Absolute Oneness believes that the relationship of God to his word is the relationship of his will to his power, so that his word is manifested in his power to fulfill his will. It is from here that all the attributes of God spring. According to Absolute Oneness also, God has no eternal relationship between persons, and thus the first time God had a relationship was with creation after he created it. In contrast, Oneness in Trinity holds that God also has a fatherly nature in himself outside of creation and without it. For the relationship of this God to his word is the relationship of a father to his son, which is the only eternal relationship in existence and is superior to any other relationship in the universe. The attributes of God spring from this relationship through the Holy Spirit. As a person, the Holy Spirit unites the attributes in a unity that secures their eternal perfection and complete harmony. The richness of the relationship between the Father and the Son in the Holy Spirit overflowed into calling the universe into existence, and into a relationship with creation manifested in incarnation in the likeness of man with the goal of the redemption of humanity.

Chapter 3 *introduces the various uses of the expression "God."* This is found only in Oneness in Trinity. Awareness of these uses protects from unnecessary confusion and misunderstanding. The Bible reveals that there are three distinct ways of using "God." The first way points to the one and only God as testified by both the Old and New Testaments, by the appearance of God in the Old Testament in special form, and by the New Testament expressions of this appearance. The second way of using "God" is to point to the Father. This appears in the New Testament. It points to the same God of the Old Testament, and to the revelation that God is not only the Father of all humankind, but a Father in a unique way to his only eternal and uncreated Son with whom he has the only eternal relationship through the Holy Spirit. As such, there is repeated mention of the Father, Son and Holy Spirit in the New Testament without defense, explanation or apology. The third way of using "God" is to point to the divine nature. This appears in the use of parallel words to "God," and in the use of "God" to refer to the Son and to the Holy Spirit, who are of equal deity with the Father. Explanation is also given for the value of the relatively infrequent use of "God" for the Son and Holy Spirit. Clarification is also made regarding the importance of the personhood of the Holy Spirit.

Chapter 4 *reveals common errors about the Trinity* that have been repeated throughout history, and gives guidelines for avoiding them. These errors include such subjects as understanding the term "person" in the Trinity and the difference between a divine person and a human person; understanding the distinction between the Father, Son and Holy Spirit, and staying away from five main errors; understanding the union of the two natures of Christ in his one person, and steering clear of five other main errors; attention to precision in expression, with examples; and the use of illustrations, with examples.

Though this study deals with the view of God according to the philosophy of Absolute Oneness, which is held by several religions and beliefs, chapter 5 makes another attempt to answer the perennial question of *whether the God proclaimed by the Qur'an is the same as the God of Oneness in Trinity proclaimed by the Bible*. To deal with this question, this chapter begins with the early use of the expression "Allah" in Arabic poems, in the Hadith and in the Arabic New Testament since the eighth century AD, and the meaning of this early use. Then an examination is made of the common root in Semitic languages, Hebrew, Aramaic and Syriac, and the meaning of this common root. Next, a conclusion is presented for the use of the expression "Allah" by Arab Christians today. Following this, the difficulty of the question is dealt with by suggesting an alternative question. This leads to a clarification of the main difference between Oneness in Trinity and Absolute Oneness by the confession of Absolute Oneness. This book refers to it as "the giant leap" in describing the attributes of God and what this means to believers and non-believers.

Chapter 6 *presents the example of a historical struggle within Absolute Oneness*. This struggle was expressed by some Arab philosophers because of their rejection of the doctrine of the Trinity, and it shows what God would be like if he were not triune, and the effect this has on humankind. Behind the expressed differences between Absolute Oneness and Oneness in Trinity lies a question that cannot be avoided. This chapter begins by presenting this question, which is in regard to how the attributes of God can be active eternally, apart from the existence of creation, without God existing in relationship. Because Absolute Oneness rejected the possibility of a relationship within God, a conflict arose in the eighth century AD between two schools of thought, the Ash'arites and the Mu'tazilites. The conflict revolved around the attributes of action (i.e. God with us) and the attributes of essence (i.e. God without us).

This chapter deals in detail with the attributes of action in regard to their source, their manifestation, the prevention from comparing them, and the resultant inconsistency. This chapter then deals in detail with the attributes of essence in regard to the separation of the attributes of action from attributes of essence, the separation of the attributes of essence from the essence, and the resultant inconsistency.

Chapter 7 *presents the answer of Oneness in Trinity to the historical conflict of Absolute Oneness.* It begins by answering the inevitable question by demonstrating that the reason why the attributes of God can be active eternally apart from the existence of creation is that he exists in relationship between persons in his oneness. The chapter then proceeds to give the answer of Oneness in Trinity regarding the source and manifestation of the attributes of action, followed by the relationship of attributes of action to the attributes of essence, and the relationship of the attributes of essence to the essence. The chapter then demonstrates the resultant coherence of Oneness in Trinity. After this, a summary is presented by illustrating Oneness in Trinity and Absolute Oneness in two parallel lines. The chapter ends with an appeal to believers and non-believers.

Chapter 8 *attempts to demonstrate the harmony of the Trinity with logic.* Though the doctrine of the Trinity came by divine revelation, it is nevertheless consistent with logic. In the spirit of "faith seeking understanding," this chapter presents four assurances for this. First, the eternal existence of God is in harmony with the eternal activity of his attributes. In support of this, the chapter seeks to demonstrate that the existence of God means the existence of his attributes, which in turn requires positive description of them, and this necessitates their activity, requiring God's self-sufficiency. Second, the eternal activity of God's attributes presupposes a relationship between persons. This is demonstrated in that the activity of God's attributes depends on a relationship, and the relationship depends on equal persons. Third, the relationship is protected by "threeness" of persons. This is shown in that it is logical for the persons to be at least, and at most, three. Fourth, the threeness of persons is guaranteed perfection through oneness. This is demonstrated in that the triune relationship requires the perfection of attributes, that the perfection of attributes requires oneness, and that this oneness depends on the perfection of attributes. In short, the eternal existence of God means the eternal activity of his attributes, which means a relationship between persons, which is protected through the perfection of threeness of persons, which in turn is guaranteed perfection through oneness. And all of this is an eternal inevitability. *This is congruent with the revelation of the Bible about the Trinity.*

A Synopsis of the Chapters of Volume 2:
The Divine Beauty of Oneness in Trinity

The eight chapters of the second book present the divine beauty of Oneness in Trinity. After answering the objection to the study of the activity of God's attributes outside creation, and after presenting categorization of the attributes of God adopted in this study, an exegetical and theological study is made of the main passages and words in the New Testament that relate to the activity of God's attributes both outside and inside creation. This is done according to both Christ and his followers. At the heart of this lies the truth that the activity and perfection of the attributes of God inside creation are an expression of their activity and perfection in himself outside creation. Then, the importance of each attribute is treated, as well as their perfection and their equal activity at all times. The book then gives the reasons why the oneness of God in the Old Testament is vastly different from Absolute Oneness. An examination is made of the significance of the names "Father," "Son" and "Holy Spirit." When understood, in these names lies the greatest good news to humanity. After this, eight declarations of Christ's submission to the Father are examined in order to show that these are the strongest and most beautiful expressions of the union of his two natures, the divine and the human, in his one person. These provide an expression inside creation of the beauty of Oneness in Trinity inside and outside creation. The book ends with the power of the Trinity in providing meaning to all of life and in influencing the individual, the family, the church, the society and the world.

Chapter 1 *examines the activity of the attributes of God outside creation, or "God without us."* This truth is the foundation of the doctrine of the Trinity. The chapter begins with answering objections to the study of the activity of God's attributes outside creation by pointing to God's desire to be known and trusted, to the danger of separating God's activity inside creation from his nature, and to God's revelation of an eternal relationship within himself. Following this, the twofold categorization of the attributes of God adopted in this study is introduced: the attributes of God active outside creation; and the attributes of God active inside creation. The major portion of this chapter then presents an exegetical and theological study of the main passages and words in the New Testament that relate to the activity of God's attributes outside creation that spring from the only eternal relationship between the Father and the Son through the Holy Spirit. This is demonstrated from what Christ revealed as well as from what his followers revealed as recorded in the New Testament.

Chapter 2 *examines the activity of the attributes of God inside creation, or "God with us."* The chapter presents evidences for the activity and perfection of the attributes of God inside creation as an expression of their activity and perfection in himself outside creation. In other words, the relationship of the one true God "with us" springs from the relationship in himself "without us." So this chapter presents an exegetical and theological study of the main passages and words in the New Testament that relate to the activity of God's attributes inside creation. This is demonstrated from what Christ revealed as well as from what his followers revealed as recorded in the New Testament. The activity of God's attributes inside creation also includes the importance of each attribute of God, their superiority and perfection, as well as their equal activity at all times, without the cessation or independent activity of any of them. It also includes explaining the activity of the negative attributes of God with regard to the presence of sin in creation.

Chapter 3 *exposes the differences between Old Testament oneness and Absolute Oneness.* Though the Old Testament holds strongly to the oneness of God, there is a huge difference between oneness in the Old Testament and Absolute Oneness. This difference lies in the presence of a theological system in the Old Testament that forms the necessary foundation for the doctrine of the Trinity. This system includes five main factors absent in Absolute Oneness.

Chapter 4 *examines the significance of the name "Father" and the name "Son."* This and the following chapter seek to demonstrate that the correct understanding of the names "Father," "Son" and "Holy Spirit" leads to the discovery that in these names resides the greatest good news to humanity. This chapter begins by showing the importance of the names in the Bible. It then proceeds to show how the names "Father" and "Son" express the superiority of the persons and of the relationship between them as far above human imagination. These names also form the foundation for the priority of love for all of existence. They also form the foundation for the necessity of order in submission with equality in all relationships. The names "Father" and "Son" communicate something valuable in the nature of God, and it is "sonship." This sonship is granted to humankind in the gift of adoption and regeneration. Furthermore, the names "Father" and "Son" furnish the only explanation for creation, incarnation and redemption.

Chapter 5 *studies the significance of the name "Holy Spirit."* This chapter begins by analyzing the 378 occurrences of the word "spirit" in the Hebrew text of the Old Testament, and the 379 occurrences in the Greek text of the New Testament, with statistics and illustrations of its varied uses in each book of the Bible. The chapter then presents evidences for several concepts, including the importance of the use of the word "spirit" to refer to something other than the Spirit of God, pointing to either an attribute or a personality; the significance of the fact that the Bible presents the Holy Spirit in two aspects, as a person equal to the Father and the Son, and as an influence or an attribute, where the word "spirit" takes the place of the word "attribute"; the significance of the dominance of the feminine gender in referring to the spirit or Spirit; and the significance of speaking of "the seven spirits of God."

Chapter 6 *deals with the manifestation of the Trinity in Christ's submission to God.* When examining the declarations of Christ's submission to God, one finds the loftiest meaning of Oneness in Trinity, which is the basis for God's incarnation as man. This chapter presents general principles regarding these declarations as springing from the relationship between the Father and the Son both outside creation and inside creation. After this, eight specific declarations of Christ's submission to the Father are examined in order to show that, in the end, these are the strongest and most beautiful expressions of the union of his two natures, the divine and the human, in his one person, as an expression inside creation of the beauty of Oneness in Trinity inside and outside creation.

Chapter 7 *studies the manifestation of the Trinity in the self-emptying of Christ.* The rejection of the doctrine of the Trinity parallels the rejection of the doctrine of the incarnation and redemption that was accomplished through the cross. One of the main attributes that causes this rejection is the divine humility that is proclaimed by Oneness in Trinity. This humility was expressed supremely in what the New Testament declares as the self-emptying of Christ. This chapter presents an exegetical and theological analysis of Paul's words in Philippians 2:6–8 in order to communicate several lasting principles, including the following: that the mind of Christ before his self-emptying reveals the nature of humility in the Trinity outside of creation; that the trials of Christ on earth coupled with his inability to sin spells the language of pain; and that the self-emptying of Christ is a description of what the true God would do in his triune nature to save humankind. Christ's self-emptying presupposes the Trinity, and the Trinity is manifested in Christ's self-emptying.

And chapter 8 *suggests practical applications in the life-transforming power of the Trinity.* Contrary to what many think, the doctrine of the Trinity has a powerful influence on the daily life of a believer, the continual activity of the church, the real impact on society, and the necessary witness to the world. Several points of application are given that climactically demonstrate that the Trinity reveals reciprocal love and humility in equality in relationships to be the essence of all life.

How to Benefit from This Book

This book can be read consecutively, from beginning to end. Alternatively, a specific topic or biblical passage can be studied by using the list of Frequently Asked Questions and the list of Biblical Passages Studied found at the beginning of this book. A complete index of all Scripture passages used is at the end of the book.

To help readers, additional information has been placed in footnotes at the bottom of the page. These footnotes include explanations of phrases in the original biblical languages as well as from specific historical or theological studies. Key points have been indicated by *the use of italics*, and italics are also used to emphasize words in the Bible passages. Important summaries are given in boxes and scrolls.

Unless otherwise indicated, the New American Standard Bible 1995 edition is used. Information in square brackets [. . .] indicates a different rendering or a necessary explanation. All emphases in Scripture quotations have been added. As to dealing with the exchange between English and non-English, the following points should also be noted:

- Capitalization of pronouns and demonstratives referring to God is avoided, except in quotations, in order to avoid confusion when discussing God as presented in Oneness in Trinity and Absolute Oneness.
- Translations of quotes from non-English sources are my own unless noted otherwise.
- Words and sentences in the biblical languages (Greek, Hebrew and Aramaic), as well as other non-English words or sentences (Arabic and Syriac), appear in the footnotes and not in the main text, and are transliterated according to sound and not according to any specific transliteration system.

May this book lead the reader in a journey to discover deeper truths about God with the goal of coming closer to him in a way he or she had not known before.

Imad Nicola Shehadeh

1

Readiness to Receive God's Revelation of Himself

Some of the main reasons why many find difficulty with the doctrine of the Trinity reside in wrong presuppositions that have accumulated over a long period of time. Added to this is being surrounded by a social and religious system that rejects the main concepts about God that form the basis for the doctrine of the Trinity. However, a person's shortcoming lies not in failing to understand the doctrine of the Trinity, but in *failing to be ready to receive God's revelation of himself.* This chapter aims to help the sincere seeker to achieve freedom from those obstacles that prevent the discovery of deeper truths about God's nature.

Several elements contribute to readiness to receive God's revelation of himself. The ones suggested here overlap, and are not necessarily given in order of importance.

1. The Fountain of All Thought about God Is the Bible

All that is taught about God in this book is based on the Bible, with the belief that the sixty-six books of the Old and New Testaments were *inspired by God*, in the sense that "men moved by the Holy Spirit spoke from God" (2 Pet 1:21) so that the words of the Bible are verbally inspired. This divine inspiration extends equally and fully to all parts: historical, poetical, doctrinal and prophetical.

The evidences for the inspiration of the Bible are enough to give the faithful person the foundation to trust the Bible *historically, culturally, theologically* and *personally*. There is no other book that combines all these traits as does the Bible. It stands as an immovable rock, such that a great chasm separates it from other religious books – a complete and eternal separation. It is not the purpose of this study to examine these evidences.[1] But it should be stressed that this belief in the inspiration of the Bible has several implications for this study.

Veracity

Belief in the inspiration of the Bible means that the Bible is truthful, accurate and completely trustworthy in the original manuscripts.[2] Though the original manuscripts do not exist today, the original text does exist in the numerous copies of the original. These copies far surpass all classical ancient texts in both the number of manuscripts and the short distance in time between the original writing and the earliest extant manuscripts. The original manuscripts have been transmitted down to the present day with high and unique accuracy and reliability to form the Bible, which is the complete written word of God. If the Bible is not truthful, then either God is not truthful, or the Bible is not the word of God. But God is truthful, and the Bible is his word. Therefore, *all that is contained in this study about God is subject to the Bible.*

Authority

Belief in the inspiration of the Bible means that the Bible has final authority in all matters of faith and practice. It is *the final arbiter* in all matters of life and teaching. For a correct understanding of God, our reason must be subject to divine revelation.

Continual Discovery

Belief in the inspiration of the Bible means that the Bible contains unending riches about God waiting to be discovered. Commitment to the inspiration, veracity and authority of the Bible gives the researcher the privilege of discovering these riches. Modern devices such as televisions, mobile phones and planes were not present during Adam's time but their constituents were, waiting to be discovered. Likewise, new depths of knowledge can be found

---

1. For a more complete treatment of the inspiration and inerrancy of the Bible, see Geisler and Nix, *General Introduction to the Bible*, 191–200; McDowell and McDowell, *Evidence That Demands a Verdict*, 15–79; Keller, *Reason for God*, 167–192.

2. Two terms are normally used to point to the veracity of the Bible: infallibility and inerrancy. "Infallibility" is technically defined as being free from error in matters of faith and practice. "Inerrancy" is defined as being free from error in all that it affirms. This work uses the positive term "veracity" to indicate belief in both infallibility and inerrancy, for it is impossible for God to lie (Num 23:19; Titus 1:21; Heb 6:18).

hidden in the crevices of the Bible. But in any new discovery of truth, the truth that was discovered previously remains unchanged and the *new discovery functions to add new depth or a new expression of the same truth.* There remains complete harmony with all truth declared previously from the Bible.

Progress of Revelation

Belief in the inspiration of the Bible means that the Bible reveals truth about God progressively. In other words, *any truth that God revealed about himself grew and developed with the progress of time* as he spoke his word through his prophets and apostles. So what he revealed in brief and limited form at one time increased in clarity, expansion and interpretation.

Complete Harmony

Belief in the inspiration of the Bible means that the Bible is totally consistent and congruent in everything it affirms. Therefore, any text about God may be explained by another text. The Bible gives the best explanation of itself.

Revalidation of Doctrine

People often overly depend on the theological and philosophical conclusions of the history of Christian doctrine without returning to examine their foundation in the Bible. There is a critical need to ascertain the precision of doctrinal declarations in new ways through fresh examination of the biblical text. Systematic theology should never be isolated from its continual need to return to the Bible.

Arguing against the dangers of consensus, Stephen Lewis writes,

> No one should discount the role of history in helping us understand how the earliest interpreters understood the Scriptures. Yet believers today must renew their commitment to the Scripture itself. The real issue must not be whether a doctrine is affirmed by every Christian everywhere, nor whether it is officially orthodox according to the historical creeds, nor whether it is unofficially orthodox according to the fashions of contemporary Christian thought . . . The only real issue is whether a doctrine or belief is BIBLICAL. There is no more sound approach to the formation of our beliefs. It is time we rescued Christian theology from the

theologians and put it back in the hands of biblical exegetes and biblical theologians.[3]

D. A. Carson expresses the same sentiment: "I have been thinking through the hiatus between careful exegesis and doctrinal formulations. We need both, of course, but unless the latter are finally controlled by the former, and seen to be controlled by the former, both are weakened."[4]

The Accompaniment of the Holy Spirit

Belief in the inspiration of the Bible means that *the Bible is the only book that is accompanied by the Holy Spirit* who aids our understanding of the mind of God in all that he reveals about himself. Thus Jesus declared,

> But when He, the Spirit of truth, comes, He will guide you into all the truth; for He will not speak on His own initiative, but whatever He hears, He will speak; and He will disclose to you what is to come. He will glorify Me, for He will take of Mine and will disclose it to you. (John 16:13–14)

Paul likewise asserted that the Holy Spirit works in the hearts of believers to enable them to grow in the knowledge of God:

> . . . that the God of our Lord Jesus Christ, the Father of glory, may give to you a spirit of wisdom and of revelation in the knowledge of Him . . . that the eyes of your heart may be enlightened. (Eph 1:17–18a)

At the same time, the Holy Spirit *convinces believers of their sonship*, cries with them during prayer, guides them, liberates them from fear, and testifies to their hearts that they are sons of God:

> Because you are sons, God has *sent forth the Spirit* of His Son into our hearts, crying, "Abba! Father!" (Gal 4:6)

> For all who are being led by the Spirit of God, these are sons of God. For you have not received a spirit of slavery leading to fear again, but you have received a *spirit of adoption as sons* by which

---

3. Stephen R. Lewis, "Greek Philosophy Tainted Early Church Theology; What About Today?" (unpublished article, Rocky Mountain Bible College and Seminary).

4. Carson, *Jesus the Son of God*, Kindle loc. 68–70.

we cry out, "Abba! Father!" The Spirit Himself testifies to our spirit that we are children of God. (Rom 8:14–16)[5]

Therefore the Bible is the fountain of all truth about God, which ever springs forth to form a picture growing in its radiance to reflect some of the eternal beauty of the true God.

2. The Christian Message Begins with the Gospel

Many Christians find difficulty, not only in understanding the doctrine of the Trinity, but also in explaining it to others. They also question the necessity of sharing this doctrine with non-Christians in the process of witnessing. The answer to this concern lies in realizing, first, that the responsibility of the Christian does not begin with *explaining the Trinity* but in *explaining the message of the gospel.* This message is a declaration of the good news of what God has done to save humanity from sin.

Second, humanity's salvation from God's judgment against sin does not come by understanding the doctrine of the Trinity but only by believing in what Christ has done on the cross to redeem us. Of course, the gospel message presupposes the doctrine of the Trinity, for it speaks of the Father sending his Son to save humanity, and of the Holy Spirit applying the message to the believer's heart.

---

5. Here the translation "testifies *to* our spirit" of v. 16 replaces NASB's "testifies *with* our spirit." "At issue, grammatically, is whether the Spirit testifies alongside of our spirit (dat. of association), or whether he testifies to our spirit (indirect object) that we are God's children. If the former, the one receiving this testimony is unstated (is it God? or believers?). If the latter, the believer receives the testimony and hence is assured of salvation via the inner witness of the Spirit. The first view has the advantage of a σύν- (*sun-*) prefixed verb, which might be expected to take an accompanying dat. of association (and is supported by NEB, JB, etc.). But there are three reasons why πνεύματι (*pneumati*) should *not* be taken as association: (1) Grammatically, a dat. with a σύν- prefixed verb does not necessarily indicate association. This, of course, does not preclude such here, but this fact at least opens up the alternatives in this text. (2) Lexically, though συμμαρτυρέω (*summartureo*) originally bore an associative idea, it developed in the direction of merely intensifying μαρτυρέω (*martureo*). This is surely the case in the only other NT text with a dat. (Rom 9:1). (3) Contextually, a dat. of association does not seem to support Paul's argument: What standing has our spirit in this matter? Of itself it surely has no right at all to testify to our being sons of God [Cranfield, *Romans*, 1:403]. In sum, Rom 8:16 seems to be secure as a text in which the believer's assurance of salvation is based on the inner witness of the Spirit. The implications of this for one's soteriology are profound: The objective data, as helpful as they are, cannot by themselves provide assurance of salvation; the believer also needs (and receives) an existential, ongoing encounter with God's Spirit in order to gain that familial comfort" (NET Bible notes). An added support to this are the parallel concepts of the leading of the Spirit (8:14) and the crying of sons (8:15).

Third, in spite of the above, the gospel message presupposes the doctrine of the Trinity, for it speaks of the Father sending his Son to save humanity, and of the Holy Spirit applying the message to the believer's heart.

Fourth, understanding the message of the gospel leads to understanding Christ, and understanding Christ leads to the beginning of a growing and unending adventure of understanding the nature of God. So first we enjoy the salvation that is ours in Christ, and then we begin to experience increasing growth in the knowledge of the nature of God.

Fifth, the doctrine of the Trinity is foundational to all other Christian doctrine: to Bibliology (the Bible), Christology (Christ), Anthropology (man), Pneumatology (the Holy Spirit), Hamartiology (sin), Ecclesiology (the church), Epistemology (knowledge), Axiology (values) and Eschatology (the future), as well as to the handling of metaphysical inquiry.

Sixth, the level of depth in discussing the Trinity with another person depends on the level of the question that is asked, the level of maturity of the inquirer and the level of his or her biblical knowledge.

3. The Doctrine of the Trinity Is Not Confined to the Word "Trinity"

Though the Bible teaches the doctrine of the Trinity strongly, the word "Trinity" is not found in the Bible. The earliest use of the term "Trinity" dates to the second century AD.[6] The word "Trinity" was meant to summarize the Bible's unique teaching about God that he is not one person but three, and not three gods but one God.

The fact that the word "Trinity" is not found in the Bible means that Christians are not obliged to use it. They may therefore innovate in the use of any expression to convey the doctrine as long as there is accuracy in the intended meaning. For example, it may be said that "God is love" in his nature. The presence of love presupposes a relationship within God that may be pursued to discover all that it means. Another expression used to refer to God as "Father." This too presupposes a mysterious relationship within God.

In like fashion, the Christian Arab philosopher, Awad Samaan, has used the expression "inclusive exclusive oneness" to point to the idea that God includes

---

6. The earliest use of the term "Trinity" to express this doctrine came from Theophilus (AD 168–183), from the Greek τριάδος (Theophilus of Antioch, *Theophilus to Autolycus*, Book II, Chapter XV). It was then used by Tertullian (AD 145–220), from the Latin *trinitas* (Tertullian, *Against Praxeas*, Chapter II). Cf. Cross and Livingstone, *Oxford Dictionary of the Christian Church*, s.v. "Triad"; "Trinity"; Hastings, Selbie and Lambert, *Dictionary of the Apostolic Church*, 1:460.

in himself all that is required for the activity of his attributes, but at the same time prevents the presence of any other god besides him.[7]

The term chosen depends upon such matters as the circumstances, the context and the need. It also depends on the ability to explain a sublime doctrine or to correct a wrong teaching about God. This often requires divine enablement and long experience.

4. The Finite Cannot See All of the Infinite

God is much bigger than can be imagined by any human being! It is impossible for a finite man or woman to comprehend all of the infinite God. Therefore it is expected that we will find difficulty when first hearing about the doctrine of the Trinity. As an illustration of this, because of our limited sight, we are unable to see both sides of a coin at the same time. We can see only one side then the other. Likewise, our limited comprehension allows us to see one side of God, then another, then another, and so on, but never to see all sides at the same time.

Another illustration is to imagine two worlds: one that is three-dimensional, with length, width and height; and one that is two-dimensional, with length and width only. The two-dimensional world sees a cube as a square, and a ball as a circle. This is because the common intersection is only two-dimensional. This is similar to what happened to Christ when he came to earth. It is impossible for human beings, who are limited in dimensions, to comprehend all of God who is infinite in dimensions.[8] We can only experience one specific aspect of

---

7. Awad Samaan, الله، ذاته ونوع وحدانيته [God, His Essence and His Kind of Unity], 3–4.

8. In a sermon delivered by Timothy Keller on the subject of "The Triune God" on 12 June 2011, he stated, "Sometimes people get hung up on the difficulty of the thought, and they try to say, 'How can it be?' One of my favorite examples of this, though, is a place where C. S. Lewis talks about the Trinity. He says to imagine a flat world in which everything is in two dimensions. There are no spheres; there are only circles. There are no cubes; there are only squares. What if, suddenly, into this two-dimensional world comes a three-dimensional being, and the person sits there and says, 'I'm three-dimensional'? The trouble is, you might say, the intersection of the three-dimensional person with the two-dimensional world would only be two-dimensional. I mean, if you actually brought a cube into the two-dimensional world, the footprint would be a square. Therefore, if you actually had a three-dimensional person coming in, there would be all kinds of things about him or her that would be pretty counterintuitive and people in the two-dimensional world couldn't understand. Whenever he would try to explain, 'But I'm a three-dimensional person,' nobody would be able to understand that. This is what we have here. This is Jesus coming into our world. This is the triune God coming into our world, coming into time, coming into a world where we can't understand it. But why should we? What makes us think we would understand it? Why would a two-dimensional world understand a three-dimensional object, or why would a three-dimensional world understand a twenty-dimensional object? We can't, but what we can understand is the beauty and power of the implications of this doctrine."

God, then another, then another, and so on. For if God was small enough to be comprehended, he would not be big enough to be worshipped.

5. What Is Necessary Is Often Unseen

The study of the doctrine of the Trinity leads the examiner to enter the depths of what might be the subconscious. A person does not often consciously or continually think to this depth. But this does not make the doctrine unimportant. Much of what we enjoy in life is preceded by many basic necessities that we may not think of consciously. But not thinking of them does not negate their importance.

As an illustration, a family enjoys life in a house and all that the house offers for comfort and delight. But few members of the family would consciously or continually be thinking of the foundations of the building they are in, the rebar, the cement, the electrical and mechanical connections, the cost, and so on. But not thinking consciously of these things does not render them unimportant. On the contrary, these things are necessary so that the family can enjoy living inside the house.

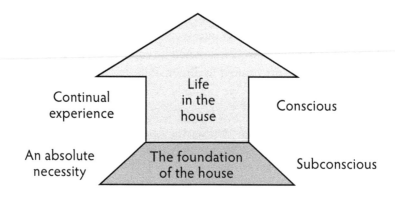

Figure 1.1: The Question of the Foundation

To use another illustration, a person may enjoy the beauty of a tree and its fruit without necessarily thinking consciously of the roots of the tree, their length, depth and function. But the person's not thinking consciously of these things does not make them unnecessary. In the same way, someone may enjoy a cooked meal without knowing the details of what it took to prepare it. A person may also drive a car without having any mechanical or electrical knowledge of how the car runs. But these people's not knowing the constituents of the meal or the car does not mean that they are not necessary.

In like fashion, a person may enjoy fellowship with God, the grace of salvation and confidence in the attributes of God without any mental effort regarding the necessary theological and philosophical requirements that make enjoyment of these fruits possible. However, *our enjoyment of knowing God does not mean that what is above our comprehension of God's nature is not necessary.*

In addition, it may be difficult to accept the truth and easy to accept error. But the first is usually built on the right foundations, while the second is usually built on the wrong foundations. People may be sincere about their religion without realizing that religion is based on wrong foundations. Conversely, people may not be sincere about their religion even though their religion may be based on the right foundations. In reality, most people do not examine the foundations upon which their beliefs are based. Therefore, one of the goals of this study is to aid people to examine the religion they follow, whether from sincerity or not.

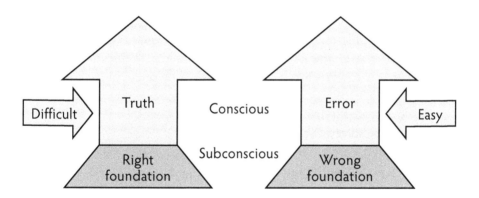

Figure 1.2: The Difficulty of Accepting the Truth

One of the factors that distinguishes the solid foundation from the corrupt foundation is to what extent it is consistent with the progress of God's revelation of himself throughout history and through his prophets and the holy Scriptures. It will be seen that the right concept of God builds on the foundation of the previous progress of revelation in the Bible, whereas the wrong concept of God rejects the previous progress of revelation.

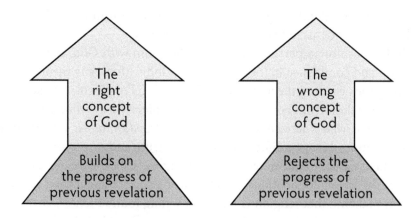

Figure 1.3: Harmony with the Progress of Revelation

6. The Trinity Is Not a Problem to Be Solved

The study of the doctrine of the Trinity does not aim at presenting a final solution to a problem as in the case of medical science. Dealing with the doctrine of the Trinity as a problem leads to ridicule, falsification, or both, in a similar way to what Satan did to Eve when he said, "Indeed, has God said . . . ?" (Gen 3:1b).

The doctrine of the Trinity is not a problem to be solved but rather a beauty to be discovered.[9] Weinandy perceptively points out that proper theological method does not rely on the dialectic method because the latter "still approaches theological issues as problems or riddles."[10] Henry Bulad asserts that a problem, like a riddle, is not clear and is a dead-end road with no answer,

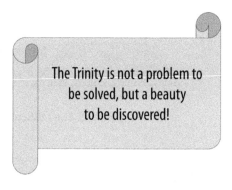

The Trinity is not a problem to be solved, but a beauty to be discovered!

---

9. This thought is a variation of a similar idea from Thomas Weinandy, who cautioned against making the goal of theological inquiry a problem to be solved rather than a mystery to be clarified. He convincingly shows that theological method, unlike science, does not seek to find a final solution to a problem, but rather seeks to clarify a mystery by penetrating more deeply into it (Weinandy, *Does God Suffer?*, 29).

10. Weinandy, 37.

whereas beauty, like a mystery, provides growing knowledge with no end. It is not a block in the way; rather, its depths and heights call for daily discovery and unending worship.[11]

The Importance of Discovery

The Old Testament gives examples of the necessity of searching to discover greater depths of divine beauty. When Moses asked God about his name, he was looking for a solution to how he was to convince the nation of his calling to be their leader. But God did not give him a solution to his problem; instead, he presented him with new information about his nature (Exod 3:13–14). Later again, when Moses asked to see God's glory, he was looking for a solution to a problem he had with understanding God's glory. But God answered him by giving him a new revelation of his nature (Exod 33:18 – 34:7).[12] In both cases, *God provided the opportunity for Moses to experience a new depth in knowledge of God's nature*, without leading him to the end of all knowledge about himself.

In an example from the New Testament, Jesus challenged the traditional and limited teaching about the Messiah held by the Pharisees by asking them a question regarding the simultaneous relationship of Christ to God and to David, pointing to their failure to seek deeper truths, a condition very similar to that of adherents of Absolute Oneness:

> Now while the Pharisees were gathered together, Jesus asked them a question: "What do you think about the Christ, whose son is He?" They said to Him, "The son of David." He said to them, "Then how does David in the Spirit call Him 'Lord,' saying, 'The Lord said to My Lord, "Sit at My right hand, until I put Your enemies beneath Your feet"'? If David then calls Him 'Lord,' how is He his son?" No one was able to answer Him a word, nor did anyone dare from that day on to ask Him another question. (Matt 22:41–46; cf. Mark 12:35–37; Luke 20:41–44)

Beauty Introduced through the Word "Mystery" The Bible uses the word "mystery" to convey a beauty waiting to be discovered. The greatest beauty is Christ, who is the chief mystery of all.

---

11. Henry Bulad, منطق الثالوث [The Logic of the Trinity], 12.

12. Weinandy gives this and other illustrations for the same concept (Weinandy, 31–37).

The New Testament uses the word "mystery" twenty-eight times to point to beauty that is to be discovered.[13] The word "mystery" does not refer to something that is vague or obscure, but to something that was not known at all, or was not fully known, *but now can be discovered.*[14]

The Kinds of Mysteries

The Bible reveals several kinds of mysteries. They begin with those related to humanity's evil in order to demonstrate the beauty of change that will take place as expressed by the rest of the mysteries. These mysteries include those related to God's purpose and those related to humanity's transformation. All these mysteries lead to the chief of all mysteries, that is, Christ himself. These mysteries are briefly introduced below.

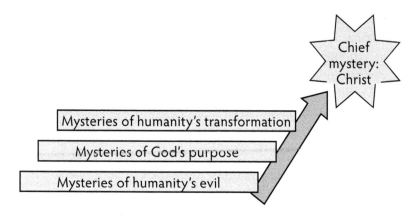

Figure 1.4: Kinds of Mysteries

---

13. The neuter noun μυστήριον (*mustarion*), translated "mystery," appears 23 times in the singular and 5 times in the plural. Of these it appears 14 times in the accusative case, 7 times in the nominative, 5 times in the genitive and 2 times in the dative. The word occurs in the OT only in the Aramaic portion of the book of Daniel, where רָז (*Roz*) is used 6 times to refer to King Nebuchadnezzar's dream (Dan 2:18–19, 27, 29, 30, 47). It was translated in the LXX with the same NT word μυστήριον (*mustarion*).

14. The meaning of the word "mystery" is presented in the lexicons as "the content of that which has not been known before but which has been revealed to an in-group or restricted constituency – 'secret, mystery'" (Louw & Nida, s.v. "μυστήριον"); "a hidden or secret thing, not obvious to the understanding . . . a hidden purpose or counsel; secret will . . . the mystic or hidden sense" (Thayer, *Greek–English Lexicon of the New Testament*, s.v. "μυστήριον"); "a secret which would remain such but for revelation" (Mounce and Bennett, *Mounce Concise Greek–English Dictionary of the New Testament*, s.v. "μυστήριον"); "the secret thoughts, plans, and dispensations of God . . . which are hidden fr. human reason, as well as fr. all other comprehension below the divine level, and await either fulfillment or revelation to those for whom they are intended" (BDAG, s.v. "μυστήριον").

1. Mysteries Related to Humanity's Evil

The Bible speaks of three kinds of mysteries related to humanity's evil that will reach a climax in the end times:

- *The mystery of lawlessness.* This points to the reality of lawlessness being currently at work until it will be unleashed in the end times with no restraint (2 Thess 2:7).
- *The mystery of the hardening of Israel.* This points to a partial and temporary hardening of Israel until a future time of true repentance (Rom 11:25).
- *The mystery of Babylon.* The city of Babylon represents the joining of all the earth against God, or "Babylonianism," and therefore is named "Mother of harlots and the abominations of the earth" (Rev 17:5).

2. Mysteries Related to God's Purpose

The purpose of God is to establish his kingdom in complete renewal of the universe and in the glorified renewal of human bodies.

- *The mysteries of the kingdom of God.* The declaration of the mysteries of God's kingdom began with Daniel's interpretation of Nebuchadnezzar's dream as revealed by God about the rise and fall of empires throughout human history, ending in the establishment of God's eternal kingdom (Dan 2:44).

  But Christ expanded the revelation by speaking about the mysteries of the kingdom. These include the coexistence of good and evil in the current age, but at the same time, the spiritual work of God in the hearts of the sons of the kingdom in anticipation of complete fulfillment in the end times (Matt 13:11; Mark 4:11; Luke 8:10). Paul reveals further that this mystery speaks of the formation of one people of Jews and Gentiles through the work of Christ on the cross (Eph 2:11–3:6).
- *The mystery of the resurrection body.* This mystery speaks of the final inheritance of every believer of a completely glorified resurrection body fit for heaven (1 Cor 15:51–55).

3. Mysteries Related to Humanity's Transformation

These mysteries speak of the inner transformation of men and women through faith and in meeting Christ in the regular assembly of believers in the local churches.

- *The mystery of faith.* This mystery refers to holding all the truths revealed by God with consistency in conduct so that there is a clear conscience (1 Tim 3:9).
- *The mystery of godliness.* This mystery declares that the hidden God becomes known to those who have faith in God and conduct pleasing to God, but remains hidden to those who do not have this faith (1 Tim 3:16).
- *The mystery of the churches and their messengers.* This mystery reveals that Christ in all his glory is present and walks in the midst of the local churches, and holds their leadership in his hands (Rev 1:12–2:1).

4. The Chief of All Mysteries, Christ Himself

Christ is presented as the chief of all mysteries in several ways. First, he is the only mystery that is a person and not a teaching, a law, a philosophy or an event. He is all of these and infinitely more. Second, Christ revealed God's triune nature as Father, Son and Holy Spirit, the one and only God. Third, as a result, Christ is given supreme descriptions, as becomes clear from the following:

- *Christ joins all divine purposes.* All the purposes of God, from eternity past to eternity future and through the present time, are gathered up into one head, that is, Christ.

    He made known to us *the mystery of His will*, according to His kind intention which He purposed in Him with a view to an administration suitable to the fullness of the times, that is, the *summing up of all things in Christ*, things in the heavens and things on the earth. (Eph 1:9–10)

- *Christ is supreme in attributes.* In Christ there is unique grace, unfathomable riches, light for all and divine manifold wisdom – and all in the eternal purpose of God.

    By revelation there was made known to me *the mystery . . . the mystery of Christ . . .* This grace was given, to preach to the Gentiles the unfathomable riches of Christ, and to bring to light what is the *administration of the mystery . . .* so that the manifold wisdom of God *might now be made known . . .* This was in accordance with the eternal purpose which He carried out *in Christ Jesus our Lord.* (Eph 3:3–4, 8–11)

- *Christ is the true spouse.* The greatness of the husband and wife relationship springs from the greatness of Christ's relationship to the church. Christ is the only true spouse!

  > This mystery is great; but I am speaking with reference to Christ and the church. (Eph 5:32)

- *Christ is the hope of glory.* Christ is the central and richest mystery, and his living in and among believers gives them the assured hope of sharing in his glory.

  > . . . the riches of the glory of this mystery among the Gentiles, which is *Christ in you*, the *hope of glory.* (Col 1:27b)

  > Geisler points to the mutual indwelling of Christ and believers as affirming sharing in his glory: "Because of . . . the riches of the glory, believers are indwelt by Christ, the hope of glory. They are thus 'in Christ' (2 Cor 5:17; Eph 1:4), and Christ is in them (cf. Rom 8:10; 2 Cor 13:5). Because of Christ, believers look forward to sharing His glory (Col 3:4; Rom 5:2; 8:18, 30; 2 Cor 4:17; Gal 5:5; 1 Pet 5:10)."[15]

- *Christ is the chief mystery of God.* The interchange of love between believers generates encouragement in the heart, and in turn engenders substantial inner change.[16] This change is from not having understanding to having the richness of the assurance in understanding or insight and perception. It also is a change from knowing the normal affairs of life to knowing the greatest mystery in existence, the greatest mystery of God, and that is Christ!

  > . . . that their hearts may be encouraged, having been knit together in love, and attaining to all the wealth that comes from the full assurance of understanding, resulting in a *true knowledge of God's mystery*, that is, *Christ Himself.* (Col 2:2).[17]

---

15. Geisler, "Colossians," 675–676.

16. The use of the preposition εἰς (*eis*) here twice points to a change in one's condition. "(An idiom, literally 'to be into'): to change from one state to another – 'to change, to become'" (Louw & Nida, s.v. "εἰς").

17. "Among what at first sight seems to be a bewildering variety of variant readings, the one adopted for the text is plainly to be preferred (a) because of strong external testimony ($\mathfrak{P}^{46}$ B Hilary Pelagius Ps–Jerome) and (b) because it alone provides an adequate explanation of the other readings as various scribal attempts to ameliorate the syntactical ambiguity of τοῦ θεοῦ,

The Beauty of Mysteries

The Bible reveals the beauty of the mysteries in several privileges. The following are the most important.

1. *The Privilege of Knowing.* No mystery is known unless the Lord reveals it. Each mystery is for human benefit. So the knowledge of the content of each mystery is a great privilege for humankind. It is a privilege to know the truth about the evil of people and nations, and that *God in the end will overcome all evil* completely. Furthermore, it is a privilege to know that people can be transformed inwardly so they can join God in overcoming evil. Human knowledge does not compare to divine mysteries, and in fact is the opposite, since it is actually foolishness compared with God's wisdom (1 Cor 3:19–4:1).

2. *The Privilege That What Was Hidden Is Available.* God not only desired to reveal his mysteries, he actually did so! What was hidden has been uncovered (Rom 16:25–27; Eph 3:3–6; Col 1:26–27).

3. *The Privilege for the Prepared Heart.* The mystery is understood by believers with prepared hearts, but remains obscure to impure and unprepared hearts, whether of believers or non-believers. Thus, "the word 'mystery'. . . describes the inner meaning of Jesus' teaching about the kingdom."[18] This is why Christ spoke in parables (Matt 13:10–13).

4. *The Privilege of Seeing the Nature of God.* Frank Thielman notes that the biblical mysteries reveal at least three aspects of God's character: (a) *God's omniscience.* Daniel thanked the Lord for revealing what was hidden in the dark with great wisdom and power (Dan 2:22–23). Paul likewise thanked God for his surpassing wisdom and ways (Rom 11:33). (b) *God's sovereignty.* Daniel demonstrated that God is sovereign over all of human history. The rise and fall of all nations is in his hands, and he will establish his eternal and final kingdom (Dan 2:44). Similarly, Paul expressed the amazing mystery fulfilling God's desire from long ages past of joining Jews and Gentiles in one body (Eph 3:9–11; Col 1:26–27). (c) *God's grace.* Hellenistic religions and cults at the time of the composition of the New Testament

---

Χριστοῦ" (Metzger, *Textual Commentary on the Greek New Testament*, on Col 2:2; for a fuller discussion see Metzger, *Text of the New Testament*, 236–238).

18. Elwell and Comfort, *Tyndale Bible Dictionary*, 926.

confined mysteries to a few, and these mysteries remained esoteric and unavailable to the majority. Yet the God of the Bible is, in his grace, pleased to make his deepest mysteries known (Amos 3:7; Rev 10:7).[19]

5. *The Privilege of Being Assured of the Final Fulfillment of God's Purposes.* All the purposes of God will reach complete fulfillment at the right time, with no delay (Rev 10:6–7).

6. *The Privilege of Proclamation of the Chief Mystery.* Those who see the nature of God and his works as beauty that is always being discovered will desire to share them with others with reverence and joy. They will do so in appreciation of their privilege and responsibility, and with the highest standards in method. This applies especially to the chief mystery, namely, Christ.

   - Appreciating the privilege of proclamation involves valuing that the mysteries are characterized by wisdom (1 Cor 2:7), grace (Eph 3:8) and enlightenment (Eph 3:9). As to appreciating the responsibility, it includes being a steward (1 Cor 4:1),[20] and having a burden to make the mysteries known, especially the chief mystery (Eph 3:10).
   - Having the highest standards in method involves love (1 Cor 13:2), boldness (Eph 6:19), striving in the power of Christ (Col 1:28–29; Col 2:1–2), and prayer (Eph 6:18–19; Col 4:3a).

Understanding Mysteries

Understanding of the divine mysteries comes from having a prepared heart, and *the heart is prepared when it believes with assurance in what Christ has done on the cross.* For he who alone has the divine nature ("the Lord of glory") and the human nature ("was crucified") took our place to absorb the divine judgment against sin, in order to redeem us and to give us salvation and eternal life. The sense of privilege of knowing and making known the beauty of God's nature and his power to transform the universe from deep evil into his glorious kingdom will grow increasingly as our hearts are prepared. And this is made

---

19. Frank Thielman, s.v. "Mystery," in Elwell, *Tyndale Bible Dictionary*, 546–547.

20. A "steward" refers to "one who has the authority and responsibility for something – 'one who is in charge of, one who is responsible for, administrator, manager'" (Louw & Nida, s.v. "οἰκονόμος"); it is "the manager of a household or of household affairs; especially a steward, manager, superintendent" (Thayer, *Greek–English Lexicon of the New Testament*, s.v. "οἰκονόμος").

possible as our joy in what Christ has done on the cross increases. This is the message of the gospel.

> We speak *God's wisdom in a mystery*, the hidden wisdom which God predestined before the ages to our glory; the wisdom which none of the rulers of this age has understood; for *if they had understood it they would not have crucified the Lord of glory.* (1 Cor 2:7–8)

> . . . that by revelation there was *made known to me the mystery . . .* when you read you can understand my *insight into the mystery of Christ . . . through the gospel.* (Eph 3:3–4, 6)

Summary Mysteries are a beauty that needs to be discovered. But the beauty of mysteries can be discovered only by prepared hearts. Such hearts discover that Christ is the chief of all mysteries. This Christ revealed the truth of the Trinity. Therefore, the Trinity is a beauty to be discovered beginning through Christ. And all this is assured at the cross!

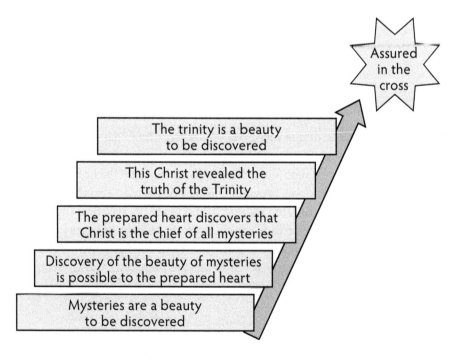

Figure 1.5: Discovering the Beauty of the Trinity

7. There Is Need for Depth behind Simplicity

The message of Christianity, the gospel that transforms people's lives, is a simple message. "Christ died for all people" seems easy to understand, but, upon questioning, it becomes apparent that there are deep truths behind it. For example, many people have died, so what makes Jesus's death different? How can one person die "for" others? What are his qualifications? In the first place, Jesus needed to be free of all sin and evil, otherwise he would have needed someone to die for him. Then, for his death to cover all people, he needed to be superior to them. Although Christ had a fully human nature, he also had what distinguished him from all other humans: what the Bible teaches as the divine nature. But what guarantee is there that his death accomplished what he came to do? His resurrection answers this question. How could he be dead on the cross and holding the universe at the same time? Clearly his nature has a greatness that needs discovering. Then what about humanity? Why did someone need to die for them? What is the human problem? What does Christ's death accomplish for all people? Is forgiveness enough? What else is needed?

These questions accumulate such that the statement "Christ died for all people" clearly *needs to be supported with deeper concepts*, which in turn form the necessary foundation for this simple message. All this would probably not be apparent upon the first declaration of the gospel message.

In sharing the Christian faith, believers begin with simple expressions and do not engage in the theological and philosophical background except when necessary and as they are able to do so. At the same time, there is a movement in the opposite direction. Researchers may be immersed in the study of theological and philosophical arguments, but they are responsible for coming up with simple statements that make an impact upon their hearers. It has been well said that if a mature believer is unable to explain a doctrine to a five-year old child, it is very likely that that believer does not actually understand it!

To offer balance on the matter, it is important to realize that having a personal relationship with the triune God is completely different from explaining philosophically and deeply what God has revealed about himself. Horrell states, "Powerful as it may be, the early church understood [that] experiencing God as tripersonal is not the same as *articulating* precisely what God has revealed of himself."[21] Explanation requires entering into the theological and logical requirements for what God has revealed about himself

---

21. Scott Horrell, "The Eternal Son of God in the Social Trinity," in Sanders and Issler, *Jesus in Trinitarian Perspective*, 46.

in the Bible. This led to the formulation of church creeds throughout history and to studies and theological expressions, all of which attempt to understand what the Bible reveals. And the challenge is continually renewed to explain what the Bible says about the doctrine of the Trinity in new ways and new forms of expression.

However, in spite of all the new and valuable explanations, *human language about God is unable fully to satisfy in describing what is infinite*. In all our attempts, we must remain humble before the greatness of the Trinity.

8. Freedom from Confining Thinking about God's Oneness

It is clear that adherents to Absolute Oneness find great difficulty in being open to other concepts of God, such as Oneness in Trinity. Conversely, many adherents of Oneness in Trinity, because they do not understand its depth of meaning, attempt to confine it within Absolute Oneness. However, upon deeper examination, the honest researcher discovers *the huge danger in confining thinking about the oneness of God*, and for several reasons.

The Danger of Expediency

Confining thinking about the oneness of God restricts the mind to what is acceptable and easy for human understanding, and rejects what is above the standard of human thinking. Again, if God is small enough for us to accept him, he will never be big enough to be worshipped.

The Danger of Subjectivity

Confining thinking about the oneness of God limits mental reasoning to what is subjective or what is built upon personal feelings, and shuts the door to what is objective. God is much greater than any person can realize.

The incongruity between Oneness in Trinity and Absolute Oneness is greater than is usually imagined. The difference lies in both the reasons and the results, that is, the presuppositions as well as the implications related to God's nature, attributes and the way he acts in history.

The Danger of Conditional Acceptance of God's Revelation

Confining thinking about the oneness of God closes the door to considering any revelation God has made about himself. For example, in spite of all the unusual evidences for the inspiration and veracity of the Bible, many accuse the Bible of having been corrupted simply because its content opposes their beliefs or preferences. The acceptance of the biblical teaching by such people is conditioned by what suits them. Therefore, these people obstruct much of what God has said about himself, and deprive their followers from knowing God in truth.

The Danger of Limiting Faith to the Existence and Oneness of God

Confining thinking about the oneness of God limits faith to being in the truth of his existence and oneness only, without any development beyond this point. Yet the Bible challenges the person who limits his or her faith to Absolute Oneness with the rebuke: "You believe that God is one. You do well; the demons also believe, and shudder" (Jas 2:19). In other words, confinement to the belief in Absolute Oneness is confinement to the same belief held by the demons about oneness! The Bible reveals much about the nature of God's oneness, including the relationality in God that is the wellspring of all of his attributes. This in turn overflows into creation, incarnation and redemption for the sake of saving humankind.

In contrast, *Absolute Oneness strongly denies relationality in the person of God.* This in turn has consequences regarding the source of God's attributes, their nature and their trustworthiness. This important issue will be studied later in greater detail.

The Danger of Indirect Belief in Polytheism

Many accuse faith in the Trinity of being polytheistic, and maintain that faith in Absolute Oneness is alone belief in the one God. But the truth is exactly the opposite. For the doctrine of the Trinity, or Oneness in Trinity, gives a clear and specific definition of the one true God that leads a man or woman to have a personal relationship with him. In contrast, and as will be seen later, *confining thinking about the oneness of God offers no clear definition of the nature of God*, and God remains vague to many, with a multiplicity of attributes that could be contradictory. It thus may lead to the adoption of a multitude of concepts about God that amounts to faith in many gods.

The Danger of the Wrong Starting Point

Confining thinking about God to Absolute Oneness leads to the wrong starting point in thinking about God. Reeves demonstrates *how erroneous it is to attempt to fit the Trinity into any other concept of God.* He states,

> The triune God simply does not fit well into the mold of any other God . . . That, ironically, is often why we struggle with the Trinity: instead of starting from scratch and seeing that the trine God is a radically different sort of being from any other candidate for "God," we try to stuff Father, Son and Spirit into how we have always thought of God. Now, usually in the West, "God" is already a subtly defined idea: it refers to one person, not three. So when we come to the Trinity, we feel like we're trying to squeeze two extra persons into our understanding of God – and that is, to say the least, rather hard. And hard things get left. The Trinity becomes that awkward appendix.[22]

Fred Sanders warns against consciously or subconsciously making the erroneous starting point that God made himself a Trinity as a means to another end. The Bible declares that God is Father, Son and Holy Spirit eternally, and he would have been so even if he had not created the world or revealed it, or even if the incarnation had never happened:

> God is God in this way: God's way of being God is to be Father, Son, and Holy Spirit simultaneously from all eternity, perfectly complete in a triune fellowship of love. If we don't take this as our starting point, everything we say about the practical relevance of the Trinity could lead us to one colossal misunderstanding: thinking of God the Trinity as a means to some other end, as if God were the Trinity in order to make himself useful. But God the Trinity is the end, the goal, the telos, the omega. In himself and without any reference to a created world or the plan of salvation, God is that being who exists as the triune love of the Father for the Son in the unity of the Spirit . . . If there had been no world, would God have been Father, Son, and Spirit? . . . If the Son of God had not taken on human nature, would he still have been the Son of God? The answer to these hypothetical questions is yes . . . God would have been Trinity with no world, and the Son of God

---

22. Reeves, *Delighting in the Trinity*, 16.

did in fact preexist his incarnation. God minus the world is still God the Holy Trinity.[23]

Thus Christianity stands unique among all religions of the world. It stands in contrast to polytheistic and pantheistic religions, as well as to religions that call for Absolute Oneness. Theodore W. Jennings expresses well how the doctrine of the Trinity emerged in the face of various forces of theological and philosophical thought:

> The distinctive character of Christianity then lay not in its assertion of the reality of the divine (more than granted by Hellenistic religion) nor the absolute unity of God as the first principle (already asserted in the philosophical schools) nor the existence and power of a single and personal God (something maintained in Judaism). In the context of these competing perspectives Christianity was compelled to articulate its own position with respect to God. This it did in the language and conceptuality of the time but in such a way as to distinguish itself from these competing perspectives. This was done by way of a doctrine of the Trinity.[24]

9. Theological Preparation in the Progress of Revelation

Many people believe in the incarnation and in the atoning death of Christ for sin without realizing that *this faith presupposes the doctrine of the Trinity*. This lack of realization has caused many to stop searching the Scriptures in more depth. If they did search the Scriptures, they would discover that the doctrine of the Trinity is the best news for humanity.

The concept of the progress of revelation discussed earlier conveys that any information that God reveals about himself is based on or is consistent with what he earlier revealed about himself. So in the beginning, God declared himself through nature, or General Revelation. He then revealed himself through the inspired Word, or Special Revelation, beginning with the prophets of the Old Testament and continuing with the apostles of the New Testament. The zenith of Special Revelation came in the incarnation.

The doctrine of the Trinity that is clearly present in the New Testament has its roots in the Old Testament. This important truth indicates that the oneness of God in the Old Testament is totally different from the Absolute Oneness

---

23. Sanders, *Deep Things of God*, 108.
24. Jennings, *Beyond Theism*, 14.

that is proclaimed by other religions.[25] The Old Testament reveals the presence of a theological system that prepares for the doctrine of the Trinity that is not present in the systems that call for Absolute Oneness. This theological system forms the necessary foundation for the doctrine of the Trinity, and it will be covered in the chapter in Volume 2 entitled "The Difference between Old Testament Oneness and Absolute Oneness." The foundation for the doctrine of the Trinity is thus not in vague mathematical or philosophical concepts, but in the eternal nature of God that has been revealed in his earthly relationship with humankind.

10. There Is Need for the Proper Use of Reason

Since the doctrine of the Trinity was not formed by human reason but came by divine revelation, what is the role of reason and logic? The answer to this question is of great importance in theological study, especially the study of the Trinity. Below are some guidelines.

The Harmony of Revelation and Reason

As mentioned earlier, in all cases human reason and logic should submit to divine revelation. The Bible is the final judge on the truth of any assertion related to God. But *the fact that the doctrine of the Trinity did not come by human reason but by divine revelation does not mean that reason contradicts revelation.* For revelation is infinite reason, and there is no revelation, if understood correctly, that contradicts reason.[26] The doctrine of the Trinity is supported by reason and logic. In spite of the inability of human reason to analyze all that came by divine revelation, solid logic agrees with divine revelation and does not oppose it. It is extremely safe to assert that any theological pursuit is built upon the foundation of logical harmony and consistency with all facets of divine revelation as it appears in the Bible.

---

25. This is expressed by Eugene Merrill (see Eugene H. Merrill, "Is the Doctrine of the Trinity Implied in the Genesis Creation Account?," in Youngblood, *Genesis Debate*, 111–116).

26. Chafer states, "The *tout ensemble* of the superhuman character of the Bible presents an almost inexhaustible array of considerations which, if observed with candor, compel one to conclude that this book could not be a human product" (Chafer, *Chafer Systematic Theology*, 1:290).

Faith Seeking Understanding

The use of reason and logic is in the spirit of the well-known principle of "faith seeking understanding" of Augustine (AD 354–430) followed by Anselm (AD 1030–1109).[27] The use of logic is not because of a lack in revelation, but for the sake of a deeper understanding, protecting, supporting, explaining and applying revelation to all of life.[28] In this there is enrichment of faith, growth in knowledge and a coming nearer to God.

The Impossibility of Doing Away with Logic

Not relying on reason in theological study is *unrealistic*. Preventing theological investigation amounts to being confined to reading the Scriptures without any comment. In such a case, there would be no ability to give any answer to the meaning of what was read.

Not relying on reason is also logically *impossible*. Though reason submits to revelation, it is impossible to do theology without reason. Geisler and Feinberg warn that "any attempt to totally disjoin reason and revelation seems unfruitful if not impossible. Even those who hold strongly to a 'revelation only' view provide arguments or reasons of some kind to support it."[29] Weinandy adds that, "while biblical revelation cannot be contradicted and while it can govern, support, and even demand specific philosophical orientations and interpretations, of itself it cannot answer the philosophical issues that arise from but are not fully addressed by it."[30] He states that the God of traditional Christian philosophy is not different from nor incompatible with the God of Christian revelation.[31] He also maintains that "reason alone cannot establish that God is a Trinity of persons. However, . . . what is established through revelation and doctrine is reinforced and in accord with what is grasped by reason, and vice versa."[32] Thus, *any theological task must be built on the foundation of the consistency and coherence of all facets of biblical and systematic*

---

27. Weinandy shows how Augustine and Anselm developed this concept (Weinandy, *Does God Suffer?*, 28, n. 2).

28. Weinandy explains that a sound theological method seeks to clarify for the sake of protecting, as well as demonstrating the reasonableness of the truth proclaimed (29).

29. Geisler and Feinberg, *Introduction to Philosophy*, 268. See Geisler and Feinberg's excellent chapter about God, analyzing the equivocal, univocal and analogical ways of talking about God (305–319).

30. Weinandy, *Does God Suffer?*, 63, n. 3.

31. Weinandy, 114.

32. Weinandy, 120.

theology. Theological method takes into account how all doctrines fit logically together, for one doctrine affects others.[33]

Difficulty Does Not Mean Illogic

The difficulty in understanding any doctrine, especially the doctrine of the Trinity, does not mean that it is illogical. Nor does difficulty give an excuse for rejection. The difficulty in comprehension should lead the serious examiner all the more to study and explore. The greater the depth of a certain truth, the greater the requirement for serious thinking and a focused heart. Then comes the discovery of the greatness and beauty of what beforehand seemed only difficult.

11. Knowing God Comes from a Pure Heart

It is unreasonable for a person to attempt to understand God's holy nature while at the same time keeping iniquity in his or her life. Christ asserts,

> Blessed are the pure in heart, for they shall see God. (Matt 5:8)

> It is written in the prophets, "And they shall all be taught of God." Everyone who has heard and learned from the Father, comes to Me. (John 6:45)

> My sheep hear My voice, and I know them, and they follow Me. (John 10:27)

Growth in the discovery of God's nature requires a pure heart. Whoever is pure in heart submits to the teaching of the Father, and this causes him or her to come to Christ and listen to his voice. Purity in heart includes repenting of sin, avoiding legalism, examining the Scriptures, seeking divine help, and humility, following the example of the first generation of believers.

Repentance from Sin

It is impossible for us to purify ourselves. The starting point is to confess our sins and trust in God to provide full forgiveness through what Christ did on the cross. Then we can ask God to expand our comprehension so that we might understand what God says about his amazing nature.

---

33. Weinandy, 29.

Avoiding Legalism

It is necessary for those seeking to know the truth about God to avoid legalism. By "legalism" is meant the *intransigent religiosity* possessed by those who presuppose their superiority to others, who boast in their adherence to all the details of the law, who think wrongly that they can earn paradise through their own efforts, who do not accept any thought other than their own, who reject any flexibility to hear, ask or give and take in discussions with fellow human beings, and who consider any who oppose them to be enemies.

Searching the Scriptures

Mind-and-heart preparedness to understand the riches of the doctrine of the Trinity demands searching the inspired Scriptures. It is not reasonable to expect to enter the things of God by settling for a cursory passing over of biblical verses. How dangerous it is for people to arrive at their conclusions on the basis of certain sayings of people in society without seriously searching the word of God that contains the riches of knowledge, especially about God!

Asking for Divine Help

Those who want to know the truth about God must ask for assistance from God. If the desire to know God is real, prayer for the fulfillment of this desire will be continual. Not only so, but since knowing God is his perfect will, as will be demonstrated later, a sincere seeker may expect that the Lord will answer this kind of prayer. The Bible declares,

> This is the confidence which we have before Him, that, *if we ask anything according to His will, He hears us.* And if we know that He hears us in whatever we ask, we know that we have the requests which we have asked from Him. (1 John 5:14–15)

Following the Example of the First Generation

Those who seek to know the doctrine of the Trinity can find encouragement in the first generation of Christians who were at the forefront of discovering the divine nature of Christ. They exhibited great humility in accepting what was revealed to them. The following are examples of these heroes of faith.

The Virgin Mary

The first example is the response of the Virgin Mary to the angel when he informed her that the Holy Spirit would overshadow her and that she would conceive the holy Son of God. Her response was one of acceptance and humility, in spite of the fact that society would consider her an adulteress for becoming pregnant outside of marriage:

> Behold, the bondslave of the Lord; *may it be done to me according*
> *to your word . . .*
> My soul exalts the Lord,
> And my spirit has rejoiced in God my Savior . . .
> He has done mighty deeds with His arm;
> He has scattered those who were proud in the thoughts of their
> heart.
> He has brought down rulers from their thrones,
> And has exalted those who were humble.
> He has filled the hungry with good things;
> And sent away the rich empty-handed. (Luke 1:38, 46–47, 51–53)

Elizabeth

In the same spirit of receptivity, Elizabeth, Mary's relative, responded by calling the child in Mary's womb her Lord, and commending Mary for accepting what was to happen to her in spite of the risk of society stigmatizing her and questioning her integrity:

> Now at this time Mary arose and went in a hurry to the hill
> country, to a city of Judah, and entered the house of Zacharias
> and greeted Elizabeth. When Elizabeth heard Mary's greeting, the
> baby leaped in her womb; and Elizabeth was filled with the Holy
> Spirit. And she cried out with a loud voice and said, "Blessed are
> you among women, and blessed is the fruit of your womb! And
> how has it happened to me, that the mother of my Lord would
> come to me? For behold, when the sound of your greeting reached
> my ears, the baby leaped in my womb for joy. And blessed is she
> who believed that there would be a fulfillment of what had been
> spoken to her by the Lord." (Luke 1:39–45)

Zechariah

With the same humble response, Zechariah, John the Baptist's father, declared that his son John had come to prepare the way for Christ, whom he called the *Anatole*, pointing to either the morning star or to the branch that was prophesied about (cf. Num 24:17; Isa 11:1–10; Jer 23:5; 33:15; Zech 3:8; 6:12). Zechariah declared,

> And you, child [John], will be called the prophet of the Most High;
> For you will go on before the Lord to prepare his ways;
> To give to His people the knowledge of salvation
> By the forgiveness of their sins,
> Because of the tender mercy of our God,
> With which the Sunrise [*Anatole*] from on high will visit us,
> To shine upon those who sit in darkness and the shadow of death,
> To guide our feet into the way of peace. (Luke 1:76–79)

Simeon

The first generation also included Simeon, who was a wonderful example in his response to the Holy Spirit, declaring that Christ was the salvation sent from God, a light to the Gentiles and the glory of Israel:

> And there was a man in Jerusalem whose name was Simeon; and this man was righteous and devout, looking for the consolation of Israel; and the Holy Spirit was upon him. And *it had been revealed to him by the Holy Spirit* that he would not see death before he had seen the Lord's Christ. And he came in the Spirit into the temple; and when the parents brought in the child Jesus, to carry out for Him the custom of the Law, then he took Him into his arms, and blessed God, and said,
>
> "Now Lord, You are releasing Your bond-servant to depart in peace,
> According to Your word;
> For *my eyes have seen Your salvation*,
> Which You have prepared in the presence of all peoples,
> *A light of revelation to the Gentiles*,
> *And the glory of Your people Israel*." (Luke 2:25–32)

Anna

In the same temple as Simeon was Anna the widow, who was advanced in years. She too accepted what was told to her about Christ, praising God and speaking of him to all:

> And there was a prophetess, Anna the daughter of Phanuel, of the tribe of Asher. She was advanced in years and had lived with her

husband seven years after her marriage, and then as a widow to the age of eighty-four. She never left the temple, serving night and day with fastings and prayers. At that very moment she came up and *began giving thanks to God, and continued to speak of Him to all those who were looking for the redemption of Jerusalem.* (Luke 2:36–38)

The Disciples

The Jews were the last people on earth to worship a human being. Yet the New Testament records that they worshipped the risen Christ in spite of the doubt they had had in the beginning. It usually takes at least one generation for such a shift in worldview to occur, but here it occurred almost overnight: "When they saw Him, *they worshiped Him*" (Matt 28:17a). After the day of Pentecost, when the Holy Spirit was poured out on them, their commitment to the deity and lordship of Christ became unshaken. Notice the words of Peter in his first sermon:

> Therefore let all the house of Israel know for certain that *God has made Him both Lord and Christ* – this Jesus whom you crucified. (Acts 2:36)

Later, upon healing the lame man, Peter rebuked the Jews, saying,

> [You] put to death *the Prince of life*, the one whom God raised from the dead, a fact to which we are witnesses . . . Therefore repent and return, so that your sins may be wiped away, in order that times of refreshing may come from the presence of the Lord; and that He may send Jesus, the Christ appointed for you, whom *heaven must receive until the period of restoration* of all things about which God spoke by the mouth of His holy prophets from ancient time. (Acts 3:15, 19–21)

The early believers also, as a result of the persecution they experienced, prayed,

> O Lord, it is You who made the heaven and the earth and the sea, and all that is in them, who by the Holy Spirit, through the mouth of our father David Your servant, said,
>
>> "Why did the Gentiles rage,
>> And the peoples devise futile things?
>> The kings of the earth took their stand,
>> And the rulers were gathered together
>> Against the Lord and against His Christ." (Acts 4:24b–26)

The radical change in the first generation is a testimony to the truth of what they believed in and their continual growth in the discovery of the truth about the nature of God.

12. Only by Accepting the True God Can There Be Life Transformation

If God were as people want him to be, he would not be able to make any impact on them because God would be of human creation. However, if people relate to God in God's own reality, as he is in himself, then God can have a strong impact on them. Only the true God can change humanity. Therefore, people must accept all that God has revealed about himself, and must also be ready for the consequent changes in their lives. The life-changing power of the triune God will be addressed later.

Conclusion

If there are no mind or heart obstacles preventing the acceptance of God's revelation of himself, people, upon their first reading of the Bible, though they do not expect to see the Trinity, find that it is not prohibited – indeed, that it is actually prepared for. They eventually discover that the Trinity is an inevitable necessity in the nature of God. They then grow to experience the life-changing power of the Trinity in their own lives, and increasingly see the magnificent beauty of the true God!

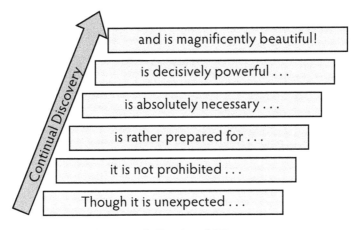

Figure 1.6: Continual Discovery

2

The Various Concepts of the Oneness of God

Introduction

This chapter presents the concepts of God in Absolute Oneness and in Oneness in Trinity and the differences between them. This prepares for the following chapter which presents the various ways of using the expression "God" which are found only in Oneness in Trinity.

God in Absolute Oneness

The concept "Absolute Oneness" refers to the belief in one necessary and sovereign creator God, without the existence of any other god or any secondary god, and without this oneness including any persons in relationship. The concept "Absolute Oneness" is not confined specifically to Islam, but is the general belief of a large portion of humanity. This is the general belief of most of humanity, and is also the conclusion of philosophy. Absolute Oneness may be explained as follows:

- God alone is the only necessary and sovereign creator God, with one essence or nature, without being composed of parts, and without the existence of any other god or any secondary god.

- The relationship of this sovereign God to his word is the relationship of his will to his power, which began to be revealed in creation.

- The word of God is a manifestation of his power.

- The word of God is the law that reveals to humanity the truth about the will of God.

- The role of the Holy Spirit is not known except by God.

- There is no eternal relationship between persons.

- The attributes of God spring from the power to fulfill his will.

- Only the will of God determines the activity of his other attributes.

- Only the will of God gives meaning to his attributes.

- Being without an eternal relationship, God called the universe into existence by his will.

- The first time God had a relationship was with creation after he created it.

- There is no work of the Holy Spirit in human beings.

God in Oneness in Trinity

The expression "Oneness in Trinity" is adopted in this book to refer to the Trinity. Other expressions used throughout history include "Triunity," "Inclusive and Exclusive Oneness," "Trinitarian Monotheism," or simply "Trinitarianism." All these expressions and other similar ones point to the same system of theology, with each expression contributing a certain emphasis.

The concept of Oneness in Trinity shares with Absolute Oneness the belief in one necessary and sovereign creator God, without the existence of any other god or any secondary god. Again, this is the general belief of most of humanity, and is also the conclusion of philosophy. But Oneness in Trinity differs in that it goes further by *believing that God revealed himself as existing in three equal but distinct persons in an unending relationship.* This is the nature of God eternally, that is, from eternity past to eternity future, outside of creation, with or without its presence. In this faith, God is one in a first sense and plural in a second sense. For he is one in the sense of essence or nature, without being composed of parts. But he is also three in the sense of persons. These persons are the Father, the Son and the Holy Spirit, whereby each of them is equally God, without separation or confusion, and each is distinct from the others. This has been the traditional way of expressing the Trinity and is represented in the following diagram:

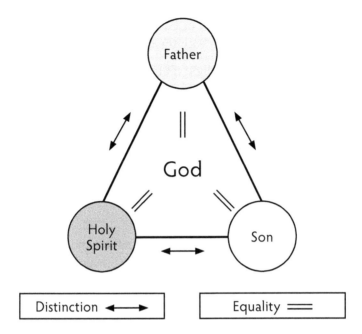

Figure 2.1: The Traditional Expression of the Trinity

The above expression stresses both the oneness of God and the diversity in this oneness in three distinct persons. However, in spite of the precision and truth of this expression, it does not explain the nature of the relationship between the Father, the Son and the Holy Spirit. The expression "Oneness in Trinity" was adopted in order to focus on the nucleus of this relationship, which will be studied in detail in the pages of this book, and may be described briefly as follows:

- God alone is the only necessary and sovereign creator God, with one essence or nature, without being composed of parts, and without the existence of any other god or any secondary god.

- This sovereign God also has a fatherly nature, not only as a father to humanity as their creator, but also an eternal fatherhood in himself, outside of creation and without it. For the relationship of this God to his word is the relationship of a Father to his Son, through whom he created the world.

- The word of God is above being only a manifestation of his power, for he is the person of the Son of God in whom is all of life.

- The word of God is the Son of God and the light that enlightens everyone who receives him with the truth about the nature of God.

- All the attributes of life and light are revealed through the Holy Spirit, who is the Spirit of the Father and the Spirit of the Son.

- The relationship of the Father and the Son is the only eternal relationship in existence, is superior to any other relationship in the universe, and is above human comprehension.

- The attributes of God spring from the relationship between the Father and the Son through their Holy Spirit, and are in ultimate perfection and complete harmony.

- The Holy Spirit reveals the attributes that are active between the Father and the Son, and as a person, unites them in real unity that secures their eternal perfection.

- The oneness of the Father, Son and Holy Spirit is never divided and is not composed of parts.

- The Father, Son and Holy Spirit have special roles that give real meaning to the attributes of God.

- The richness of the relationship between the Father and the Son in the Holy Spirit overflowed into calling the universe into existence.

- The richness of the relationship between the Father and the Son in the Holy Spirit overflowed also into a relationship with creation manifested in the incarnation in the likeness of man with the goal of the redemption of humanity.

- The Holy Spirit himself, who is active between the Father and the Son, becomes active with humanity to bring them into a relationship with the Father and the Son.

The Differences between Oneness in Trinity and Absolute Oneness

In order to clarify the concepts further, the following table presents the difference between Oneness in Trinity and Absolute Oneness, noting that many of the concepts expressed will be delineated in detail in the rest of the book.

Table 2.2: The Differences between Oneness in Trinity and Absolute Oneness

Oneness in Trinity	Absolute Oneness
Sovereign and Father	Sovereign
The relationship of God to his word is the relationship of a Father to his Son.	The relationship of God to his word is the relationship of his will to his power.
The word of God is above being only a manifestation of his power to being the person of the Son of God in whom is all of life.	The word of God is a manifestation of his power.
The word of God is the Son of God and the light that enlightens everyone who receives him with the truth about the *nature* of God.	The word of God is the law that reveals to humanity the truth about the *will* of God.
All the attributes of life and light are revealed through the Holy Spirit, who is the Spirit of the Father and the Spirit of the Son.	The role of the Holy Spirit is not known except by God.
The relationship of the Father and the Son is the only eternal relationship in existence.	There is no eternal relationship between persons.
The attributes of God spring from the relationship between the Father and the Son through their Holy Spirit.	The attributes of God spring from the power to fulfill his will.
The Holy Spirit as a person *unites* the attributes active between the Father and the Son in real unity that secures their eternal perfection.	Only the will of God *determines* the activity of his other attributes.
The oneness of the Father, Son and Holy Spirit is never divided and is not composed of parts.	The oneness of God is never divided, and is not composed of parts.
The special roles of the Father, Son and Holy Spirit give meaning to the attributes of God.	Only the will of God gives meaning to his attributes.

The richness of the relationship between the Father and the Son in the Holy Spirit overflowed into calling the universe into existence.	Being without an eternal relationship, the will of God called the universe into existence.
The richness of the relationship between the Father and the Son in the Holy Spirit overflowed also into a relationship with creation manifested in the incarnation with the goal of redemption.	The first time God had a relationship was with creation after he created it.
The Holy Spirit himself becomes active with humanity to bring them into a relationship with the Father and the Son.	There is no work of the Holy Spirit in human beings.

3

The Various Uses of the Expression "God"

Introduction

This study now presents the various ways of using the expression "God," which are found only in Oneness in Trinity. The Bible reveals that there are three distinct ways for using "God." Realizing this protects from confusion and misunderstanding.

"God" Pointing to the One and Only God

The first use of "God" is to identify him as the Creator and the only necessary and eternal being, excluding the presence of any other like him. Everything else that exists was created by him and is dependent on him for remaining in existence.[1] Abundant verses in both the New and the Old Testaments are clear and insistent that there is only one true God.

1. The Testimony of the Old Testament about the Only God

The following are sample verses from the Old Testament that speak of God as the one and only God:

---

1. Several words are used to translate the title "God" in the Hebrew Old Testament: אֱלֹהִים (Elohim); אֵל (El); אֱלוֹהַּ (Eloah); אֱלָהּ (Elah). It is also translated in the Aramaic portions of the Old Testament: אֱלָהָא (Elaha). It is translated in the Greek New Testament θεός (Theos). The use of the names אֶהְיֶה (ehyeh) and יְהוָה (yahweh) and their adoption in the NT will be examined in Volume 2, in the chapter "The Activity of the Attributes of God Inside Creation."

[Moses the prophet wrote:] In the beginning God created the heavens and the earth. (Gen 1:1)

[Moses the prophet wrote:] You shall have no other gods before Me. (Exod 20:3)

[Moses the prophet wrote:] To you it was shown that you might know that the Lord, *He is God; there is no other besides Him.* (Deut 4:35)

[Moses the prophet wrote of the Lord speaking:] See now that I, I am He, and *there is no god besides Me.* (Deut 32:39a)

[Moses the prophet wrote:] Hear, O Israel! The Lord is our God, *the Lord is one!* (Deut 6:4)

[David wrote:] The heavens are telling of the glory of God; and their expanse is declaring the work of His hands. (Ps 19:1)

[Solomon wrote:] The conclusion, when all has been heard, is: fear God and keep His commandments, because this applies to every person. (Eccl 12:13)

[Isaiah the prophet wrote of God speaking:] They will make supplication to you [Israel]: "Surely, God is with you, and there is *none else, no other God.*" (Isa 45:14b)

[Isaiah the prophet wrote of God speaking:] *I am God, and there is no other; I am God, and there is no one like Me.* (Isa 46:9b)

2. The Testimony of the New Testament about the Only God

The following are sample verses from the New Testament that speak of God as the one and only God:

Jesus answered, "The foremost [commandment] is, 'Hear O Israel! *The Lord our God is one Lord;* and you shall love the Lord your God with all your heart, and with all your soul, and with all your mind, and with all your strength.'" . . . The scribe said to Him, "Right, Teacher; You have truly stated that He is One, and there is no one else besides Him." (Mark 12:29–30, 32)

Jesus spoke these things . . . "This is eternal life, that they may know You, the only true God, and Jesus Christ whom You have sent." (John 17:1, 3)

[Luke wrote about the apostle Paul's words:] The God who made the world and all things in it, since He is Lord of heaven and earth, does not dwell in temples made with hands; nor is He served by human hands, as though He needed anything, since *He Himself gives to all people* life and breath and all things; and He made from one man every nation of mankind to live on all the face of the earth, having determined their appointed times and the boundaries of their habitation, that they would seek God, if perhaps they might grope for Him and find Him, though *He is not far* from each one of us. (Acts 17:24–27)

[The apostle Paul wrote:] For the *wrath of God is revealed* from heaven against all ungodliness and unrighteousness of men who suppress the truth in unrighteousness, because that which is known about God is evident within them; for *God made it evident* to them. For since the creation of the world His invisible attributes, His eternal power and divine nature, have been clearly seen, being understood through what has been made, so that they are without excuse. (Rom 1:18–20)

[The apostle Paul wrote:] We know that there is no such thing as an idol in the world, and that *there is no God but one . . .* For us there is but one God, the Father, from whom are all things and we exist for Him; and one Lord, Jesus Christ, by whom are all things, and we exist through Him. (1 Cor 8:4b, 6).

[The apostle Paul wrote:] . . . being diligent to preserve the *unity of the Spirit* in the bond of peace. There is one body and *one Spirit,* just as also you were called in one hope of your calling; *one Lord,* one faith, one baptism, *one God and Father* of all who is over all and through all and in all. (Eph 4:3–6)

[The apostle James wrote:] You believe that *God is one.* You do well. (Jas 2:19a)

3. Appearance of the Only God in the Old Testament in Special Form

Both Testaments of the Bible add another dimension to the use of the expression "God" that introduces the only God in a more specific way. The Old Testament reveals special appearances of God in the form of an angel, a man or another being. One of these amazing appearances was to Moses when God permitted him to see a glimpse of his glory:

Then the LORD said, "Behold, there is a place by Me, and you shall stand there on the rock; and it will come about, while My glory is passing by, that I will put you in the cleft of the rock and cover you with My hand until I have passed by. Then I will take My hand away and *you shall see My back*, but My face shall not be seen."

The LORD descended in the cloud and stood there with him [Moses] as he called upon the name of the LORD. Then the LORD passed by in front of him . . . *Moses made haste to bow low toward the earth and worship* . . . "It is a fearful thing that I am going to perform with you . . ."

It came about when Moses was coming down from Mount Sinai . . . that Moses did not know that the skin of his face shone because of his speaking with Him. So when Aaron and all the sons of Israel saw Moses, behold, the skin of his face shone, and *they were afraid to come near him*. (Exod 33:21–23; 34:5–6, 8, 10, 29–30)

The word "back" refers to a glimpse of something, or to the last part of it, as opposed to seeing the whole thing.[2] This view of God affected Moses so powerfully that he bowed to the ground and worshipped. God described what he was about to do as "fearful." As a result of Moses's encounter with God, the skin of his face shone, causing the people to be afraid.

Many years before Moses's experience, the same thing happened to Hagar, when the Lord appeared to her as an angel, identified later as the Lord himself. From this astonishing meeting with God, she called the God who spoke to her "the one who sees":

Then she called the name of the LORD who spoke to her, "You are a God who sees"; for she said, "Have I here seen the back of Him who sees me?" Therefore the well was called Beer-lahai-roi. (Gen 16:13–14, personal translation)

In the form of a rhetorical question expecting a positive answer, Hagar declares that at that place she was given the privilege to see the back of the One who paid attention to her.[3] She was shown exactly what Moses saw, that is, the "back" of

---

2. The word for "back" in the genitive construction is אַחֲרָי (*acharaih*), and it is used here to refer to "the hind side, back part" (*BDB*, "אָחוֹר").

3. Wellhausen proposes that the verse from הֲגַם (*hagam*) should be amended to mean "Did I see God yet remain alive?" This reading is unlikely, for two reasons. First, it involves too many changes in the MT. Second, it betrays the context, which stresses the fact that God sees the affliction of his people and condescends to comfort them, as he did with Hagar. Cf.

God![4] Hagar expressed her gratitude to the Lord by using a word twice in two different grammatical paintings. The first time she called the Lord who spoke to her "you are the one *who sees*" in general (Gen 16:13), while the second time she called the well where she met him "the well of him *who sees me*" (16:14).[5]

In the same way, the Lord appeared to Jacob in the form of a man who wrestled with him. After this experience, Jacob called the name of the place "Peniel," meaning "the face of God."[6]

> So Jacob named the place Peniel, for he said, "I have seen God face
> to face, yet my life has been preserved." (Gen 32:30)

> In these examples, the appearance of God was intermittent and unexpected. In addition to these appearances, there is repeated mention of God's attributes and promises. They all communicated God's desire to reveal deeper truths about his nature one day.

More examples of the appearances of God, his attributes and his promises will be covered in Volume 2 in the chapter entitled "The Difference between Old Testament Oneness and Absolute Oneness."

4. NT Expressions of the Appearance of God in Special Form

The New Testament speaks of God in the same way as the Old Testament. However, it adds a revelation of God's penetration of creation to complement the appearances of the Old Testament as well as to vindicate his attributes and fulfill his promises. Thus, the appearances that were intermittent became a

---

Speiser, *Genesis*, 118–119; T. Booij, "Hagar's Words in Genesis 16:13b," *Vetus Testamentum* 30 (1980): 1–7.

4. There are four possible meanings for the MT reading אַחֲרֵי (16:13) often translated as "after." First, it could be used as an adverb, either of place or of time. Second, it could be used as a preposition of place or of time. Neither of these two uses seems to fit the context. The third use is to take the word to mean "another." This fits the context well, with a negative answer expected to the question, "Have I here seen another who sees me?" However, because of the clear use of the same word in the Lord's communication to Moses in Exod 33:23, the most likely option for the word is to take it as a substantive meaning "hind part," or "back." It seems that Hagar was awarded the same honor that Moses was given!

5. There is a change from the participle רָאִי (*rai*) meaning "the one who sees" to the proper name רֹאִי (*roi*) with the personal pronoun meaning "the one who sees me." There is no valid reason to adopt the reading of either the Samaritan Pentateuch or the Septuagint.

6. "The face of God" (Freedman, *Anchor Bible Dictionary*, s.v. "פְּנוּאֵל").

permanent presence, and what they pointed to became promises fulfilled. This took place climactically through the incarnation and redemption in Christ.

However, it is important to note that, although the New Testament explains in detail how the incarnation and redemption were accomplished through the new revelation of the Father, Son and Holy Spirit, it nevertheless includes many expressions that point to the incarnation and redemption as being the work of God without emphasizing the work of the Son or the Holy Spirit, and often without directly mentioning them.

Using the same expression "God" of the only God like whom there is no other, and in a startling way, the New Testament points to God's involvement in the human condition, the revelation of the gospel of God for the joy of humanity, the salvation of God for all peoples, the appearance of God in the flesh, the work of the grace and mercy of God, the manifestation of the righteousness of God, the hope of the fulfillment of the word of God, the ownership of the universal church of God and the work of the local churches of God, all *without immediate explanation of how these works of God came to be.* The following are sample verses:

- *God's Involvement in the Human Condition:*

  "Behold, the virgin shall be with child and shall bear a Son, and they shall call His name Immanuel," which translated means, "God with us." (Matt 1:23)

  What then shall we say to these things? If God is for us, who is against us? (Rom 8:31)

- *The Gospel of God for the Joy of Humanity:*

  I preached the gospel of God to you without charge. (2 Cor 11:7b)

  We had the boldness in our God to speak to you the gospel of God amid much opposition . . . Having so fond an affection for you, we were well-pleased to impart to you not only the gospel of God but also our own lives, because you had become very dear to us. For you recall, brethren, our labor and hardship, how working night and day so as not to be a burden to any of you, we proclaimed to you the gospel of God. (1 Thess 2:2b, 8–9)

  . . . according to the glorious gospel of the blessed God, with which I have been entrusted. (1 Tim 1:11)

For it is time for judgment to begin with the household of God; and if it begins with us first, what will be the outcome for those who do not obey the gospel of God? (1 Pet 4:17)

In the days of the voice of the seventh angel, when he is about to sound, then the mystery of God is finished, as He preached [proclaimed the gospel] to His servants the prophets. (Rev 10:7)

- *The Salvation of God for All Peoples:*

Glory to God in the highest, and on earth peace among men with whom He is pleased. (Luke 2:14)

Therefore let it be known to you that this salvation of God has been sent to the Gentiles; they will also listen. (Acts 28:28)

. . . in the hope of eternal life, which God, who cannot lie, promised long ages ago, but at the proper time manifested, even His word, in the proclamation with which I was entrusted according to the commandment of God our Savior. (Titus 1:2–3)

. . . the kindness of God our Savior and His love for mankind appeared. (Titus 3:4b)

- *The Appearance of God in the Flesh:*

By common confession, great is the mystery of godliness: He [God] who was revealed in the flesh, was vindicated in the Spirit, seen by angels, proclaimed among the nations, believed on in the world, taken up in glory. (1 Tim 3:16)[7]

---

7. The reading of the Byzantine text of 1 Tim 3:16, along with a few other witnesses, is θεός rather than ὅς. However, the relative pronoun ὅς has earlier and stronger support. "Externally, there is no question as to what should be considered original: The Alexandrian and Western traditions are decidedly in favor of ὅς. Internally, the evidence is even stronger. What scribe would change θεός to ὅς intentionally?" (NET Bible notes). The NET Bible also argues against looking for an antecedent for ὅς, as is commonly done, because, beginning with ὅς, the verse "appears to form a six-strophed hymn. As such, it is a text that is seemingly incorporated into the letter without syntactical connection." Nevertheless, the relative pronoun must point to a referent, and the immediate prior context clearly refers to God: "the household of God" and "the church of the living God." Thus the passage intends to point to Christ as God appearing in the flesh. This is why some scribes added the word "God" in the transcription of some manuscripts.

- *The Work of God's Grace and Mercy:*

  And now I commend you to God and to the word of His grace, which is able to build you up and to give you the inheritance among all those who are sanctified. (Acts 20:32)

  What if God, although willing to demonstrate His wrath and to make His power known, endured with much patience vessels of wrath prepared for destruction? And He did so to make known the riches of His glory upon vessels of mercy, which He prepared beforehand for glory, even us, whom He also called, not from among Jews only, but also from among Gentiles. (Rom 9:22–24)

  [After the teaching on justification and regeneration:] For God has shut up all in disobedience so that He may show mercy to all. Oh, the depth of the riches both of the wisdom and knowledge of God! How unsearchable are His judgments and unfathomable His ways! (Rom 11:32–33)

  For the grace of God has appeared, bringing salvation to all men. (Titus 2:11)

  This is the true grace of God. Stand firm in it! (1 Pet 5:12b)

- *The Manifestation of the Righteousness of God:*

  But now apart from the Law the righteousness of God has been manifested, being witnessed by the Law and the Prophets. (Rom 3:21)

  Indeed God who will justify the circumcised by faith and the uncircumcised through faith is one. (Rom 3:30)

- *The Hope of the Fulfillment of the Word of God:*

  And now I am standing trial for the hope of the promise made by God to our fathers. (Acts 26:6)

  . . . the hope laid up for you in heaven, of which you previously heard in the word of truth, the gospel which has come to you, just as in all the world also it is constantly bearing fruit and increasing, even as it has been doing in you also since the day you heard of it and understood the grace of God in truth. (Col 1:5–6)

For this reason we also constantly thank God that when you received the word of God which you heard from us, you accepted it not as the word of men, but for what it really is, the word of God, which also performs its work in you who believe. (1 Thess 2:13)

For it is for this we labor and strive, because we have fixed our hope on the living God, who is the Savior of all men, especially of believers. (1 Tim 4:10)

- *Ownership of the Universal Church of God:*

  It is purchased by his blood: Be on guard for yourselves and for all the flock, among which the Holy Spirit has made you overseers, to shepherd the church of *God* which He purchased with His own blood. (Acts 20:28)

Acts 20:28 makes a strong declaration about the blood used in purchasing the church.[8] The translation "with his own blood" appears in the major English translations.[9] However, it is possible to translate the last part of the verse in various other ways.

1. The first possible translation is "The church of God [i.e. of Jesus, referring to him as "God"; see the study later in this chapter about calling Jesus "God"]. However, Murray Harris observes that, when describing the redemptive work of Christ, the NT does not mix descriptions of deity with words pertaining to what is human (like blood).[10] This is why there are no expressions like "the cross of God"

---

8. The phrase τὴν ἐκκλησίαν τοῦ θεοῦ, ἣν περιεποιήσατο διὰ τοῦ αἵματος τοῦ ἰδίου (*tane eklessia tu theou, hane perepoiesato dia tu haimatos tu idieu*) is considered here to be the correct reading. For further information, see Metzger, *Textual Commentary on the Greek New Testament*, 425; and NET Bible notes on Acts 20:28.

9. The translation "with his own blood" appears in the New American Standard Bible (NASB), the New International Version (NIV), the New King James Version (NKJV), the English Standard Version (ESV), the Holman Christian Standard Bible (HCSB), Young's Literal Translation (YLTG), the American Standard Version (ASV) and the New Living Translation (NLT).

10. Harris observes, "New Testament descriptions of Christ's redemptive death as well as of his life always avoid blending unqualified affirmations of deity (such as θεός) with terms that can be related only to his humanness (such as αἷμα)" (Harris, *Jesus as God*, 137).

(rather, "the cross of Jesus," as in John 19:25; Gal 6:14), "they crucified God" (rather, "they crucified Jesus," as in John 19:18) or "God died" (rather, "Jesus died," as in 1 Thess 4:14).[11]

2. The second possible translation is "The church of God [the Father] which Jesus [as the subject of the verb] purchased with his blood." However, changing the subject from "the Father" to "Jesus" is a presupposition without strong evidence.

3. The third possible translation is "The church of God [the Father] which he purchased with the blood of his own [i.e. Jesus]."[12] Accordingly, the expression "his own" is understood as a title for Christ, and points to his uniqueness, as does the title "one and only" or "only begotten." It would then be parallel to "the righteous one," "the beloved one" and "the chosen one."[13] However, the weakness of this translation is that the expression "his own" is not in the masculine gender but in the neuter, modifying the expression "his blood," which is also in the neuter.[14] Furthermore, the New Testament never points to Christ using "his own" as a title. The expression in its various forms is rather a general expression used in various ways. It appears 114 times in the NT, of which sixteen are in the book of Acts, pointing to what a person owns or is special to him or her, including authority, language, place, power, people, things, generation, time, wife, religion or home.[15]

4. The fourth possible translation is "The church of God [the one and only God] which he purchased with his own blood." This translation, in its simplicity, mysteriousness and beauty, is most likely the correct translation. It declares the amazing work of the one and only true

---

11. Harris, 137.

12. The New English Translation (NET) adds the specification "the blood of his own Son."

13. The expression "his own" in the original is the genitive τοῦ ἰδίου (*tu idieu*) and the nominative ὁ ἴδιος (*ho idios*). The expression "one and only" or "only begotten" is μονογενής (*monogenase*; John 1:14, 18; 3:16, 18; 1 John 4:9). The expression "the righteous one" is ὁ δίκαιος (*ho dikaios*; Acts 3:14; 7:52; 22:14). The expression "the beloved one" is ὁ ἀγαπητός (*ho agapatos*; Matt 3:17; 12:18; 17:5; 2 Pet 1:17). The expression "the chosen one" is ὁ ἐκλεκτός (*ho eklektos*; Luke 23:35).

14. The neuter τοῦ ἰδίου (*tu idieu*) modifies the neuter τοῦ αἵματος (*tu haimatos*).

15. Acts 1:7, 19, 25; 2:6, 8; 3:12; 4:23, 32; 13:36; 21:6; 23:19; 24:23–24; 25:19; 28:30.

God through blood that was special to him and owned by him.[16] This parallels what was mentioned earlier in this chapter about the occasional NT pattern of referring to the incarnation and redemption as being the work of God without direct mention of the work of the Son or the Holy Spirit. So the one and only God is described with reference to his involvement in the human condition, his gospel for humanity, his salvation for all peoples, his appearance in the flesh, his church on earth, his blood as a price of purchase, and so on, and all this without direct explanation of how this was done.

So God chose one blood with which to purchase his church, blood that is superior to any other blood, whether of a human being or of other creatures. This special blood, owned by the one and only God, is the same special blood owned by the Son, as expressed in the parallel verse in the letter to the Hebrews: "and not through the blood of goats and calves, but through His own blood, He entered the holy place once for all, having obtained eternal redemption" (Heb 9:12).[17]

On this basis, Paul's exhortation to the church elders was to remind them of the privilege they had received from the Holy Spirit to shepherd the church. It was the same God of the OT who purchased this church through special blood owned by him according to a plan special to him, which his Son executed by becoming flesh in order to die. So it is "the church of God which he purchased with his own blood."[18]

---

16. The meaning of special ownership or importance has the support of key lexicons: "pertaining to being the exclusive property of someone" (Louw & Nida, s.v. ἴδιος; cf. Thayer, *Greek–English Lexicon of the New Testament*); "pert. to belonging or being related to oneself, one's own" (BDAG, s.v. ἴδιος).

17. The expression τοῦ ἰδίου αἵματος (*tu idieu haimatos*) of Heb 9:12 is rendered "his own blood" by all the translations mentioned above for Acts 20:28, i.e. New American Standard Bible (NASB), the New International Version (NIV), the New King James Version (NKJV), the English Standard Version (ESV), the Holman Christian Standard Bible (HCSB), Young's Literal Translation (YLT), the American Standard Version (ASV), the New Living Translation (NLT) and even by the New English Translation (NET).

18. For further discussion of various other views, see Harris, *Jesus as God*, 131–141.

It is centralized locally: To the church of God which is at
Corinth . . . in every place. (1 Cor 1:2; cf. 2 Cor 1:1)

There is a responsibility to care for it and not cause offense: If
a man does not know how to manage his own household,
how will he take care of the church of God? (1 Tim 3:5)

Give no offense . . . to the church of God. (1 Cor 10:32)

It can be persecuted: For I am the least of the apostles, and
not fit to be called an apostle, because I persecuted the
church of God. (1 Cor 15:9; cf. Gal 1:13)

It is the house of God where the truth is: . . . so that you will
know how one ought to conduct himself in the household
of God, which is the church of the living God, the pillar
and support of the truth. (1 Tim 3:15)

- *The Work of the Local Churches of God:*

  Contentiousness must be avoided in it: But if one is inclined
  to be contentious, we have no other practice, nor have the
  churches of God. (1 Cor 11:16)

  It can experience persecutions and afflictions: Therefore,
  we ourselves speak proudly of you among the churches
  of God for your perseverance and faith in the midst of
  all your persecutions and afflictions which you endure.
  (2 Thess 1:4)

- *The Sovereignty of God:*

  The last enemy that will be abolished is death. For He [i.e.
  God the Father] has put all things in subjection under His
  [i.e. the Son's] feet. But when He says, "All things are put
  in subjection," it is evident that He is excepted who put all
  things in subjection to Him. When all things are subjected
  to Him, then the Son Himself also will be subjected to the
  One who subjected all things to Him, so that God may
  be all in all. (1 Cor 15:26–28)

  And I saw the holy city, new Jerusalem, coming down out
  of heaven from God, made ready as a bride adorned for
  her husband. And I heard a loud voice from the throne,

saying, "Behold, the tabernacle of God is among men, and He will dwell among them, and they shall be His people, and God Himself will be among them." (Rev 21:2–3; cf. Rev 21:10–11; 22:18–19)

> In all the examples above from the Old and New Testaments, the Bible declares that the one and only God penetrates creation in a specific way and in a specific time and place. This he accomplishes in his gospel, his salvation, his appearance in the flesh, his grace, his mercy, his manifestation of righteousness, his fulfillment of his word, and for the benefit of his church. All this was fulfilled through the work of the Father, Son and Holy Spirit that is hidden latently in some texts of the Bible, but is revealed clearly in other texts. All of this is for the glory of the one and only true God in his beautiful nature.

On this basis, the Christian believer in Oneness in Trinity may use "God" to state the following: "God *created me*, then God became a human being *like me*. God took my place by bearing the penalty of my sins through his death on the cross, and he rose from the dead victoriously. He then gave me new life and now he *lives in me*."

> Adherents of Absolute Oneness may wish to experience what adherents of Oneness in Trinity experience, but they unfortunately want to stay within the confines of rigid monotheism. But when we ask how these rich experiences of Oneness in Trinity are possible, the New Testament answers by declaring a second use for "God" as signifying the Father.

"God" Pointing to the Father

The New Testament declares that the reason for the appearances and works of God for the salvation of humanity is that he exists eternally as a Father in an eternal relationship with his only eternal and uncreated Son through the Holy Spirit. So the second use of "God" is identify him as the Father.

The closest reference in the Old Testament to God as Father to a Son is the prefiguring of Christ in the Davidic king:

> When your days are complete and you lie down with your fathers,
> I will raise up your descendant after you, who will come forth from

you, and I will establish his kingdom. He shall build a house for My name, and I will establish the throne of his kingdom forever. I will be a father to him and he will be a son to Me. (2 Sam 7:12–14a)

I will surely tell of the decree of the LORD:
He said to Me, "You are My Son,
Today I have begotten You." (Ps 2:7)

He will cry to Me, "You are my Father,
My God, and the rock of my salvation." (Ps 89:26)

But most of the uses of "God" to signify Father in the Old Testament are in reference to his *fatherhood in relation to creation*, in three primary ways: (1) as a father to *angels* (Gen 6:2; Job 1:6; 2:1; 38:7; Pss 29:1; 89:6); (2) as a father to the nation *Israel* (Exod 4:22; Deut 32:6, 18, 20; 1 Chr 29:10; Isa 63:16; 64:8; Jer 3:19; 31:9; Hos 11:1; Mal 1:6; 2:10); (3) as a father to *orphans* (Ps 68:5).

The revelation of the use of the expression "God" to refer to the Father comes in the New Testament and in most of the times that "God" is used. There are several important considerations here.

1. The Same OT God

The dominant use of "God" in the New Testament to refer to the Father indicates that he is the *same one and only God of the Old Testament*. Everything revealed in the New Testament remains firmly under this overarching principle.

2. God Has a Son

The use of "God" to refer to the Father reveals that *the one and only God is an eternal Father with an eternal and uncreated Son*. This fatherhood of God is different from his fatherhood of people as their creator. It is rather an eternal fatherhood. In addition, the use of the expression "God" to refer to the Father does not necessarily require mentioning "the Father" each time. So when it is said that *God* sent his Son, the meaning becomes that *the Father* sent his Son. And when "God" is mentioned without definition, the Father is signified, as in the following examples:

For God so loved the world that he gave his one and only [or "only begotten"] Son. (John 3:16a, NIV)

For us there is *one God, the Father*, from whom are all things and we exist for Him; *and one Lord, Jesus Christ*, by whom are all things, and we exist through Him. (1 Cor 8:6)

The grace of the Lord Jesus Christ, and the *love of God*, and the fellowship of the Holy Spirit, be with you all. (2 Cor 13:14)

The *God of our Lord Jesus Christ*, the Father of glory . . . (Eph 1:17a)

Through Him we both have our access in *one Spirit to the Father*. (Eph 2:18)

There is one body and *one Spirit*, just as also you were called in one hope of your calling; *one Lord*, one faith, one baptism, *one God and Father* of all who is over all and through all and in all. (Eph 4:4–6)

May our *Lord Jesus Christ Himself* and *God our Father*, who has loved us and given us eternal comfort and good hope by grace . . . (2 Thess 2:16)

[Christ's reference to the Father:] *My God, My God* . . . (Matt 27:46b; Mark 15:34)

[Christ's reference to the Father:] I ascend to *My Father* and your Father, and *My God* and your God. (John 20:17)

Blessed be the *God and Father of our Lord Jesus Christ*. (1 Pet 1:3a)

[In what was said about Christ:] *God, Your God*, has anointed You with the oil of gladness above Your companions. (Heb 1:9b)

[In what was said about Christ:] He has made us to be a kingdom, priests to *His God and Father*. (Rev 1:6a)

3. The Only Eternal Relationship

The New Testament also reveals that the use of "God" to signify the Father means there is a relationship between the Father and his Son, and that this relationship is the only eternal relationship in existence, is superior to any other relationship in the universe and is above human comprehension. There are a couple of considerations in this regard:

1. The title "one and only" (or "only begotten") used to refer to the Son confirms that the eternal relationship between the Father and the

Son is the only one in existence through their Holy Spirit.[19] This title occurs five times (John 1:14, 18; 3:16, 18; 1 John 4:9). There is no other person in existence who has this relationship with the Father.

2. The Bible declares that glory springs from this one and only eternal relationship between the Father and the Son:

> We saw his glory, glory as of the one and only [or "only begotten"] to the Father, full of grace and truth. (John 1:14b, personal translation)[20]

This glory is not found in any relationship except the one between the Father and the Son. Christ described this glory when he addressed his Father, saying,

> . . . the glory which I had with You before the world was. (John 17:5b)

What is amazing is that the Old Testament records that Ezekiel witnessed this same glory when he saw what resembled a throne over the heads of the cherubim, and on the throne the figure of the appearance of a man. He mentions the glory of the Lord sixteen times in his book.[21] Ezekiel writes about the glory of this man:

> Now above the expanse that was over their [the four living creatures'] heads there was something resembling a throne, like lapis lazuli in appearance; and on that which resembled a throne, high up, was *a figure with the appearance of a man* . . . Such was the *appearance of the likeness of the glory of the LORD*. And when I saw it, I fell on my face and heard a voice speaking. (Ezek 1:26, 28b)

The above texts and others related to the glory of the relationship between the Father and the Son will be examined in more detail in Volume 2 in the chapter entitled "The Activity of the Attributes of God Outside Creation."

---

19. The meaning of the title μονογενής (*monogenase*) will be examined when John 1 is studied in Volume 2 in the chapter entitled "The Activity of the Attributes of God Outside Creation."

20. Again, this verse will be studied later in more detail in the chapter in Volume 2 entitled "The Activity of the Attributes of God Outside Creation."

21. The glory of the Lord is mentioned in the book of Ezekiel in 1:28; 3:12, 23; 8:4; 9:3; 10:4, 18–19; 11:22–23; 39:21; 43:2 [twice], 4–5; 44:4.

4. The Role of the Holy Spirit

All the attributes of perfection are related to the Holy Spirit, who is the Spirit of the Father and the Spirit of the Son. So all that takes place between the Father and the Son is related to the Holy Spirit. This means that when the relationship between the Father and the Son is described without mention of the Holy Spirit, the context is richly filled with the divine attributes which are exchanged between the Father and the Son and which overflow into creation. For *the Holy Spirit is present in the activity of these attributes.*[22]

> So, while the Bible declares that the relationship between the Father and the Son is the only eternal relationship in existence, it also declares that the person of the Holy Spirit, who is the Spirit of the Father and the Spirit of the Son, reveals the beauty and perfection of this eternal relationship through his dynamic presence in the activity of the attributes between the Father and the Son.

Therefore, the use of "God" to refer to the Father was a revelation of the Son, which in turn became a revelation of the relationship between the Father and the Son. This then also became a revelation of the activity of the attributes between them through the Holy Spirit. Taken together, this is the revelation of three persons in the one being of God. Thus the revelation of the Father is a revelation of the Trinity!

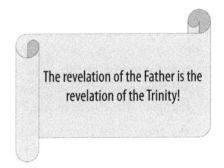

The revelation of the Father is the revelation of the Trinity!

5. The Repeated Mention of the Persons of the Trinity

The three persons of the Trinity are repeatedly mentioned in the New Testament. This fact draws those with a pure heart to seek more knowledge and understanding, which in turn leads to deeper worship.

---

22. The relationship between the Father and the Son through their Spirit will be covered in detail in the chapters in Volume 2 dealing with the significance of the names "Father," "Son" and "Holy Spirit."

> The astonishing fact is that there are about 120 New Testament passages in which the persons of the Trinity are mentioned together in simplicity, without defense, without explanation and without apology! Why? Because it is *a beauty beyond description!*

Below are a few examples of the mention of the Father, Son and Holy Spirit in the same passage. Each person is referred to by name, or by other titles or attributes, as indicated by *the emphasis* (for a longer list of such verses, see appendix 1):

The angel answered and said to her, "The *Holy Spirit* will come upon you, and the power of *the Most High* will overshadow you; and for that reason *the holy Child* shall be called the *Son of God*." (Luke 1:35)

And *the Holy Spirit* descended upon *Him* in bodily form like a dove, and a voice came out of heaven, "*You* are *My beloved Son*, in You *I am* well-pleased." (Luke 3:22)

But *the Helper*, *the Holy Spirit*, whom *the Father* will send in *My* name, *He* will teach you all things, and bring to your remembrance all that *I* said to you. (John 14:26)

However, you are not in the flesh but in *the Spirit*, if indeed *the Spirit of God* dwells in you. But if anyone does not have *the Spirit of Christ*, he does not belong to *Him* . . . But if *the Spirit of Him* who raised *Jesus* from the dead dwells in you, *He* who raised *Christ Jesus* from the dead will also give life to your mortal bodies through *His Spirit* who dwells in you. (Rom 8:9, 11)

The grace of *the Lord Jesus Christ*, and the love of *God*, and the fellowship of *the Holy Spirit*, be with you all. (2 Cor 13:14)

But when the fullness of the time came, *God* sent forth *His Son*, born of a woman, born under the Law, so that He might redeem those who were under the Law, that we might receive the adoption as sons. Because you are sons, *God* has sent forth *the Spirit* of *His* Son into our hearts, crying, "Abba! *Father!*" Therefore you are no longer a slave, but a son; and if a son, then an heir through *God*. (Gal 4:4–7)

There is one body and one *Spirit*, just as also you were called in one hope of your calling; one *Lord*, one faith, one baptism, one *God and Father* of all who is over all and through all and in all. (Eph 4:4–6)

. . . how much more will the blood of *Christ*, who through the *eternal Spirit* offered Himself without blemish to *God*, cleanse your conscience from dead works to serve the living *God*? (Heb 9:14)

. . . according to the foreknowledge of *God the Father*, by the sanctifying work of *the Spirit*, to obey *Jesus Christ* and be sprinkled with His blood: May grace and peace be yours in the fullest measure. (1 Pet 1:2)

But you, beloved, building yourselves up on your most holy faith, praying in the *Holy Spirit*, keep yourselves in the love of *God*, waiting anxiously for the mercy of our *Lord Jesus Christ* to eternal life. (Jude 20–21)

6. Mention of the Three Persons with Oneness

The above mentions of the three persons of the Trinity were without direct reference to the oneness of God. The reason for this is that the oneness of God is always presupposed as the uniform teaching of the Bible. However, though it was shown earlier that many verses in the Old and New Testaments strongly declare the oneness of God, there are other verses that mention the three persons of the Trinity and the oneness of God at the same time. The following are some examples:

Go therefore and make disciples of all the nations, baptizing them in the *name of the Father and the Son and the Holy Spirit*. (Matt 28:19)[23]

My Father, who has given them to Me, is greater than all; and no one is able to snatch them out of the Father's hand. *I and the Father are one*. (John 10:29–30)[24]

And Jesus cried out and said, "He who believes in Me, does not believe in Me but *in Him who sent Me*. He *who sees Me sees the One who sent Me* . . . For I did not speak on My own initiative, but *the Father Himself who sent Me* has given Me a commandment as to what to say and what to speak. (John 12:44–45, 49)

---

23. This verse will be explained in Volume 2 in the chapter entitled "The Activity of the Attributes of God Inside Creation."

24. The word ἕν (*hen*) meaning "one" in Greek is in the neuter. This indicates that the Son is not the Father, or else John would have used the masculine εἷς (*hase*). The use of the neuter means that there is unity in work, will or nature. However, more likely it is the nature that is intended here, as proven by the response of the Jews who wanted to stone him because, they said, he made himself to be God (John 10:33b).

Jesus said to him, "I am the way, and the truth, and the life; no one comes to the Father but through Me. If you had *known Me, you would have known My Father* also; from now on *you know Him, and have seen Him.*" Philip said to Him, "Lord, show us the Father, and it is enough for us." Jesus said to him, "Have I been so long with you, and yet you have not come to know Me, Philip? *He who has seen Me has seen the Father;* how can you say, 'Show us the Father'? Do you not believe that *I am in the Father, and the Father is in Me?* The words that I say to you I do not speak on My own initiative, but *the Father abiding in Me* does His works." (John 14:6–10)[25]

Yet for us there is but *one* God, the Father, from whom are all things and we exist for Him; and *one* Lord, *Jesus Christ*, by whom are all things, and we exist through Him. (1 Cor 8:6)[26]

Grace to you and peace, *from* Him [the Father] who is and who was and who is to come, and *from* [the Holy Spirit] the seven Spirits [attributes] who are before His throne, and *from Jesus Christ*, the faithful witness, the firstborn of the dead, and the ruler of the kings of the earth. To Him who loves us and released us from our sins by His blood – and He has made us to be a kingdom, priests *to His God and Father* – to Him be the glory and the dominion forever and ever . . . "I am the Alpha and the Omega," says the *Lord God*, "who is and who was and who is to come, the Almighty." (Rev 1:4–6, 8)

In summary, the expression "God" became a revelation that the one and only God is a Father who has a Son in a relationship with a glory that surpasses any relationship in existence. This takes place through attributes associated with their Spirit, who is the Spirit of the Father and the Spirit of the Son. The repeated mention of the Father, Son and Holy Spirit in amazing unity is a solemn invitation to those with pure hearts to an ever greater discovery of the power of this revelation and the beauty of this God. This leads to *the enjoyment of the true worship* of which he is worthy.

25. Notice here the movement from plurality (14:6, 10) to unity (14:7, 9).

26. This verse is Paul's expression of the Shema of the Old Testament: "Hear, O Israel! The LORD is our God, the LORD is one!" (Deut 6:4). Paul's words in 1 Cor 8:6 are also expressed in the Nicene Creed, as indicated by the emphasis: "We believe in *one God*, the Father Almighty; maker of heaven and earth, and of all things visible and invisible, and in *one Lord*, Jesus Christ . . . *by whom all things were made.*"

"God" Pointing to the Divine Nature

The reason for the eternal relationship between the Father and the Son through the Holy Spirit is that the Son and the Holy Spirit have the same divine nature as the Father. So the third use of "God" is to identify the divine nature. When "God" is used of the one and only God, it refers to his being, or *who* he is. But when "God" is used of the Father, Son or Holy Spirit, it refers to his nature, or *what* he is.[27] In this third use, several matters are to be noted.

1. Parallel Words to "God"

The New Testament uses parallel words to "God" that refer to the divine nature. For example, both Paul and Peter alternate between "God" and three words referring to the divine nature.[28] The first word is used to refer to what *pertains to the divine nature* (Acts 17:29; 2 Pet 1:2–4a).[29] Likewise, the second word refers to the *attributes related to divinity* (Rom 1:20).[30] But the third word refers to more than the divine nature; it points to the "state of being God" (Col 2:9).[31] The literal translation is "the fullness of being God."[32] The verses indicated are:

> Being then the children of *God*, we ought not to think that the *Divine Nature* is like gold or silver or stone, an image formed by the art and thought of man. (Acts 17:29)

> Grace and peace be multiplied to you in the knowledge of *God* and of Jesus our Lord; seeing that His *divine* power has granted to us everything pertaining to life and godliness, through the true

---

27. When discussing later the infrequency of references to Christ as "God," Harris adds, "The very rarity of the designation of Jesus as 'God' is evidence that θεός never becomes a proper name when used of Jesus but remains a descriptive title" (Harris, *Jesus as God*, 274).

28. There is movement from θεός (*theos*) meaning "God" to words in various grammatical forms pointing to the divine nature. This can be seen in the use of the neuter accusative adjective θεῖον (*theon*) from the root θεῖος (*theos*) in Acts 17:29 and of the feminine genitive adjective θείας (*theas*) from the same root θεῖος (*theos*) twice in 2 Pet 1:2–4a. The root feminine nominative θειότης (*theiotase*) is used in Rom 1:20, and the feminine genitive noun θεότητος (*theotatos*) from the root θεότης (*theotase*). So three root words are used: θεῖος, θειότης and θεότης.

29. "Pertaining to that which belongs to the nature or status of deity" (BDAG, s.v. "θεῖος").

30. "Divinity, divine nature" (Thayer, *Greek–English Lexicon of the New Testament*, s.v. "θειότης"); "the quality or characteristic(s) pert. to deity, divinity, divine nature, divineness" (BDAG, s.v. "θειότης").

31. "The state of being God" (Thayer, *Greek–English Lexicon of the New Testament*; BDAG, s.v. "θεότης"); "the nature or state of being God" (Louw & Nida, s.v. "θεότης"); "Godhead . . . as essence differs from quality or attribute" (Thayer, s.v. "θεότης").

32. "In him [Christ] there dwells in bodily form the total plentitude of deity [πᾶν τὸ πλήρωμα τῆς θεότητος]" (Harris, *Jesus as God*, 287–288).

knowledge of Him who called us by His own glory and excellence. For by these He has granted to us His precious and magnificent promises, so that by them you may become partakers of the *divine nature.* (2 Pet 1:2–4a)

. . . that which is known about *God* is evident within them; for *God* made it evident to them. For since the creation of the world His invisible attributes, His eternal power and *divine nature,* have been clearly seen, being understood through what has been made, so that they are without excuse. (Rom 1:19–20)

. . . a true knowledge of *God's* mystery, that is, Christ Himself . . . For in Him all the fullness of *Deity* dwells in bodily form. (Col 2:2b, 9)

Based on the above, "God" is used in parallel with references to all that makes God to be God.

2. The Use of "God" of the Son

Though the expression "God" is used to refer to Christ, it *does not in these cases refer to the Creator* because creation came from the Father through the Son and with the Holy Spirit. Furthermore, the expression "God" used to describe the Son or the Spirit *cannot refer to the Father* because there is distinction between the Father and the Son. This affirms that whenever "God" is used to describe the Son, it is referring to the divine nature.

Though much of the New Testament reveals the deity of Christ through his actions without using "God," nevertheless, it does also at times use "God" for Christ. Thus the New Testament uses "God" to refer to Christ *directly* in John 1:1, 18; 20:28; Romans 9:5; Titus 2:13; Hebrews 1:8; 2 Peter 1:1. The New Testament uses "God" to refer to Christ *indirectly* in Matthew 1:23; Ephesians 5:5; Colossians 2:2; 2 Thessalonians 1:12; and 1 John 5:20.[33] As to the direct references to Christ, the following are the most important verses:

The Word [that became flesh and dwelt among us] was *God.* (John 1:1b)

[Jesus Christ] The one and only [or "only begotten"], who is *God.* (John 1:18b, personal translation)[34]

---

33. For a complete analysis of these passages, see Harris, 51–268.

34. John 1:1, 18 will be studied in detail in Volume 2 in the chapter entitled "The Activity of the Attributes of God Outside Creation."

Thomas answered and said to Him, "My Lord and my *God!*" (John 20:28)[35]

... who are Israelites, to whom belongs the adoption as sons, and the glory and the covenants and the giving of the Law and the temple service and the promises, whose are the fathers, and from whom is the Christ according to the flesh, who is over all, *God* blessed forever. (Rom 9:4–5)[36]

Our *God* and Savior, Jesus Christ. (2 Pet 1:1b)

Our great *God* and Savior, Christ Jesus. (Titus 2:13b)[37]

Your throne, *O God* . . . (Heb 1:8b)[38]

---

35. There are several reasons why Thomas's expression "My Lord and my God!" in John 20:28 was not one of astonishment and praise to God. (1) Limiting the meaning to astonishment does not give any meaning to the prior statement "Thomas answered and said to Him . . ." (2) If Thomas's statement was one of praise, why did he not say, "Blessed be my Lord and my God" or "My Lord and God, how great is your power"? (3) The context clarifies that the discussion was between Christ and Thomas. Verse 27 states, "He [Jesus] said to Thomas . . ." Then verse 29 states, "Jesus said to him . . ." So why would verse 28, which says "Thomas answered and said to Him . . .," not be addressed to Jesus? (4) John 20:29 clarifies that the object of faith is the one whom Thomas saw. (5) Every use of the word "Lord" in John 20 refers to Christ (John 20:2, 13, 15, 18, 20, 25). And the presence of the word "Lord" with the word "God" indicates that more than "Lord" is intended here. For here is an address to Jesus, not one about Jesus. (6) The relative pronoun requires the article, and Christ distinguishes himself from the Father (John 20:17). For the words "Lord" and "God" function as titles of Christ without making Jesus the same as the Father (the mistake of modalism). (7) The relative pronoun transforms doctrine (that Christ is Lord and God) to personal faith (my Lord and my God). So it can be concluded that John 20:28 crowns John's Gospel by declaring that Christ is God. For more explanation, see Harris, 105–129.

36. The phrase in Rom 9:5 "from whom is the Christ according to the flesh" points to the coming of Christ in his human nature from the Israelites, whom Paul mentions in the previous verse. This phrase expects another parallel phrase that clarifies another feature about Christ, which is that he is "over all," or ἐπὶ πάντων θεὸς (*epi pantown theos*). It is more natural grammatically for the participle ὁ ὢν (*ho own*) to be connected to the name ὁ Χριστὸς (*ho Christos*), which precedes it, than to θεὸς (*theos*), which comes after it. This means that Paul declares that the reason for his deep pain is the nature and preeminence of the person whom the Israelites have rejected. For though Christ according to the flesh is from the Israelites, he is at the same time over all the universe and its creatures, including the Jews who have rejected him, because in his nature he is God, and he is the object of worship forever. Therefore Paul called Christ "God."

37. The interpretation of both Titus 2:13 and 2 Pet 1:1 employs the Granville Sharp rule, which states that, when descriptions of the same kind are joined together (including nouns [except if one is a proper name], adjectives, participles, attributes or titles) through the conjunction καὶ (*kai*), the repetition of the article points to different elements (e.g. Acts 26:30; 1 Cor 3:8), and non-repetition points to one element (e.g. Acts 15:23; Eph 4:11). On this basis, "Savior" and "God" point to the same person. Had Paul believed that Christ was not God, he would have used a different construction, but he did not (cf. Granville Sharp, "Remarks on the Uses of the Definitive Article," 3, quoted by Wallace, *Greek Grammar Beyond the Basics*, 271).

38. The translation "Your throne, O God" of Heb 1:8 is based on the following. (1) The Old Testament (including the LXX) supports this interpretation. (2) This translation reflects more precisely and simply the word order in the original text: ὁ θρόνος σου ὁ θεὸς (*ho thrones*

Murray Harris concludes that use of the expression "God" to refer to Christ had spread throughout the known world at the time when the New Testament was being written. This expression appeared in Asia Minor (the Gospel of John and the letter to Titus), in European Rome and Achaia (the letters of Romans and 2 Peter), and in Middle Eastern Judea (if the letter to the Hebrews was written there). The recipients were believers that were both Jews (the Gospel of John and the letters of Hebrews and 2 Peter) and Gentiles (the letters of Romans and Titus). Jesus was also referred to by the expression "God" *before* his incarnation (John 1:1, 18; Heb 1:8), *during* his incarnation (John 20:28) and *after* his incarnation (Rom 9:5; Titus 2:13; 2 Pet 1:1).[39] The main leaders of the early church shared the conviction that Christ is called "God": Peter; Paul; the writer to the Hebrews; and John. Furthermore, because the date of using "God" for Jesus was different from the date of writing about it, Thomas would have been the first to use it – that is, in AD 30 or 33 – though the Gospel of John was written in AD 85–95.[40] The date of the use of "God" for Jesus in the other cases would be the date of the writing of the books by the authors themselves.[41] On this basis, the chronological order for the uses of "God" for Jesus is as follows:

John 20:28   in AD 30 or 33

Romans 9:5   about AD 57

---

su ho theos). So, if the intention was "your throne is God" or "God is your throne," the order would be different. (3) It would be inconceivable and unacceptable to conceive of God as a throne. (4) With the repeated use of the second person when speaking of Christ in Heb 1, verse 8 should be "to the Son . . ." and not "of the Son . . ." This is in contrast to verse 7: "of the angels . . ." Angels are not addressed by God, but the Son is addressed as God. (5) The context of Heb 1–2 speaks of the superiority of Christ over angels because of his supremacy in nature, office and divine rank. Actually, the supremacy of Christ is the subject of the whole book. Therefore, the designation "God" is consistent with the first two chapters and with all the book of Hebrews. In conclusion, Heb 1:8–9 addresses Christ with the title "God" with the purpose of communicating how tragic it is not to treat him according to this truth. For more information, see Harris, *Jesus as God*, 205–227.

39. See Harris, 273, 298.

40. "It is assumed that the date of the first use of θεός as a title of Jesus may be determined by its first literary occurrence: because θεός is first applied to Jesus in Romans 9:5 [about AD 57], the christological use of the title is thought to have begun in the mid-50s. It is axiomatic in all literary study, however, that a clear distinction must be drawn between the date of the composition of a book and the date of the material contained in it. The point does not seem to have been given the attention it warrants, for it implies that no definitive *terminus a quo* may be placed on the christological use of θεός solely on the basis of literary occurrence" (Harris, 276).

41. Harris, 278.

Titus 2:13	about AD 63
2 Peter 1:1	about AD 65
Hebrews 1:8	in the 60s AD
John 1:1	in the 90s AD
John 1:18	in the 90s AD

3. Reasons for the Infrequent Use of "God" for Christ

The expression "God" is used in the original language 1,315 times in the New Testament. Of these, it is used only seven times to refer to Christ! The question is: If the New Testament writers were convinced of the deity of Christ, why were they so reserved about using "God" to refer to Christ? Care must be taken not to draw *wrong conclusions* as to the causes, which may include the following:

1. Harris states that the reason for the infrequent occurrence of "God" to point to Christ is *not* because the early believers did not have a developed enough Christology to harmonize their faith with Jewish monotheism, since "God" was actually used at times, especially by the leaders of the church. He says,

    > The sparse use was not because at this point faith was outstripping reason and the early Christians felt unable to accommodate the new christological data within the consistent theological framework of hereditary monotheism. The presence of *any* examples of the usage in the early church's documents discounts this explanation. If the early church was embarrassed by the ascription of θεός to Jesus or if the ascription was regarded as heterodox by some elements in the church, it is strange that four NT writers (John, Paul, the author of Hebrews, and Peter) should have examples.[42]

2. The same author indicates that the reason for the infrequent occurrence of "God" to point to Christ is *not* because the early believers thought that "God" was a sacred title and they must be reserved in using it, or, conversely, that it was used of humans and it would be demeaning to use it for Christ. In response, Harris affirms

---

42. Harris, 281–282.

that "both of these criteria . . . if valid, would have also excluded the christological use of κύριος, a title which occurs frequently throughout the epistles in reference to Jesus."[43]

3. Murray also states that the reason for the infrequent occurrence of "God" to point to Christ is *not* because the title "Lord" could replace "God" to point to the deity of Christ. However, this view does not stand because the two words are not interchangeable; "Lord" is a functional title referring to sovereignty, while "God" is an essential title referring to deity.[44]

However, there are *right reasons* for the infrequent occurrence of "God" to point to Christ.

1. The New Testament's general use of "God" is in reference to the Father, as mentioned above. Accordingly, if Jesus were to be referred to repeatedly as "God," there would be great obscurity.[45]

2. The New Testament preserves the distinction between the Father and the Son in a consistent way. This appears strongly in the following examples: "the God of our Lord Jesus Christ" (Eph 1:17); "His God and Father" (Rev 1:6); in Jesus's saying "My God" (Matt 27:46; Mark 15:34; John 20:17; Rev 3:2, 12); in addressing Christ as "Your God" (Heb 1:9); in Christ referring to God as "My Father" (John 5:17); in the statement that it was the Word, not God, that became flesh (John 1:14).[46]

3. The New Testament also preserves the subordination of the Son to the Father. For though they share the same divine nature, because the expression "God" is used of the Father, it is the uniform testimony of the New Testament that the Son submits to the Father and not the Father to the Son.[47] It is for this reason that "one finds the expression

---

43. Harris, 282.

44. Harris, 282.

45. Harris maintains that, when θεός is used to refer to the Father, "Father" becomes a proper name. Therefore, his emphasis on the confusion that would result from repeatedly calling Jesus θεός is correct. He states that, "since πατήρ refers to a particular person (not an attribute), the identity between ὁ θεός and ὁ πατήρ *as proper names* referring to persons must be numerical: 'God' is to be equated with 'the Father.' If Jesus were everywhere called θεός . . . linguistic ambiguity would be everywhere present" (282).

46. Harris, 283.

47. It is subordination without subordinationism. The subject of the subordination of the Son will be studied in Volume 2 in the chapter entitled "The Significance of the Names 'Father and Son.'"

'the Son of God' where God is the Father, but never 'the Father of God' where God is the Son."[48] Therefore, if the expression "God" was used of Christ continually, it would alienate the attribute of humility from God's nature, the very attribute that led to the incarnation and redemption.

4. If "God" was used to refer to the Father and to the Son equally, it would have led the Jews of the time to wrongly conclude that Christianity proclaims two gods. It would then provide enemies of Christianity with an excuse for attack. So the New Testament's insistence on proclaiming the one and only God and not many gods is another reason for the infrequency of using "God" to refer to Christ.[49]

5. The New Testament emphasis on using the designation "God" to refer to the Father protects the reality of Christ's human nature. This was necessary in the face of the docetic heresy, which believed that Christ only appeared to be, but was not actually, in the flesh. It was also necessary in the face of the monophysite heresy, which claimed that Christ had only one nature, the divine. The docetic and monophysite heresies preceded the Arian heresy which believed in the opposite, that is, in Christ's human nature not the divine.[50]

6. It protects the expression "God" from any polluted meanings drawn from society or from erroneous religions and heresies. At the time of the writing of the New Testament, the expression "God" "may [have referred] to a particular god (or even goddess), to the supreme god, Zeus, or to a deity in general . . . famous heroes, politicians, philosophers, patriarchs, renowned rulers, self-styled servants of God."[51] The same is true in every age, even today. In addition, even the title "Elohim," most often translated as "God" in the Old Testament, was also used to refer to a variety of beings, including angels, heroes and false gods. Yet it was used to point to Yahweh, the only true and covenantal God. Therefore, to shield from the wrong understanding of "God," the New Testament resorted to focusing on

---

48. Though Harris uses the term "subordinationism," he surely does not imply inequality in nature between the Father and the Son (see Harris, 283).

49. See Harris, 283.

50. Harris, 283.

51. Harris, 270.

the works of Christ, demonstrating that what Christ did is what only God can do. In this regard, there are several important observations:

a.   The New Testament functional concentration appears in that, even when using "God" to refer to Christ, the context adds a description of his role as an agent in creation (John 1:1–4), revealer of God (John 1:18), righteous in his rule (Heb 1:8), savior (Titus 2:13; 2 Pet 1:1) or Lord over all (John 20:28; Rom 9:5). So, though Christ is described as "God," there is an added description of his role.

b.   The works of Christ are not confined to being the works of God. Likewise, the words of Christ are not confined to being the words of God. Rather, the works and words of Christ spring from him because he is God in his nature. He is God both in nature and in function.

c.   What Christ does within creation depends on the activity of all of his attributes outside creation. So what Christ does functionally presupposes who Christ is ontologically, that is, in the nature of his being. *Functional Christology presupposes ontological Christology*. Christ works because Christ is God in nature. Logically, ontology precedes function. Temporally, function presupposes ontology. These matters will be explained more clearly later in this book.

d.   Ontological thinking is not absent from the New Testament. But there must be recognition of Christology from *above*, that is, from the heavenly perspective in pointing to Christ, in his divine nature, coming to earth to be among humanity (e.g. John 1:1, 14, 18; Col 1:15–19; Heb 1:1–4). There must also be recognition of Christology from *below*, that is, from the earthly perspective in pointing to Christ in his human nature being exalted and elevated to heaven to be with God (e.g. Matt 11:4–5; John 5:36; 10:25, 32, 37, 38; 14:11).

7.   A further reason for the infrequent occurrence of "God" to point to Christ is to protect the role of the Holy Spirit. Since "God" is used mostly of the Father, and since "God" for the Son is used to point to his divine nature, if "God" was applied continuously to the Son, it would undermine the importance of the meaning of the divine nature common between the Father and the Son. This divine nature springs from the attributes exchanged between them, which are related to the Holy Spirit. Therefore, if "God" was used repeatedly

of the Son, it would diminish the role of the Holy Spirit, who is the Spirit of the Father and the Son, the *Spirit of God.*[52]

4. Equality of the Son's Deity to the Father's

Even if the expression "God" were not used to refer to Christ, his deity is strongly affirmed in the New Testament in a variety of ways. Christ's possession of a full divine nature, without surrendering the full human nature he assumed in the incarnation, is the foundation for his uniqueness and for the distinctive identity of Christianity. The truth of Christ's deity makes him greater than any prophet, priest, king, ruler, teacher, philosopher, doer of great works or human personality.

As to the revelation of Christ's deity, *the New Testament provides a strong testimony* that includes the divine works and attributes of Christ in his relationship to creation, his relationship to people and his relationship to the Father. It includes the use of Yahweh's description in the Old Testament to refer to Jesus in the New Testament. It also provides the divine titles and attributes declared by Christ and ascribed to him (for a comprehensive outline of the New Testament witness to the deity of Christ, see appendix 2).

The Bible leaves the door wide open for those whose hearts are prepared to discover and experience the beauty of the deity of Christ in growing personal experience.

5. Reasons for the Infrequent Use of "God" for the Holy Spirit

The use of "God" to refer to the Holy Spirit is found only in one indirect reference when it is stated that lying to the Holy Spirit is lying to God (Acts 5:3–5). But if the writers of the New Testament were convinced of the deity of the Holy Spirit, why did they not use "God" more often to refer to the Holy Spirit? Again, it is important to avoid the wrong conclusions mentioned above in regard to Christ. Right reasons for the infrequent occurrence of "God" to point to the Holy Spirit include the following:

1. The deity of the Holy Spirit was assumed and accepted because he is the Spirit of God.

---

52. The relation of God's attributes to the Holy Spirit is covered in greater detail in Volume 2 in the chapter entitled "The Significance of the Name 'Holy Spirit.'"

2. The dominant use of "God" in the New Testament is to refer to the Father, as mentioned above. Accordingly, if "God" was used repeatedly to refer to the Holy Spirit, it would cause confusion.

3. The New Testament consistently preserves the distinction between the Father, Son and Holy Spirit. Its dedication to using "God" mostly to refer to the Father protects this distinction.

4. The New Testament safeguards the order between the persons of the Trinity. For though they share equally in the divine nature, the Holy Spirit submits to the Son, who in turn submits to the Father.

5. The infrequent occurrence of "God" to point to the Holy Spirit emphasizes the divine nature that is common between the Father and the Son. This nature springs from the attributes exchanged between them, which are related to the Holy Spirit, who is the Spirit of the Father and the Son, the Spirit of God.[53]

6. The Personhood and Deity of the Holy Spirit

The Bible declares that the Holy Spirit is a person who has a divine nature equal with the Father and the Son.

The personhood of the Holy Spirit is affirmed by the use of pronouns and demonstratives that belong to rational beings, and by his *having a will* of his own, *having emotions* characteristic of persons, being *engaged in relationships*, *performing works* belonging to rational beings and being the *other comforter* alongside the Son (for an expanded treatment of the personhood of the Holy Spirit and its importance, see appendix 3 and also the chapter in Volume 2 entitled "The Significance of the Name 'Holy Spirit'").

The deity of the Holy Spirit is affirmed in that he *belongs* to the Father and the Son, has *divine attributes*, what he says is *what God says*, what was ascribed to God is *ascribed to him*, his works are the *works of God and the works of Christ*, he is *the medium in which Christ baptizes* believers, the *same honor* is bestowed on him as was bestowed on the Father and the Son, he continues to *work in the* hearts of people, *worship and prayer* are requested and expected to him, and he is *in the presence of the Father and the Son* in heaven (for an expanded treatment of the deity of the Holy Spirit, see appendix 3).

---

53. Again, the relation of God's attributes to the Holy Spirit is covered in greater detail in Volume 2 in the chapter entitled "The Significance of the Name 'Holy Spirit.'"

Table 3.1: The Various Ways "God" Is Used In Oneness in Trinity

"God" Pointing to the One and Only God	"God" Pointing to the Father	"God" Pointing to the Divine Nature
Old and New Testaments	New Testament	New Testament
God's Appearances and Works The Bible reveals intermittent appearances of the one and only God in the OT, and his appearance in the flesh in the NT, with works to save humanity.	**The Reason for God's Appearances and Works** The reason for the appearances and works of the one and only God for the salvation of humanity is that he exists eternally as a Father in an eternal relationship with an only eternal and uncreated Son through the Holy Spirit.	**The Reason for the Eternal Relationship** The reason for the eternal relationship is that the Son and the Holy Spirit have the same divine nature as the Father.
God's Desire to Reveal His Nature The intermittent appearances of the one and only God of the OT point to his desire to reveal deeper truths about his nature.	**His Nature Springs from the Glory of the Relationship** Deeper truths are revealed in the NT unveiling the preeminent glory of the nature of God springing from the relationship between the Father and his Son through the Holy Spirit, who is the Spirit of the Father and the Spirit of the Son.	**The Glory of the Relationship Is Affirmed** The glory of the relationship between the Father and the Son through the Holy Spirit is affirmed by the use of parallel words to "God" to point to the divine nature, by the use of "God" to refer to the Son and to the Holy Spirit, and by the provision of sufficient evidence of their deity before and after the incarnation of the Son.

Appearances without Explanation	Appearances Explained in the Outpouring of the Eternal Relationship	The Outpouring of the Eternal Relationship Springing from Submission
The NT points to the climactic appearances of God in the OT by speaking of his salvation, his appearance in the flesh, his grace, his mercy, his righteousness, his Word, his universal church, and his local churches, without direct explanation of how this came to be.	Direct explanation is given for the climactic appearances of God in the OT through repeated declaration in the NT of the accomplishment of the incarnation and redemption by the Son as an expression of the outpouring of the rich eternal relationship between the Father and the Son through the Holy Spirit.	The outpouring of the rich eternal relationship springs from the submission of the Son to the Father and the submission of the Holy Spirit to the Father and the Son, a submission that appears through the dominant use of "God" to refer to the Father.

Summary

The grandeur of using the expression "God" in three different ways of Oneness in Trinity reaches its climax at the cross. For the one and only true God revealed that he is the Father in the only eternal relationship with his Son in utmost beauty and perfection through the Holy Spirit, who is the Spirit of the Father and the Son, whereby the Father, Son and Holy Spirit each have God's same divine nature. This relationship overflowed to creation by the Father sending his Son through incarnation in the likeness of human beings in order to redeem humanity from sin through the death of his Son for them on the cross and through his resurrection that vindicated his claims and granted newness of life to all who believe in him. All this begins and ends in the one God beside whom there is no other.

4

Avoiding Common Errors about the Trinity

Introduction

While the first chapter dealt with challenges facing Christians and non-Christians, this chapter is primarily for Christian believers, though it has great value for non-Christians as well. The concern here is that many Christians can immerse themselves in serious errors about the Trinity that have been repeated throughout history. The most important of these errors are still common today and are covered here in order to help Christians avoid them.

Understanding the Use of "Person" in the Trinity

The critical issue with the term "person" is to distinguish between divine persons and human persons.[1] There are several important points in this regard.

First, when used of *human persons*, there is distinction and separation between them, so that each human person has his or her own essence, and the existence of each human person is independent of the existence of any other human person. However, when used of the *divine persons*, although there is distinction between the persons, there is no separation, so that they

---

1. There is more difficulty in the Arabic language because it uses the non-Arabic word أقنوم ('uqnum) that comes from the transliterated Syriac word ܩܢܘܡܐ (qnomeh) to refer to the persons of the Trinity. The meaning of the word is not known to most Arabic-speaking people. Though it means "person," "personality," "self" or the like, its use as a vague word to Arab Christians only serves to distinguish between divine persons and human persons. For full discussion of this term, see the third chapter of the Arabic version of this book, Imad Shehadeh, الله معنا وبدوننا. الجزء الأول. الوحدانية بثالوث مقابل مقابل الوحدانية المُطلقة [God With Us and Without Us: Volume 1 – Oneness in Trinity versus Absolute Oneness], 76–81.

share one and the same essence, and the existence of one person is eternally interdependent on the existence of the other persons.

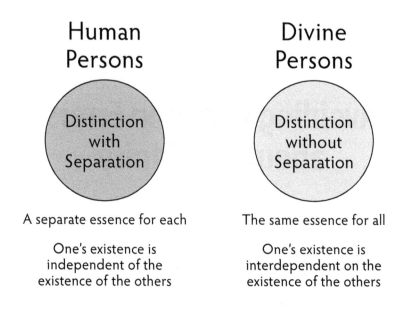

Human Persons

Distinction with Separation

A separate essence for each

One's existence is independent of the existence of the others

Divine Persons

Distinction without Separation

The same essence for all

One's existence is interdependent on the existence of the others

Figure 4.1: Distinction between Human and Divine Persons

Second, the use of the term "person" for the divine persons is necessary and important, yet it is insufficient and incomplete. It is necessary and important in that the word "person" communicates that there is a true and real relationship between real persons. This in turn points to the fact that *relationality* – that is, the reality of a relationship between persons – is most important to the being of God, and in turn central to all of existence. At the same time, using the term "person" to refer to the divine persons is insufficient and incomplete. The reason for this is that using the term "person" alone to refer to the Father, Son or Holy Spirit without further indication as to the uniqueness of this use does not convey the reality of the connection of each of the persons to the one divine and common nature between them. So it is necessary and important to use the term "person" of the Father, Son and Holy Spirit, but not to use it alone. An addition must be made to clarify that, though they are distinct from one another, just as human persons are, yet, unlike human persons, they are never separate from one another, they share the same essence, and the existence of each person is interdependent on the existence of the other persons. It could simply be said that they are *three persons in one deity*. *This is a distinction unique to God alone; it is not shared by any creature.*

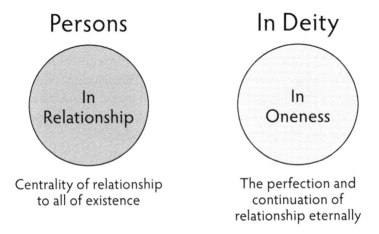

Persons

In Relationship

Centrality of relationship
to all of existence

In Deity

In Oneness

The perfection and
continuation of
relationship eternally

Figure 4.2: Persons in One Deity

Understanding the Distinction between the Persons

An accurate understanding of what the Bible says about the Trinity – especially as related to the distinction between the persons – is necessary for enriching spiritual life and giving greater power in proclamation. Five main errors on this subject have appeared in history, and their effects persist until today. These must be avoided.

The First Error: Confining Faith to the Existence of God Only

The first error is to think that correct doctrine is confined to faith in the existence of God only (Jas 2:19; as was covered in ch. 1). The Bible proclaims that correct doctrine adopts faith not only that God exists, but that he exists in relationship. This relationship is the spring for the activity of his attributes, which overflow into creation, incarnation and redemption.

The Second Error: Belief in Three Gods

The second error to avoid is to think that the Trinity means three gods. The Bible insists that there is only one God, and strongly rejects polytheism. The three persons exist in the one and only God.

The Third Error: Modalism

The third error is to think that the Trinity refers to three aspects or modes, that is, to think that the Father is himself the Son who is also himself the Holy Spirit. This teaching is known as Modalism or Sabellianism, after Sabellius who propagated this thought. The Nicene Creed rejected Modalism based on the teachings of the Bible that proclaim distinction between the persons. So there are three distinct persons and not three modes.

The Fourth Error: Subordinationism

The fourth error is to think that the Trinity holds to subordinationism between the persons, that is, that the Father is greater in essence or worth than the Son, and the Son is greater in essence or worth than the Holy Spirit. However, the Bible teaches order, not subordinationism, emphasizing the equality of the persons, who share the same essence. So at the Council of Nicea in AD 325, Athanasius stressed that the Father and the Son are of the same essence, in response to Arius who spoke of a different essence, and to others who spoke of a similar essence.[2] Later in the same century, the Cappadocian Fathers (Basil the Great, Basil's younger brother Gregory of Nyssa, and Gregory of Nazianzus, known as the Three Cappadocians), explaining the doctrine of the Trinity, also stressed that the Holy Spirit is of the same essence as the Father himself.[3] The beauty of this is that, while the persons are equal, there is genuine humility in the one God. This attribute appeared in the incarnation and redemption to save mankind.

The Fifth Error: Independence

The fifth error is believing in the independence of the persons from one another, that is, their separation, division or isolation from one another. The Bible is clear that there is no work done by one of the persons without the active participation of the other persons. Moreover, there is mutual indwelling of the persons of the Trinity, so that the Father is in the Son, the Son is in the Father, both are in the Spirit, the Spirit is in the Father and the Son, and so on

---

2. In Greek, the word ὁμοούσιος (homoousios) is used to refer to the same essence, the word ἑτεροούσιος (heteroousios) is used to refer to a different essence, and the word ὁμοιούσιος (homoiousious) is used to refer to a similar essence.

3. The Cappadocian Fathers used the word οὐσία (ousia; in Latin substantia) to refer to the essence, and the word ὑπόστασις (hupostasis; in Latin persona) to refer to each person.

(mutual indwelling will be covered in Volume 2 in the chapter entitled "The Activity of the Attributes of God Outside Creation").

Conclusion in Regard to the Distinction between the Persons

The true God exists not only in oneness, but also in relationship. This relationship is between the three persons within the oneness of God, so that there are not three gods. But these persons are not modes, but are rather distinct persons from one another. These persons share in the same essence without subordinationism, and mutually indwell one another without ceasing. So the true God combines all these aspects together.

The five-sided diagram (pentagon) in figure 4.3 illustrates the differences between the right and wrong beliefs. The words at the angles of the pentagon represent the wrong conceptions, while the sides opposite each angle represent the true doctrine, that is, the truth. The circle touches the five sides at the same time to point to the fact that the one true God exists in relationship between equal but distinct persons. This is the fountainhead for the beauty and power of the Trinity, as will be expanded upon in this book.

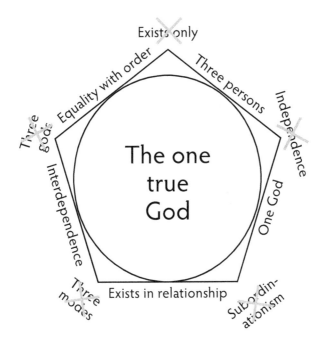

Figure 4.3: Distinction between the Father, Son and Holy Spirit

Understanding the Unity of Christ's Two Natures

Just as it is necessary to have an accurate understanding of what the Bible says about the distinction between the persons, it is also necessary to have an accurate understanding of the unity of Christ's two natures in his one person. An accurate understanding of this subject provides deeper understanding of the work of Christ in his incarnation and redemption to save humankind. Five main errors about Christ's divine and human natures have appeared in history, and their effects still persist today. These too must be avoided. The explanation below builds on the declaration of the Council of Chalcedon in AD 451, which expresses in summary form the biblical teaching of the hypostatic or essential union of the two natures of Christ "unconfusedly, unchangeably, indivisibly, inseparably."[4]

The First Error: Change in the Divine Nature

The first error is the belief that the incarnation brought about change in the divine nature, so that God transformed from being God to becoming man. This is a grave error for several reasons. First, one of the distinctive features of God's divine nature is that *he does not undergo change*. Second, in John 1:14, where it is declared "And the Word became flesh, and dwelt among us, and we saw His glory," the verb "became" refers to adding a new condition without eliminating the first condition, as in "the king became a shepherd" while remaining king.[5]

Third, in John 1:14 also, the Word remains the subject of the verse, so that the Word refers to the one who "dwelt among us" and whose "glory" "we saw."[6] So when the Word became flesh, he added the human nature while keeping the divine nature. The process here is a process of *addition and not change* such

---

4. The summary text of the Chalcedonian Creed states, "We, then, following the holy Fathers, all with one consent, teach men to confess one and the same Son, our Lord Jesus Christ, the same perfect in Godhead and also perfect in manhood; truly God and truly man, of a reasonable [rational] soul and body; consubstantial [coessential] with the Father according to the Godhead, and consubstantial with us according to the Manhood; in all things like unto us, without sin . . . to be acknowledged in two natures, unconfusedly, unchangeably, indivisibly, inseparably; the distinction of natures being by no means taken away by the union, but rather the property of each nature being preserved, and concurring in one Person and one Subsistence, not parted or divided into two persons, but one and the same Son" (Lang, *Creeds, Confessions and Catechisms*, paragraph 86).

5. When the verb "became" from the Greek γίνομαι (*ginomai*) is used with the neuter noun, the meaning is a change in the nature of the subject, as in "the water became wine." But when the verb "became" is used with a masculine noun, the change is of the outward shape and not of the inner identity (see Godet, *Commentary on the Gospel of John*, 269).

6. Schnackenburg, *Gospel According to St John*, 1:266.

that his glory was evident to those who knew him. The person of the Word became able to work through the two natures, the divine and the human.[7]

The Second Error: Temporal Union

The second error is to think of the union of the divine and human natures as a temporal and temporary union confined to the period of the incarnation on earth. The biblical teaching, however, emphasizes that this union is forever! One day believers shall see him in his *human nature*, but engulfed by the glory of his *divine nature*. This is the hope of the revelation of his appearing!

The Third Error: Mixing the Natures

The third error is found in mixing or confusing the natures. This takes place by reducing the divine nature and elevating the human nature, elevating the divine nature and reducing the human nature, or reducing both natures together. The mistake in reducing the divine nature and elevating the human nature is in assuming that the divine nature loses some of its divinity when united with the human nature, and that the human nature assumes an elevated status when united with the divine nature. *The truth is that the divine nature maintains its fullness, and the human nature its limitedness.*[8] In addition, the word "became" in the declaration "the Word became flesh" (John 1:14) cannot mean that the Word only appeared in the mask of flesh and blood. The verb "became" does not allow for this meaning.[9]

The mistake in elevating the divine nature and reducing the human nature is that it causes great difficulty in understanding the appearance of Christ in a human body, the reality of his death to redeem humankind, and the eternal glory prepared for believers in real, though glorified, bodies.[10]

The mistake in reducing both the divine and human natures is that the two natures of Christ become a mixture of part of one nature or part of both natures together; it thereby combines the two previous errors, resulting in greater contradiction with the Chalcedonian Creed mentioned above.

---

7. Crawford, "Relation of the Divinity and the Humanity in Christ," 238.

8. Cf. Chafer, *Chafer Systematic Theology*, 1:385.

9. The word "became" is γίνομαι (*ginomai*). Cf. Schnackenburg, *Gospel According to St John*, 1:266.

10. Cf. Chafer, *Chafer Systematic Theology*, 1:385.

The Fourth Error: Separating the Natures

The fourth error is to think that the fact of two natures means two persons. The difficulty with this view is that the New Testament's portrayal of Christ *is always and consistently as one person*, though he exhibited contrasting attributes belonging to their respective natures.[11] Hodge states that the Son of God did not unite Himself with a human person, but with a human nature.[12]

The Fifth Error: the Independence of the Natures

The fifth error is to think of the natures as functioning independently of one another. One of the manifestations of this error is to conclude that, though Christ never sinned, it was possible for him to sin. However, *the union of the two natures without separation guarantees the impeccability of Christ* (the subject of the impeccability of Christ will be covered in Volume 2 in the chapter entitled "The Manifestation of the Trinity in the Self-Emptying of Christ"). So there is complete harmony and agreement between the two natures so that neither nature functions independently of the other nature.

Conclusion on the Union of the Two Natures of Christ

The divine nature of Christ without his human nature cannot redeem, and the human nature without the divine nature cannot save.[13] In the end, without the union of the two natures there can be no hope for humankind to reach glory as Christ did in his two natures.[14] In any of the errors above, there is loss to the most important features of human salvation.

To help understand the differences between the right and wrong beliefs, the pentagon in figure 4.4, like the previous diagram illustrating the distinction between the persons of the Trinity, illustrates the unity of Christ's two natures in his one person. The words at the angles of the pentagon represent the wrong conceptions, while the sides opposite each angle represent the true doctrine, that is, the truth. The circle touches the five sides at the same time to point to the fact that the union of the two natures of Christ is an eternal union without change, confusion, separation or independence. This is the fountainhead for

---

11. Chafer, 1:385.
12. Hodge, *Systematic Theology*, 2:391.
13. Cf. Chafer, *Chafer Systematic Theology*, 1:385; Walvoord, *Jesus Christ Our Lord*, 120–121.
14. Cf. Walvoord, 121–122.

the beauty of the Trinity and of the person of Christ, as will be expanded upon in this book.

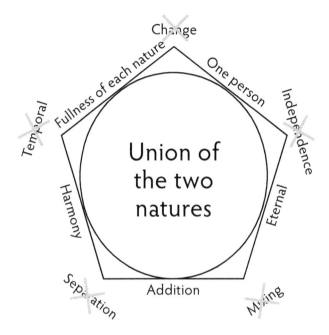

Figure 4.4: The Union of the Two Natures in the One Person of Christ

Attention to Precision in Expression

It is necessary to pay attention to precision in speaking on this subject in order to avoid confusion and misunderstanding. For example, the expression "the Son of God" really means "the Son of God the Father" or simply "the Son of the Father." So, although Christ is referred to as "God" and also as "the Son of God," it would be contradictory to mention both expressions in the same sentence without explanation. Therefore, if mentioned in the same sentence, it is more precise to say that Christ is "the Son of God the Father" and is "God in nature."

In the same way, the expression "the Spirit of God" means "the Spirit of God the Father," "the Spirit of God the Son," or simply "the Spirit of the Father" or "the Spirit of the Son." So, although the Holy Spirit is referred to as "God" and also as "the Spirit of God," it would be contradictory to say "the Spirit of God" and "God" in the same sentence without explanation. Therefore, if mentioned in the same sentence, it is more precise to say that the Holy Spirit is "the Spirit of the Father" or "the Spirit of the Son" and is "God in nature."

Another example of contradiction is the saying that "God is one and three," as if "God" is a fourth person! It is more accurate to say that God is one in one sense and three in another sense. For he is one in essence or nature, and three in person. In this way contradiction disappears.

Avoiding Exaggeration in the Use of Illustrations

Many attempt to explain the Trinity through illustrations, pictures and examples, such as those described below. Though there may be some value in these methods, none of them is actually able to explain this doctrine. The Christian Arab philosopher Awad Samaan maintains that God is not compound and the persons are not parts in him that can be compared to anything in existence.[15]

The Pattern of the First Family

Eve was created out of Adam's rib. Then through their physical union they had offspring. So Adam, Eve and their descendants form three elements, when they were originally one. However, in the Trinity, there was no temporal order in the presence of the persons, there was no causation for any of them, and *there was no time when God was not a Trinity.*

The Pattern of the Head of the Family

The head of the family is used in his triple role as father to his children, son to his parents and husband to his wife. But the problem in using this pattern for the Trinity is that it communicates modalism and not the Trinity.

The Pattern of Soul, Body and Spirit

The problem with using the illustration of soul, body and spirit to illustrate the Trinity is that it implies that God is composed of parts, when he is simple and not compound.

---

15. Samaan, الله، ذاته ونوع وحدانيته [God, His Essence and His Kind of Unity], 43.

The Triple Point Pattern

There is a condition called the "triple point" whereby, under specific pressure and at a certain temperature, water exists as ice, liquid and vapor at the same time. Three distinct conditions thereby exist in one essence (H_2O). However, the problem in using this illustration for the Trinity is that there is a change from one nature to the other, and this change requires certain conditions, not to mention the absence of the personal element. None of these features can be found in the Trinity.

The Pattern of the Sun: Its Rays, Heat and Light

One of the best-known illustrations of the Trinity is the nature of the sun, with its rays, heat and light being three elements of one entity. There have been variations in the sun illustration. The Greek Gregory of Nazianzus of the fourth century AD spoke of the Trinity not as the sun with its rays, but as three suns combined in one ray.[16] The Arab Ammar Al Basri of the ninth century AD stated that, just as the soul with its spirit and word did not become three souls, and fire with its heat and light did not become three fires, and the sun with its light and heat did not become three suns, so God with his Spirit and Word did not become three gods. *Threeness does not nullify oneness, and oneness does not nullify threeness.*[17]

While these pictures provide great benefit, especially in supporting plurality in unity, it must be noted that they give only one aspect of the Trinity and not the whole. Moreover, they of course lack the element of persons in relationship.

Conclusion about the Use of Illustrations

If there is any benefit in using illustrations, it is not in explaining the Trinity, but at best in illustrating that there can be plurality in one respect and unity in another. But that is very far from explaining the Trinity. All a person can experience is to discover one of the many aspects of the Trinity, then another and yet another, all the days of his or her life. The greatest obstacle in these illustrations lies in preventing this discovery.

---

16. Gregory of Nazianzus stated that "the Godhead is, to speak concisely, undivided in separate Persons; and there is one mingling of Light, as it were of three suns joined to each other" (Schaff and Wace, *Nicene and Post-Nicene Fathers*, Second Series, Vol. 7, 14:32).

17. Ammar Al Basri, كتاب البرهان [The Book of Evidence], 48–49.

Conclusion on Avoiding Common Errors about the Trinity

The above explanation of errors common today can help in seeing other errors that prevent us from experiencing the beauty and power of the Trinity. For the New Testament reveals the Trinity in simplicity, without explaining it and without apology for proclaiming it. Believers do not deal with a distant God who is uncaring about his creation, but they are *related to God as a Father who loves them, in the name of the Son who redeemed them, and in the intercession of the Holy Spirit who lives within them.* The New Testament is filled with prepositions that express God's care for the world personally and deeply in his three persons, as Robert Jensen expresses aptly:

> The gospel-insight is that if we only pray to God, if our relation to God is reducible to the "to" and is not decisively determined also by "with" and "in," then it is some distant and timelessly uninvolved divinity whom we have envisaged. We pray indeed to the Father, and so usually address the Father simply as "God." But we address this Father in that and only in that we pray with Jesus in their Spirit. The particular God of Scripture does not just stand over against us; he envelops us. And only by the full structure of the envelopment do we have this God.[18]

Believers discover infinite beauty gradually and continually by meditating on the Scriptures and submitting to the teaching of the Holy Spirit.

---

18. Jenson, *Triune Identity*, 51.

5

Is It the Same God?

Introduction

As expressed earlier, this study deals with what is said about God by the philosophy of Absolute Oneness, which is held by several religions and beliefs. But before entering discussion on the ramifications of this philosophy, this chapter makes another attempt at answering the perennial question of whether the God proclaimed by the Qur'an is the same as the God of Oneness in Trinity proclaimed by the Bible.

The focus of this chapter is on the Arabic language's use of "Allah" to refer to God and the strong association of "Allah" with Absolute Oneness. Adherents of Absolute Oneness claim that they speak of the same God spoken of by the Bible as the one and only God, Creator, necessary being, uncaused cause, sovereign over all of creation, omnipotent, omniscient and omnipresent.[1] They base this on several declarations of qur'anic surahs which instruct Muslims to treat Christians on this basis:

> Say, "We believe in that which has been revealed to us and revealed to you. And our God and your God is one; and we are Muslims [in submission] to him." (Surah Al ankaboot 29:46; Saheeh International translation)

Qur'anic surahs also claim that inspiration occurred exactly as with the prophets of the Old Testament:

---

1. Cf. المنجد [Al-Munjid], s.v. "إله"; Al-Sabzawari, الجديد في تفسير القرآن المجيد [The New in the Explanation of the Glorious Qur'an], 2:502; Al-Baydawi, أنوار التنزيل وأسرار التأويل [The Lights of Revelation and the Secrets of Explanation], 227; 'Abduh, *Risalat al Tawhid* [The Theology of Unity], 29–52; Phillip Hatti, تاريخ العرب [The History of the Arabs], 48.

Indeed, we have revealed to you, [O Muhammad], as we revealed
to Noah and the prophets after him. And we revealed to Abraham,
Ishmael, Isaac, Jacob, the Descendants, Jesus, Job, Jonah, Aaron,
and Solomon, and to David we gave the book [of Psalms]. (Surah
Al Nissa 4:163; Saheeh International translation)

The qur'anic surahs further assert that the same God declared his will to all
nations, though each nation may approach him differently:

And for all religion we have appointed a rite [of sacrifice] that they
may mention the name of Allah over what he has provided for
them of [sacrificial] animals. For your god is one God, so to him
submit. And, [O Muhammad], give good tidings to the humble
[before their Lord]. (Surah Al Haj 22:34; Saheeh International
translation)[2]

To answer the question whether the God of Absolute Oneness is the same
as the God of Oneness in Trinity, the following subjects will be addressed in
this chapter: the early use of the expression "Allah," the common root in Semitic
languages, the use of "Allah" by Arab Christians today, and dealing with the
difficulty of the question.

The Early Use of the Expression "Allah"

There is no doubt that worship of a moon god existed in the Arabian peninsula
before the rise of Islam in the late sixth century AD. But "a moon god" is
different from "Allah," who was considered to be supreme over other deities.
The *Encyclopaedia of Islam* indicates that the term "Allah" was well known to
Arabs prior to Islam. Accordingly, the epithet or title became to them a proper
name, and is presupposed in the qur'anic surahs without reference to its origin:

Allāh was known to the pre-Islamic Arabs; he was one of the
Meccan deities, possibly the supreme deity and certainly a creator-
god (cf. Kur'ān, xiii, 16; xxix, 61; xxxi, 25; xxxix, 38; xliii, 87). He
was already known, by antonomasia [the substitution of an epithet
or title for a proper name], as *the God, al-Ilāh* . . . But the vague
notion of supreme (not sole) divinity, which *Allāh* seems to have
connoted in Meccan religion, was to become both universal and

---

2. The Qur'an prohibits the worship of the moon or of any of the planets or stars on the
basis that Allah is their creator (Surah Fussilat 41:37; Yunis 10:5; Al-Rad 13:2; Ibrahim 14:33;
Luqman 31:29).

transcendental; it was to be turned, by the Kur'anic preaching, into the affirmation of the Living God, the Exalted One.[3]

The view that the term "Allah" developed through a contraction of the definite article *al* with the word *elah* for "a god" is not certain. There have been considerable differences of opinion on this issue. However, since the expression *al elah*, meaning "the God," does not appear in the qur'anic text, it is probable that the expression "Allah" replaced *al elah*.[4] The following are some examples of the use of "Allah" before Islam as evidenced by Arabic poems, the Hadith and early translations of the New Testament into Arabic.

Arabic Poems

The use of "Allah" before Islam occurs in the famous seven poems known as *Almu'alaqat*, in which Allah is presented as the giver of the attributes of moral excellence without hesitation, the object of faith and of right religion, the judge, the one who elevates human beings, the object of prayer, the hope of immortality in paradise, the owner of the earth, the source of wealth, the knower of the secrets of hearts and the master of the destiny of all human beings.[5]

The Hadith

In addition, the understanding of the true God came through the influence of Jews and Christians on the Muslim community and not the reverse. In an admission by the Hadith, Bukhari asserts that "The People of the Book used to read the Torah in Hebrew and explain it to Muslims in Arabic."[6] Bukhari

---

3. Bearman et al., *Encyclopaedia of Islam*, s.v. "Allah." See also Hatti, 141; F. V. Winnett, "Allah Before Islam," *Muslim World* 28 (1938): 246–247.

4. "By frequency of usage, *al-ilah* was contracted to Allah, frequently attested in pre-Islamic poetry . . . , and then became a proper name (*ism 'alam*). But whilst the form *al-ilah* is not found in the Kur'an, *allah* seems in some cases to have preserved the same meaning . . . *Ilah* is certainly identical with אֱלוֹהַּ . . . The Arab philologists discussed at great length the etymology of the words *ilah* and *allah* . . . The Basrans established no direct connection between *ilah* and *allah* . . ., but most regarded the proper name Allah as a derivative (*mushtakk, mankul*), a contraction of *al-ilah*, and endeavored to attach *ilah* to a trilateral root" (Bearman et al., *Encyclopaedia of Islam*, s.v. "Ilah").

5. Al-Zuzuni, شرح المعلقات السبع [The Explanation of the Seven Suspended Poems], 81, 163, 165.

6. Bukhari 65 (2):11:150. For more on the phrase "The People of the Book" as referring to the Jews and the Christians, see Al Fakhr Al-Razi, تفسير الفخر الرازي [The Commentary of Al-Razi], 11:194; Al-Sabzawari, 2:439.

also adds that "Waraqah bin Nūfal, the cousin of Khadijah, who had been a Christian before the development of Islam, was accustomed to copying the Injīl from Hebrew."[7]

The New Testament

The words of the Hadith above point to the absence of Arabic Bible manuscripts prior to the sixth century AD. However, extant Arabic palimpsests (manuscripts or pieces of writing material on which the original writing has been effaced to make room for later writing, of which traces remain) from the seventh and eighth centuries AD point to the existence of earlier manuscripts.[8]

Further evidence comes from the oldest extant Arabic manuscript of the New Testament known as Vatican 13 and dated to the eighth century AD.[9] It contains most of the Synoptic Gospels, all of the letters of Paul and the letter to the Hebrews. Careful comparison of this translation with other translations reveals that it was most likely translated from the Greek New Testament. But what is most obvious is that there is no evidence of Islamic influence on this manuscript, yet it uses "Allah" throughout.

But this was not the case with the translation that came a century after Vatican 13, which is the Mt Sinai Arabic Codex 151, dated from the ninth to the eleventh century. It contains the letters of Paul, the book of Acts and the General Epistles, with numerous colophons of explanations.[10] There is clear evidence of the influence of Islamic thinking on this codex – not in the actual translation, but in the comments made in the colophons about it. For example, all but three of the New Testament books begin with the common introduction of qur'anic surahs, "In the Name of Allah, the Merciful and Compassionate." Only three New Testament books in the manuscript (Acts, Romans and 2 Corinthians) begin instead with "In the name of the Father, Son, and Holy Spirit" (Romans and Acts add "one God").[11]

---

7. Bukhari 1:3:3. Kahdijah was Muhammad's first wife, and the Injīl is the New Testament.

8. Atiya, "Arabic Palimpsests of Mount Sinai," 112–113. Cf. Kenneth Bailey, "The Arabic Versions of the Bible: Reflections on Their History and Significance" (unpublished paper, 1979).

9. *Vat. Arabo 13* (Biblioteca Apostolical Vaticana). Cf. Guidi, "Le traduzioni degli Evangelii in Arabo e in Etiopien," 5–37.

10. Staal, *Mt Sinai Arabic Codex 151*, ix.

11. Islamic influence on Codex 151 is seen in other ways. For example, it uses the dating system of AH (after the hijrah of Muhammad to Medina) instead of AD. The earliest colophon dates the writing of the Pauline Epistles to the month of Ramadan 253 AH (or AD 867), which encompasses most of the epistles. The next period of copying appears in three colophons reflecting the two dates of the month of Dhu al-Hijjah 412 AH (AD 1030) and the month of

It is a glaring fact that there was never an avoidance of the use of the expression "Allah" to refer to God in any of the extant Christian Arabic Bibles from their earliest appearance in history. Any mention of God consistently used "Allah."

> It is safe to conclude that the expression "Allah" was used before the eighth century AD by Jews and Christians with a biblical understanding.

The Common Root in Semitic Languages

The term "Allah" is attested through a number of Semitic languages which have the same root of *a, l,* and *h.* The Arabic language shares this root with Hebrew, Aramaic and Syriac.

Hebrew

The Hebrew singular *Elah* and *Eloah* and the plural *Elohim* share the same root.[12] The expression *El* is a contraction of the previous expressions.[13]

Aramaic

Following the Babylonian exile, Aramaic naturally became the language used by the Jews. In fact, Aramaic was the lingua franca of the Near East in biblical and post-biblical times[14] and it ceded to Arabic only in the ninth century AD, two full centuries after the rise of Islam. Middle Eastern Jews and Christians came to use the Aramaic designation for God frequently, and it would often have been heard. The official (Masoretic) text of the Aramaic portions of Daniel and Ezra uses the word *Elaha* thirty-one times, employing the Hebrew

---

Safar 416 AH (AD 1034). Furthermore, it uses qur'anic terminology to refer to Christians as *al-mutanasirun* and its derivatives (Staal, 45, 116, 212, etc.).

12. The singular אֱלָהּ (*Elah*) and אֱלוֹהַּ (*Eloah*) and the plural אֱלֹהִים (*Elohim*) have the root אלה (a, l and h). See *BDB*, s.v. "אלה"; *TDOT*, s.v. "אֱלֹהִים." Some think that the Arabic اللهم (*allahumma*) is a derivative of אֱלֹהִים (*Elohim*), but most think that it is a vocative form of "Allah" and has no relationship to *Elohim.* The expression (*allahumma*) occurs as a vocative five times in qur'anic surahs and twenty-one times in the common Arabic Van Dyke translation.

13. The expression is אֵל (*el*).

14. See 2 Kgs 18:26; Ezra 4:7; Isa 36:11; Dan 2:4; John 5:2; 19:17, 20; 20:16; Acts 21:40; 22:2; 26:14.

transliteration of the Aramaic to refer to "the God."[15] Accordingly, following the Aramaic, the final letter serves as the definite article, thus yielding "the God."[16] The anarthrous *Elah* in construct with another word, becoming "God of . . .," is used eighty-six times.[17] The plural, meaning "gods," is used nine times.[18]

The Use by Christ

Jesus spoke mostly Aramaic, although sometimes he spoke Hebrew and may have spoken Greek and Latin on some occasions.[19] If Jesus spoke Aramaic, then *Elah/Elaha* would have been one of the words Jesus would have used to refer to God. Matthew records Christ's words on the cross as "Eli, Eli" (Matt 27:46), while Mark records them as "Eloi, Eloi" (Mark 15:34). Carson comments, "Matthew keeps 'Eli, Eli' . . . representing a Hebrew original, and Mark 'Eloi, Eloi,' representing an Aramaic original."[20]

Syriac

Syriac was born out of Aramaic, and became the main language among Christian communities. As Aramaic served the Assyrian and Persian empires, its successor, Syriac, inherited the cultural heritage to become the dominant language in the Arabian Peninsula and northern Mesopotamia. This was before Arabic became the dominant language.[21] The zeal of faith of the Assyrian people caused them to seek education. That is why their writings are filled with

---

15. The word אֱלָהָא (*Elaha*) occurs in Dan 2:20; 3:26, 32 [4:2 in the English Bible]; 5:3, 18, 21, 23, 26; 6:21, 27; Ezra 4:24; 5:2 [2 times], 8, 13, 14, 15, 16, 17; 6:3, 5 [2 times], 7 [2 times], 8, 12 [2 times], 16, 17, 18, 24.

16. The word אֱלָה (*elah*) would mean "god," and the final א (*a*) in אֱלָהָא (*Elaha*) serves as the definite article, following the Aramaic, meaning "the God" or "God."

17. The anarthrous אֱלָה (*elah*), meaning "a god" or "God" in construct, is used between Dan 2:18 and 6:26, and between Ezra 4:24 and 7:26.

18. The plural אֱלָהִין (*elahin*), meaning "gods," is used in Dan 2:11, 47; 3:25 (2 times); 4:5–6 [4:8–9 in the English Bible]; 4:15 [4:18 in the English Bible]; 5:11 [2 times], 14.

19. John J. Parsons, "Did Jesus Speak Hebrew? Disputing Aramaic Primacy," Hebrew4Christians, accessed 19 January 2016, http://www.hebrew4christians.com/Articles/Jesus_Hebrew/jesus_hebrew.html.

20. Carson, *Matthew*, on Matt 27:46. Metzger comments that "the reading ηλει ηλει . . . represents the Hebrew אֵלִי ('my God'), and has been assimilated to the parallel in Matthew (27:46). The great majority of uncials and minuscule manuscripts read ελωι ελωι, which represents the . . . Aramaic אֱלָהִי ('my God'), the ω for the a sound being due to the influence of the Hebrew אֱלֹהַי . . . Thus, in the text preferred by the Committee the entire saying represents an Aramaic original, whereas the Matthean parallel is partly Hebrew and partly Aramaic" (Metzger, *Textual Commentary on the Greek New Testament*, on Mark 15:34).

21. قاموس كلداني-عربي [The Chaldean–Arabic Dictionary], 3–21.

Greek expressions. The Syriac translation of the New Testament, the Peshitta (meaning "simple"), spread by the end of the third century AD. The Syriac script uses *elah* for both "a god" and "God." When the definite article (*a*) is added, as in its mother language, Aramaic, it comes at the end of the word so that the word becomes *elaha* meaning "the God."[22] The Peshitta renders Christ's words on the cross "Eli, Eli" (Matt 27:46) and "Eloi, Eloi" (Mark 15:34) as "Eli Eli." But it only gives the interpretation of the Markan version as "Elahi, Elahi," which exactly parallels the Arabic *elah* with the first person pronoun.[23]

> It may be concluded that the root that "Allah" has in common with other Semitic languages and which refers to God demonstrates a shared understanding and a developing theology that grows towards submission to the biblical revelation about the true God.

The Use of "Allah" by Arab Christians Today

Arab Christianity has existed from the day of Pentecost – when Arabs are mentioned last on the list of those who came to Jerusalem for Pentecost (Acts 2:11) – right up to the present day. Today there are over forty Arabic translations of the Bible or parts of it, and from Genesis to Revelation they all use the word "Allah" for God.

The various versions of the Arabic Bible demonstrate variety in translating the Hebrew singular *Elah* and *Eloah*, and the plural *Elohim*, as well as the Greek *Theos* of the New Testament. Each term is used to refer to both the true

---

22. The Syriac script of the Aramaic uses ܐܠܗ (*alah*) for both "a god" and "God." When the definite article ܐ (*a*) is added, it comes at the end of the word, not at the beginning, so that the word becomes ܐܠܗܐ (*alaha*), meaning "the God." The plural is ܐܠܗܐ (*aloha*). Cf. *TDOT*, s.v. "אלה"; قاموس كلداني-عربي [The Chaldean–Arabic Dictionary], s.v. "ܐܠܗ."

23. The Syriac New Testament Peshitta renders both the Matthean ηλι ηλι (*eli eli*) and the Markan ελωι ελωι (*Elowi Elowi*) as ܐܠܝ ܐܠܝ (*Eli Eli*) but only gives the interpretation of the Markan version ὁ θεός μου ὁ θεός μου (*ho theos mou ho theos mou*) as ܐܠܗܝ, ܐܠܗܝ, (*Elahi Elahi*), which exactly parallels the Arabic إلٰه (*Elah*) with the first person pronoun.

God[24] and pagan gods,[25] reflecting the same phenomenon in the whole Bible. However, the Arabic "Allah" is always used to refer to the God described in the Bible as the Creator, uncaused cause and necessary being who is omniscient, omnipresent, omnipotent, existing in three persons, Father, Son and Spirit, and incarnated in the Son in order to redeem humanity.

Figure 5.1 illustrates the differences in both Testaments in the most commonly used Bible in the Arab world today, the Bustani–Van Dyke translation.

The pagan god	The true God			Both
'Alihah (198 times)	Al 'Elah (147 times)	Allahumma (21 times)	Allah (2,330 times)	'Elah (1,140 times)

Figure 5.1: The True and Pagan Gods in the Arabic Van Dyke Translation

It may be concluded that, whatever the origin of the expression "Allah," the Arab Christian concept of "Allah" since its early use, its sharing of the same root with other Semitic languages and the ascribing to it the same biblical attributes of the true God, have made "Allah" the accepted and common expression used by Christians in all translations of the Arabic Bible, in Christian systematic theology and in full submission to biblical revelation.

---

24. The Arabic Van Dyke Bible translates the singular אֱלָהּ (*Elah*) and אֱלוֹהַּ (*Eloah*) to refer to the true God using *Al 'elah* (e.g. Deut 32:15), *Allah* (e.g. Deut 32:17; Hab 3:3) and *'Elah* (e.g. Isa 44:8; Hab 1:11; Pss 18:13; 114:7). The expression θεός (*theos*) in the New Testament is used to refer to the true God (e.g. John 3:16; Heb 1:1). The plural אֱלֹהִים (*Elohim*) referring to the true God is translated as *Al 'Elah* (e.g. Gen 2:4), *Allah* (e.g. Gen 1:1; Ps 82:1), *'Elah* (e.g. Deut 10:17), *'Alihah* (e.g. Deut 4:7), *Allahumma* (e.g. Num 12:13; Ezra 9:6; Ps 44:1). *Allahumma* was also used to translate θεός (*theos*) in the New Testament two times (Luke 18:11, 13).

25. The Arabic Van Dyke Bible translates the singular אֱלָהּ (*Elah*) and אֱלוֹהַּ (*Eloah*) to refer to a pagan god using *'Elah* (e.g. 2 Kgs 17:31; Hab 1:11) and *Alihah* (e.g. Deut 32:17; Dan 11:37). The expression θεός (*theos*) in the New Testament is also used to refer to pagan gods (e.g. Matt 10:34; Acts 14:11; 1 Cor 8:5). The plural אֱלֹהִים (*Elohim*) of the Old Testament, referring to a pagan god, is translated as *Alihah* in the plural (e.g. Exod 32:24; Deut 10:17; Ps 82:1) and *Alihah* in the singular (e.g. Exod 32:4–8; Deut 4:7).

"Allah," then, is simply the Arabic word for God, just as it is *Dieu* in French, *Gott* in German, *Dios* in Spanish, and so on.

Dealing with the Difficulty of the Question

The question whether it is possible that the God that the Qur'an proclaims is the same as the God that Oneness in Trinity proclaims may not be the right question to ask. A "yes" or "no" answer may offend the adherents of one group or the other. Duane Litfin asserts that this question is incapable of providing an adequate answer:

> The question appears incapable of generating a satisfactory answer, and when well-intentioned people try to answer it anyway, as they often do, the typical result is turmoil and confusion. How could it be otherwise? Any question that can only be answered with a "Maybe, maybe not" . . . is doomed from the outset . . . How much "sameness" is required to answer yes? How much difference to answer no?[26]

Therefore, rather than a question about *sameness*, a better question to ask is about *difference*. In other words, what belief does Oneness in Trinity hold that Absolute Oneness rejects? The difference lies in two words: *the gospel*. Applying this again to Islam and Christianity, Duane Litfin states, "This is the decisive difference between these two faiths. All the other differences stem from this one."[27]

This difference can be explained at two levels. The first level is in regard to the requisite for the activity of God's attributes, and the second level is in regard to the assurance of these attributes.

The Natural Requisite for the Activity of God's Attributes

The first level of difference is in regard to the natural requisite for the activity of God's attributes. What is unique about Oneness in Trinity is that it does not stop with the proclamation of God's existence and God's oneness. It goes further than Absolute Oneness by revealing a requisite that makes the activity of God's attributes possible, for every attribute naturally presupposes and requires the presence of a relationship. As will be seen repeatedly throughout

---

26. Litfin, "The Real Theological Issue."
27. Litfin.

this book, this natural requisite gives meaning to life and existence. It reflects the wondrous and unique nature of the oneness of God, which is that *God exists eternally in a relationship between persons within oneness.* Thus, there is a relationship between the Father and the Son, and this relationship is active eternally in the exchange of perfect attributes between them through the person of the Holy Spirit, who is the Spirit of the Father and the Spirit of the Son, the Spirit of God. This is traditionally called the doctrine of the Trinity.

The rejection of the Trinity had a certain evolution. It began with the rejection by qur'anic surahs of an erroneous concept of the Trinity that Christianity also rejects, namely polytheism. Qur'anic surahs declare,

> They disbelieve who say "God is one of three, for there is no god except one God." (Al-Maida 5:73; personal translation)

> And God said, "O Jesus the son of Mary! Did you tell people, 'Take me and my mother as two gods apart from God?' He said, 'Glory to you! Never could I say what is not rightfully mine.'" (Al-Maida 5:116; personal translation)

True Christianity does not believe in three gods (as in the expression "God is one of three"), and it totally rejects giving Mary divine status. The "Trinity" that is attacked here more likely refers to that of father, mother and son.[28]

The rejection by qur'anic surahs of this wrong view about the Trinity led Absolute Oneness later to reject another wrong view which Christianity also rejects, namely, the concept that God is composed of parts. This is expressed in the writings of Muhammad 'Abduh, who died in 1905 and who is quoted and revered as the father of Muslim thinking in the Arab world.[29] Defending the simplicity of God as the necessary being, 'Abduh asserted that God cannot be composed of parts because reason requires that necessity to the whole includes necessity to the parts – that is, each of the parts becomes divine as God is divine – and to him, that was unacceptable.[30]

---

28. Cf. Al-Sabzawari, 2:502; Al-Razi, 12:64; 'Ibn Kathir, تفسير القرآن العظيم [Explanation of the Great Qur'an] 2:77; Jalal Al Din Muhammad Bin Al Mahali, Jalal Al Din Al Suyuti, تفسير الجلالين [The Explanation of the Two Jalals], 158.

29. See C. C. Adams, "Mohammed 'Abduh, the Reformer," *Muslim World* 19 (1929): 264–273; Osman Amin, "Mohammed 'Abduh, the Reformer," *Muslim World* 36 (1946): 153–155; Suhail Ibn Salim Hanna, "Biographical Scholarship and Muhammad 'Abduh," *Muslim World* 59 (1969): 300–307; Assad Nimer Busool, "Shahkh Muhammad Rashid Rida's Relations with Jamal Al-Din Al-Afghani and Muhammad 'Abduh," *Muslim World* 66 (1976): 272–286; and Nabeeh A. Khoury, "Muhammad 'Abduh: An Ideology of Development," *Muslim World* 69 (1979): 42–52.

30. 'Abduh, *Theology of Unity,* 45–46 (see 51). This in fact is the point in affirming the Trinity: the persons of the Godhead share in the quality of necessity of the one God.

This has finally led Absolute Oneness to an explicit and unwavering denial of the true doctrine of the Trinity.[31] It is maintained that three can never be one, and one can never be three.[32] Al-Razi states that there is nothing more wicked and vain than the claim of three persons and one essence.[33] Therefore, some have preferred the term "oneness" over "unity" for fear that the latter may imply unifying several persons or gods into one. Badawi says, "For Muslims, monotheism does not mean simply the unity of God, because there can be different persons in unity. Monotheism in Islam is the absolute Oneness and Uniqueness of Allah, which precludes the notion of persons sharing in Godhead."[34]

The opposite of Absolute Oneness is in Arabic called *shirk*, meaning the association of others with God. *Shirk* is said to include polytheism, dualism, pantheism and "all forms of God-incarnate philosophies."[35] The development of the rejection of the Trinity is summarized in figure 5.2.

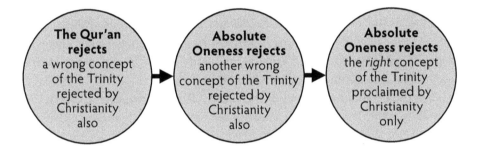

Figure 5.2: The Development of Rejection of the Trinity

The qur'anic verses denying the Trinity and the incarnation of Christ were among the main verses inscribed on the outside and inside of the octagonal arcade of the Dome of the Rock in Jerusalem, which was completed in 692 AD.

---

31. See Mohammed Sadiq, "A Moslem on the Trinity," *Muslim World* 10 (1920): 410–411; and William Shepard, "Conversations in Cairo: Some Contemporary Muslim Views of Other Religions," *Muslim World* 70 (1980): 175–177. However, Basetti-Sani declares that the Qur'an does not condemn the doctrine of the Trinity but only a false tritheism of God, Jesus and Mary, as well as the heretical Nestorian and Monophysite ideas on the incarnation (Julius Basetti-Sani, "For a Dialogue Between Christians and Muslims," *Muslim World* 57 [1967]: 189). Yet the entire weight of Islamic tradition is against his interpretation.

32. Cf. Sadiq, "A Moslem on the Trinity," 410–411. The small sect of Islamic Sophism departed from traditional Islam and some of its main leaders adopted the concept that God "became" a Trinity as an expression of his love. This will be dealt with in the chapter entitled "The Activity of the Attributes of God Outside Creation."

33. Al-Razi, 12:64.

34. Badawi, *Bridgebuilding*, 4.

35. Badawi, 4.

The Joyful Assurance in the Nature of God's Attributes

The second level of difference is in regard to the assurance of the nature of God's attributes. The adherents of both Absolute Oneness and Oneness in Trinity may speak of the *same subject*, "God," but they ascribe *different attributes* to him to the point that it seems the two sides are speaking about two completely different subjects. As Carl Henry asserts, "The importance of the discussion of divine attributes is apparent from the fact that one often alters a subject by applying different predicates to it."[36] At a different time, Irenaeus spoke similarly of the Gnostic Valentinians of the second century AD, describing an artist making an image of a king using precious jewels, but then being followed by another artist who rearranges the jewels to form an image with a totally different form, but tries to convince people that it is the same king![37]

The attributes of God proclaimed by Oneness in Trinity, as revealed in both Old and New Testaments, differ widely from those proclaimed by Absolute Oneness. In fact, *the nature of these attributes is the very reason why the oneness of God in the Old Testament is very different from Absolute Oneness.* This will be dealt with in the chapter in Volume 2 entitled "The Difference between Old Testament Oneness and Absolute Oneness."

But the height of assurance of the nature of God's attributes comes in the New Testament. The relational nature of the one and only true God as Father, Son and Holy Spirit overflowed into two actions in history that generate joyful assurance of the nature of his attributes. These are an expression of his grace and the great love with which he loves humankind. The first action was the coming of God in the incarnation, and the second action was the redemption of God at the cross vindicated by resurrection.

1. The Coming of God in the Incarnation

One of the fundamental beliefs of Christianity is that God assumed human nature, becoming a human being in the incarnation. This will be elaborated on later in different ways in various chapters of the two parts of this study.

Adherents of Absolute Oneness use the qur'anic denial of the deity of Christ to deny the incarnation (for the denial of the deity of Christ, see surahs Al Maida 5:17, 72, 75–77, 110; Al Emran 3:59; Maryam 19:88–93). Adopting

---

36. Henry, *God Who Stands and Stays*, 128.

37. Irenaeus, *Against Heresies*, 1.8.1. The Valentinians believed that God is incomprehensible and cannot be known directly nor given accurate description, but that he is androgynous, i.e. partly male and partly female, acting in conjunction to bring forth the Son, who in turn manifests himself in aeons that seek to find their origin in a journey of suffering through sophia (wisdom). Irenaeus points to them to illustrate how they speak of a different God.

the Qur'an's assumption that Christ's sonship meant God's cohabitation with Mary (Al An'am 6:101; Az-zukhruf 43:15–16), Yusuf Ali asserts that sonship pertains to the needs of the human physical condition, and that ascribing it to God is sourced in pagan mythology:

> Begetting a son is a physical act depending on the needs of men's animal nature. God Most High is independent of all needs, and it is derogatory to him to attribute such an act to him. It is merely a relic of pagan and anthropomorphic materialist superstitions . . . In 15:29, similar words are used with reference to Adam. The virgin birth should not therefore be supposed to imply that God was the father of Jesus in the sense in which Greek mythology makes Zeus the father of Apollo by Latona or of Minos by Europa. And yet that is the doctrine to which the Christian idea of "the only begotten Son of God" leads.[38]

Likewise, Gary Miller states that sonship and deity do not mix:

> Sonship and divine nature would be two attributes which are incompatible, because sonship describes someone who receives life while divine nature describes someone who receives life from no one. To be a son is to be less than divine and to be divine is to be no one's son.[39]

Miller further states that "All quotations that are cited by Christians in order to put in the mouth of Jesus the claim of deity are implicit, which means interpretation is required."[40] It is also maintained by some that, just as the virgin birth does not prove the deity of Jesus, neither do his miracles.[41] Räisänen claims that the early Christians believed much in the same way as qur'anic surahs do.[42] 'Ibn Kathir states that the curses of God will fall on all Christians until the day of resurrection for calling God "Christ."[43]

---

38. Yusuf Ali, 751, n. 2487; 1495, n. 5552.

39. Miller, "Deification of Jesus," 1.

40. Miller, 3.

41. See Räisänen, "Portrait of Jesus in the Qur'an," 126–127; C. George Fry, "The Qur'anic Christ," *Concordia Theological Quarterly* 43 (1979): 211.

42. Räisänen, 128; cf. Hick, "Jesus and the World Religions," 171.

43. 'Ibn Kathir, تفسير القرآن العظيم [Explanation of the Great Qur'an], 2:33.

2. The Redemption of God at the Cross Vindicated by the Resurrection

One of the main teachings of Christianity is that the incarnation was for the purpose of redeeming humanity. This redemption took place through the death of Christ on the cross in the place of human beings, followed by his resurrection from the dead to confirm all that he said about himself and all that he promised. Therefore, all those who believe in him will be granted forgiveness of sin, and the Lord will count his righteousness to them. Furthermore, just as Christ was raised from the dead, so believers will experience new life, and the Spirit of God will reside in them.

Adherents of Absolute Oneness use the rejection by qur'anic surahs of the need for atonement (Al Isra 17:13; Al Baqarah 2:284; Annisa 4:110; Hud 11:114) to reject the cross completely. Badawi comments,

> The Quran teaches that God is both Just and Merciful. But since he created humankind and knows its weaknesses, he does not require bloodshed to forgive. One who sincerely repents and inculcates a relationship of love for God, and obedience and submission to him, can be assured of God's loving forgiveness . . . If the All-Merciful and Loving God wanted to forgive, what prevents him from doing so in a *direct, simple and straightforward manner?* (emphasis his)[44]

Qur'anic surahs strongly reject the death of Christ. The Qur'an declares,

> That they said (in boast), "We killed Christ Jesus the son of Mary, the messenger of Allah"; but they killed him not, nor crucified him, but so it was made to appear to them, and those who differ therein are full of doubts, with no (certain) knowledge, but only conjecture to follow, for of a surety they killed him not, but Allah raised him up unto himself, and Allah is exalted in power, wise. (An Nisa 4:157–158; Yusuf Ali translation; his parentheses)

These qur'anic verses teach two things: (1) The death of Jesus is only in the minds of those who claim it; (2) Belief in his death is only an opinion based on no evidence. The ultimate act of God's saving Jesus from the Jews is said to be God delivering him from being crucified.[45] In addition, the idea of crucifixion is rejected by Absolute Oneness because God, in the eyes of its adherents, would

---

44. Badawi, "Jesus: Beloved Messenger of God," 2. Cf. Abd Al-Fadi, الخطية والكفارة في الإسلام والمسيحية [Sin and Atonement in Islam and Christianity], 33–40.

45. Cf. Al-Jalalayn, 166; 'Ibn Kathir, تفسير القرآن العظيم [Explanation of the Great Qur'an], 2:109; Al-Sabzawari, 2:536; Al-Razi, 12:135.

never condescend in incarnation or redemption, as this would lower his worth. The idea of Christ suffering is repudiated because it is shameful in their eyes that a prophet of God should suffer. In contrast, the Christian understanding is the total opposite: had Christ, who is God incarnate, not been willing to be humiliated, spat on, cursed, beaten, and to endure pain to the point of death, there would be no salvation for humanity.

The Giant Leap

It is clear that adherents of Absolute Oneness strongly reject what is essential to the concept of God in Oneness in Trinity. Though these adherents claim to proclaim the same one and only God proclaimed by Oneness in Trinity and with similar attributes, they strongly reject the unique proclamation of Oneness in Trinity. Absolute Oneness makes the giant leap from *proclaiming the one and only God to proclaiming the activity of his attributes*, completely rejecting the natural requisite for the activity of his attributes and the joyful assurance of the nature of his attributes. Figure 5.3 illustrates this.

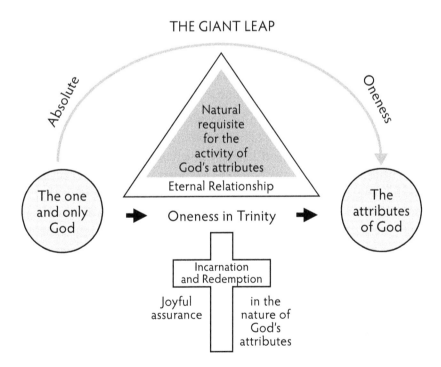

Figure 5.3: The Giant Leap between God and His Attributes

This giant leap leads in the end to an untrue concept of God, regardless of the religion adopted, and to ascribing to him attributes that are either untrue or without any meaning that can be trusted. This will be the subject of study in the rest of this book.

Appeal to Believers and Non-Believers

Many who believe in Oneness in Trinity avoid the subject in one way or another, and in their thoughts and speech focus more on the existence and attributes of God in general. They thereby ignore the natural requisite that gives life to his attributes. This shortcoming appears especially in ignoring the importance of what happened in history in the incarnation and redemption. They thus limit their thoughts and speech about Christ to his being only a prophet, teacher and exemplary man. In other words, believers in Oneness in Trinity may in practice but mistakenly make the same giant leap! Colin Gunton asserts that speaking of God's attributes apart from the Trinity is an error that springs from making human conclusions about God without hearing what God says about himself:

> To speak of the attributes apart from the Trinity – as is often done – is a mistake . . . We are concerned, rather, first of all with who God is, not what we attribute to him . . . It is not a matter of what we attribute, but of what he reveals himself to be.[46]

As to those who do not believe in Oneness in Trinity, especially adherents of Absolute Oneness, there is here a door of communication. A person may begin with the same expression "God" used by different religions, but instinctively start to believe in the true attributes of God apart from whatever religion he or she follows. This might start with belief in God as an eternal Father. The person might then ask about the nature of this Father and what makes him act with these attributes. This could lead to a path of communication between believers and unbelievers for the sake of reaching the truth. There is more in this study that aims to guide the reader in a journey of discovery of the nature of the true God. That is the appeal of this book.

---

46. Gunton, *Act and Being*, Kindle loc. 31, 95, 105.

6

The Historical Conflict of Absolute Oneness

Introduction

This chapter presents an example of the historical struggle of Absolute Oneness. As mentioned earlier, the concept of "Absolute Oneness" is the belief not of just one religion but of several, and it is also the conclusion of philosophy. The historical struggle studied in this chapter arose in the eighth century AD, two centuries after the rise of Islam. It is expressed by some Arab philosophers because of their rejection of the doctrine of the Trinity. They may or may not be followers of a particular religion or belief. *This struggle shows what God would be like if he were not triune, and the effect this has on humanity.* The struggle of Absolute Oneness is presented in this chapter and the answer of Oneness in Trinity in the following chapter.

Defining the Conflict

The conflict within Absolute Oneness commenced with defining the attributes of God and their activity. This is manifested in its difficulty in answering the inevitable question that springs from acknowledging the activity of God's attributes.

The Inevitable Question

Behind the expressed difference between Absolute Oneness and Oneness in Trinity lies a question that cannot be avoided. It is the question behind every question related to the nature of God. It is also a theological inquiry that all religions and faiths must answer. The question is: How can the attributes of God be active eternally apart from the existence of creation without God existing in relationship?

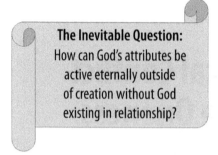

The Inevitable Question: How can God's attributes be active eternally outside of creation without God existing in relationship?

The question can be explained using the example of love. If love is one of God's eternal attributes, it requires the presence of the lover and the one loved (or beloved), in addition to love itself. Simply put, how can love be active eternally without a relationship?

However, if the object of God's love is outside of himself, this leads to two options. The first option is that God is in relationship with another eternal being like himself. But this is rejected because it opens the door to polytheism; for there is only one God with no partners. The second option is that God is in an eternal relationship with creation. But this is also rejected because it makes creation eternal like God, and it also makes the necessary being (God) dependent on what is contingent (creation).

Using the attribute of love again, if the object of God's love is within himself, this also leads to two options. The first is that God is compound. This option is rejected at once because of God's simplicity, that is, that he is not divisible and is not made up of parts. The second, and the last, option is plurality in unity, or that God exists in a relationship within himself, implying at least a duality in his one essence. Since God is independent of anything outside of himself, the three elements (lover, beloved and love) must exist in himself eternally. The same applies to all his moral attributes.[1]

> The question then becomes: If Absolute Oneness proclaims the eternal activity of God's attributes, how can it at the same time deny any relationship for the activity of these attributes?

---

1. As Macdonald puts it, to say that God is knower must mean that he either knows something within himself, implying duality, or that he knows something outside himself, implying dependence (Macdonald, "God: A Unit or a Unity?," 13).

Two Opposing Schools of Thought within Absolute Oneness

The conflict within Absolute Oneness began when it strongly rejected all the above options. It was thus put in a place where it was forced to compose a theological system that answered the questions and challenges that arose. However, the concept of Absolute Oneness was formed as a result of a long struggle in history.[2]

A theological and philosophical conflict arose between two major Arab schools of thought: the traditional and the rational.[3] The traditional school, led by the Ash'arites, stressed that what they viewed as inspired writings should be above reason, and that faith and surrender were therefore required.[4] Interpretation of the text was to be either limited or forbidden, and ignorance must be admitted.[5] The mind was considered as merely a tool to understand.

On the other hand, the rational school, represented by the Mu'tazilites, recognized the necessity of reason. They placed reason above the text, and viewed the mind as a tool to reach the truth.[6] They believed that when a discrepancy occurred between mind and revelation, interpretation was required.[7]

The Mu'tazilites were anathematized around the eleventh century AD and the Ash'arites came to be recognized as orthodox.[8] But an examination of the conflict in thought between the two schools highlights very important principles to help avoid a similar conflict about the attributes of God.

Classification of the Attributes

The conflict between the Mu'tazilites and the Ash'arites revolved around explaining the ninety-nine names of God declared in the Qur'an and in the

---

2. Fadi Abu Deeb, "جذور الوحدانية الإسلامية" [The Roots of Islamic Oneness] (unpublished paper for the course on Trinitarianism, Jordan Evangelical Theological Seminary, 2012), 9.

3. Other controversies arose unrelated to the subject at hand, including determinism and free will, the roles of science and Greek ideas in establishing dogma, the union of the body and the soul, and the union of a divine spirit with human beings (see L. Massignon, "Hulul," in *Shorter Encyclopedia of Islam*, ed. Gibb and Kramers, 141). The Sufi mystical school of thought represents a minority development (see D. B. Macdonald, "Allah," in *Shorter Encyclopedia of Islam*, ed. Gibb and Kramers, 37–40; Olari, *Arab Thought and Its Role in History*, 155–177).

4. Cf. Kamal Al-Yaziji, معالم الفكر العربي في العصر الوسيط [Highlights of the Arab Thought in the Middle Ages], 152; 'Abduh, *Theology of Unity*, 29–40.

5. Al-Yaziji, 157.

6. Al-Yaziji, 156–157.

7. Al-Yaziji, 157.

8. See Thomson, "Al-Ash'ari and His Al-ibanah," 253.

Hadith. "The most beautiful names belong to Allah: so call on him by them" (Surah 7:180; cf. 17:110; 20:8; 59:24; Hadith 8:97:64).[9] The Hadith also supports this and promises that those who recall these names will enter paradise.[10]

Exemplary Attributes

Theologians insist that the number ninety-nine does not necessarily define the limit of God's attributes.[11] Therefore, the list of ninety-nine names is only an exemplary collection and is not exhaustive.[12] They state that these names were selected to praise God, and that the Hadith does not mention all the ninety-nine names.[13]

Varied Classification of Attributes

As in any religion, there are various ways of classifying God's attributes. At the start, the ninety-nine names were classified into the metaphysical and the anthropomorphic.[14] However, due to the difficulty that Absolute Oneness had with relating anthropomorphic attributes to God, a number of other categorizations appeared in the literature. *The Encyclopaedia of Islam* presents a classification according to the attributes of essence, self-expression, qualification and action.[15] Another classification distinguished between two kinds of attributes: the philosophical attributes, which are deduced by reason and pertain to the amoral qualities of the one and only necessary being; and the

---

9. See also 17:110; 20:8; 59:24; Bukhari 8:97:64.

10. See Bukhari 8:97:164, 169.

11. Jeffrey, *Islam, Muhammad and His Religion*, 93.

12. See 'Abd Al-Mughni Sa'id, الجديد حول أسماء الله الحسنى [A New Treatment of the Most Beautiful Names of God], 7.

13. 'Abd Al-Mughni Sa'id, 9–10.

14. Rahbar prefers the classification "dispositional" (having the power or authority to arrange, settle, manage or control) and "non-dispositional" rather than "anthropomorphic" and "non-anthropomorphic" (i.e. metaphysical). He states, "Names like the Avenging, the Merciful, the Just King, the Forgiving . . . are *dispositional* attributes alluding to the moods in which God may be said to be *disposed toward men*. On the other hand the names the Eternal, the Reality, the Omnipotent, the Omniscient, the Willer, the Self-sufficient, are the ones which do not describe a disposition" (Daud Rahbar, "Relation of Muslim Theology to the Qur'an," *Muslim World* 51 [1961]: 46).

15. *The Encyclopaedia of Islam* supplies four categories of attributes. The first category relates to the attributes of essence. The second category is attributes related to self-expression, which are subdivided into negative (emphasizing transcendence) and positive attributes. The third category relates to the attributes "of qualification." The fourth category relates to the attributes of action (L. Gardet, "Allah," in Bearman et al., *Encyclopaedia of Islam*, 1:411).

moral attributes, which cannot be deduced by reason and are related to God's actions with humanity throughout history.[16] However, in the end, categorization is determined by the subject or the goal of study. It is understandable that the parties involved in the debate, the Mu'tazilites and the Ash'arites, classified the attributes into those related to God's actions and those related to God's essence, because the conflict revolved around *the attributes related to God's dealings with creation, and the attributes related to God himself apart from creation*. It is this last classification that will be used in this study.

The Conflict Regarding the Attributes of Action

The attributes of action are related to God's dealings with creation in time and space as experienced by humankind. The conflict regarding the attributes of action revolved around their source, their manifestation, their prevention from comparison and the resultant inconsistency.

1. The Source of the Attributes of Action

The issue of the source of the attributes came to the forefront in the theological struggle between the Mu'tazilites and the Ash'arites. The struggle was triggered by the eternality of the attributes of action and their relationship to God.

The Mu'tazilites

The Mu'tazilites maintained that only the attributes of essence (such as life, power and knowledge) are necessary and eternal and can be described in positive terms. But the Mu'tazilites insisted that it would be blasphemous to acknowledge the attributes of action (such as creation, love, will, beneficence, speech, mercy and justice) as defining what God is like.[17] The Mu'tazilites maintained that the attributes of action are not eternal, but created, and therefore contingent, unnecessary and changing.[18] They even extended this to include the moral attributes. On this basis, the source of the attributes of action is unknown. Sweetman calls this "reverent agnosticism."[19] Based on this,

---

16. 'Abduh, *Theology of Unity*, 45, 53.

17. Al-Yaziji, معالم الفكر العربي في العصر الوسيط [Highlights of the Arab Thought in the Middle Ages], 160. The word for "blasphemy" is إشراك (*Ishrak*).

18. Al-Yaziji, 161. Cf. Majid Fakhry, تاريخ الفلسفة الإسلامية: من القرن الثامن حتى يومنا هذا [The History of Islamic Philosophy: From the Eighth Century to the Present Day], 113.

19. Sweetman, *Islam and Christian Theology*, 2:22.

Fadi Abu Deeb asserts that the Mu'tazilites fell into the trap of making God subject to change and development.[20]

But the question remained: If the attributes of action do not describe the nature of God, what is their source? It is here that the Ash'arites provided their answer.

The Ash'arites

The Ash'arites accepted the eternality of God's attributes of action, but since Absolute Oneness rejects the existence of any eternal relationship in God as a source of his attributes, the conclusion was that the attributes of action stem from his will. So, according to Absolute Oneness, God's attributes of action stem, not from anything in his nature, but rather from his will to do anything he chooses. In other words, his attributes do not communicate his personal qualities, as he is in himself, but rather point to the freedom of his will. The divine will became a dominant factor in all thought of Absolute Oneness. Accordingly, a revealed action of God "deals with the will of Allah and not Allah himself."[21] Similarly, the Arab thinker Al-Farūqi stresses that guarding God's transcendence comes at the expense of his self-revelation:

> The will of God is . . . the nature of God in so far as I can know anything about him. This is God's will and that is all we have . . . But God does not reveal himself to anyone. Christians talk about the revelation of God himself – by God of God – but that is the great difference . . . You may not have complete transcendence and self-revelation at the same time.[22]

God's oneness in Islam is thus represented by his absolute, all-encompassing will. He is seen as alone determining every human act. Macdonald asserts,

> Allah creates us and he creates all that we do, immediately, directly, without secondary causes. The unity of Allah, therefore, is a basis for his essential difference from all other beings, and also for his being absolutely the only real agent in existence. Second causes, the idea of nature, the existence of a power to do this or that

---

20. Abu Deeb, "جذور الوحدانية الإسلامية" [The Roots of Islamic Oneness], 12.

21. Arne Rudvin, "Islam: An Absolutely Different Ethos?," *International Review of Mission* 71 (1982): 59.

22. Isma'il Al-Faruqi, "On the Nature of Islamic Da'wah," *International Review of Missions* 65 (1976): 405.

created in things, man's having by Allah's will any part in an action – all these are denied.[23]

Thus, Absolute Oneness may be defined as "unity in essence and qualities and acts, both internal and external."[24]

2. The Manifestation of the Attributes of Action

The manifestation of God's attributes of action in Absolute Oneness is accomplished through his unlimited power to fulfill his free will. "The idea of absolute sovereignty and ruthless omnipotence . . . are at the basis. For the rest, his character is impersonal – that of an infinite eternal vast Monad."[25] Again, the two schools, the Mu'tazilites and the Ash'arites differed in their views on the manifestation of God's attribute of power.

The Mu'tazilites

The Mu'tazilites believed that humankind is able to distinguish good from evil. At the same time, as mentioned earlier, they considered attributes of action, including moral attributes such as love, will and justice, to be contingent and not eternal as God, unlike attributes of essence. Therefore, the Mu'tazilites maintained that God is committed through reason to shepherd what is of benefit to his creation.[26] Abu Deeb states that, because the Mu'tazilites did not accept the idea that an omnipotent God could act against principles of justice and goodness, they considered God to be bound by absolute justice.[27] He is thus said to act according to human logic in all his dealings with humanity, and he is unable to have mercy or to forgive.

The Ash'arites

The Ash'arites considered that the source of human knowledge of the difference between good and evil comes only from God by his decree that determines what is good and what is evil. According to the Ash'arites, God is under no obligation to fulfill any action that is believed to be appropriate of him. This is because his attributes are viewed as subject to his will and not to his nature. So,

---

23. Macdonald, "God: A Unit or a Unity?," 16.

24. Macdonald, 16.

25. Zwemer, *Moslem Doctrine of God*, 30.

26. Fakhry, تاريخ الفلسفة الإسلامية: من القرن الثامن حتى يومنا هذا [The History of Islamic Philosophy: From the Eighth Century to the Present Day], 336–337.

27. Abu Deeb, "جذور الوحدانية الإسلامية" [The Roots of Islamic Oneness], 12, quoting Ayoub, *Islam: Faith and History*, 164.

while the Mu'tazilites proclaimed that God works in ultimate justice according to human expectations, the Ash'arites proclaimed that God works in ultimate power to fulfill his will.

One of the main tenets of the Ash'arites is the consolidation of the power of God in the ninety-nine names. "These attributes and names point to the ability of God in being unique in his power and greatness."[28] There are three aspects that emphasize the consolidation of the source of power: the reinforcement of the attributes; the contrariness of the attributes; and the unboundedness of the attributes.

1. *The Reinforcement of the Attributes.* The emphasis on the power of God is reflected in the many similarities in the names given to him.[29] For example, eight names characterize his *knowledge* (the wise, the skilled, the guide, the one who counts, the one who sees, the one who observes, the one who witnesses and the one who knows); nine names characterize his *ability* (the mighty one, the able one, the one who subdues, the powerful, the resourceful, the one who has all power, the secure, the avenger and the one who inherits); six names characterize his *justice* (the one who humiliates, the one to whom all are accountable, the ruler, the one who gives the right judgment, the judge and the one who gathers); ten names characterize him as the *mover* (the grantor of victory, the one who leads conquest, the one who preserves, the one who protects, the ruler, the guardian, the one who answers, the one who responds, the one who guides and the one who repeats); nine names characterize his *self-sufficiency* (the one, the unique one, the eternal, the one who remains, the self-subsisting one, the first, the last, the living one and the self-sufficient one); eighteen names characterize him as the only *source of benevolence* (the light, the truth, the peace, the righteous, the holy, the compassionate, the merciful, the sympathetic, the oft returning, the patient one, the forgiver, the one who bestows forgiveness, the gracious, the kind, the loving one, the one to appreciate, the one who forbears and the one worthy of praise); thirteen names characterize his *sovereignty* (the supreme, the exalted one, the mighty one, the one who has glory and honor, the great one, the one lifted up, the great, the king, the owner of all, the glorious one, the elevated one, the

28. Muhammad Majdi Murgan, الله واحد أم ثالوث [God One or Trinity], 60.

29. See Sa'id, الجديد حول أسماء الله الحسنى [A New Treatment of the Most Beautiful Names of God], 12.

honored one and the transcendent one); three names characterize him as the only *source of provision* for humankind (the one who extends, the sustainer and the giver); and six names characterize him as the *originator* of all things (the one who begins, the creator, the evolver, the innovator, the one who disposes and the one who paints). These lists emphasize that God is able to do anything he chooses. But *they are what he can do, and not what he is.*

2.   *The Contrariness of the Attributes.* Not only are similar attributes reinforced, but contrary attributes are strongly held in opposition to one another. Thus God is said to be both the one who causes death and also resurrects and brings back; humiliates and brings shame and also exalts and lifts up; is evident and also is hidden; harms and also benefits; withholds and also gives; eradicates and also gathers; defers and also brings forward; is the first and also the last. The contrariness of the attributes supports the freedom of God to do all he wishes with no limits.[30] They emphasize God's power to fulfill his will. There is nothing good or bad that he cannot do according to his free will.

3.   *The Unboundedness of the Attributes.* Stress was made on the unbounded quality of the attributes, that is, the independence of God's power from any other attribute. Emphasis was placed upon the phenomenon that there is never a promise given by God in the Qur'an that is not accompanied by a statement stressing his freedom and power to act according to how he chooses. Accordingly, God's love for his creatures lacks a relationship of fellowship.[31] This is because, according to them, humankind is made primarily for worship rather than relationship. "Ultimate in relationship is willing submission rather than interaction."[32] Glaser adds,

> God's love may cause him to have mercy on his creatures, even to the extent of communicating with them; but it is a love that condescends in beneficence rather than a love that shares in relationship. God may love us if he so

30. See Sa'id, 12; Sweetman, *Islam and Christian Theology*, 2:23.
31. See Glaser, "Concept of Relationship as a Key," 60.
32. Glaser, 59.

chooses, but his relationship with the objects of his love is very different from that envisaged in the Christian faith.[33]

In Surah Al-Maida 5:118, Christ is said to deny requesting worship for himself and his mother. Commenting on this verse, Al-Razi maintains that the reason why Jesus made this statement was to ascribe to God the *power and freedom* to do whatever he wishes. This, he says, is because of the following: "It is possible according to our religion that God may send blasphemers to paradise and the righteous and worshipers to [eternal] fire, because ownership belongs to him and no one can stop him!"[34]

In the same vein, Sayyid Qutub specifies God's absolute freedom for these actions such that he is *bound by no law or promise*. He states,

> Every time the Qur'an states a definite promise or constant law, it follows it with a statement implying that the Divine will is free of all limitations and restrictions, even those based on a promise from Allah or a law of his. For his will is absolute beyond any promise or law.[35]

'Abduh similarly asserts that God *does not do any action out of necessity from his essence*:

> None of his deeds proceed from him of necessity as he essentially is. All the attributes of his acts, creation, provision, granting and forbidding, chastisement and beneficence, are affirmed of him by the special option of power. The intelligent mind, in allowing that all God's actions are by his knowledge and will, would emphatically never entertain the idea that any of his deeds were essentially necessary of his nature, as is the case for example in respect of the necessary qualities of things or of Divine attributes which have to be necessarily posited of him.[36]

Majid Fakhry adds that the Ash'arites rejected humanity's ability to distinguish between good and evil, and held on to the belief that *God alone* does so to the point that he has full freedom to punish those who are innocent and forgive those who are evil:

---

33. Glaser, 58.

34. Al-Razi, 12:144. My translation.

35. Qutub, في ظلال القرآن [In the Shades of the Qur'an], 6:30:3889.

36. 'Abduh, *Theology of Unity*, 57.

As they [the Mu'tazilites] believed that man is capable through reason of distinguishing good from evil, before the coming of revelation, the Asha'rites held to the moral system built on the belief in the absolute divine will. So that good is what God commanded and evil is what God prohibited. And in harmony with this priority of will, they denied that this kind of mental knowledge has any credit in the understanding of the nature of normal action, as ruled by [a] moral standard. So the power of God and sovereignty dominates everything; even the meaning of justice and oppression is related to his decrees. And justice and oppression or good and evil have no meaning outside his decrees. Therefore, God was not bound, as the Mu'tazilites believed, to shepherd what is better for his creation, or maintain their moral and religious interests – if the expression is accurate – but rather he is absolutely free to punish the innocent and forgive the guilty. And if he wished to create a world completely different than the world he created, there is nothing to prevent him from creating this world or any of its parts.[37]

Majid Fakhry's above perspective of *God's will and power* is supported by Ahmad Bin Taymiyah of the fourteenth century saying about fatalism:

Everything in existence is created for him. He created it by his will and power, and what he willed came to be and what he did not will did not. And he is the one that gives and excludes, demotes and promotes, empowers and denigrates, enriches and impoverishes, leads astray and guides, brings happiness and brings misery, gives sovereignty to whom he wills and withdraws it from whom he wills, opens hearts to Islam or causes the heart to be restrained . . . ; he also overturns hearts; there is no heart from the hearts of worshipers except that it is between the two fingers of the merciful one, if he willed he will raise it, and if he wills to lead astray he will do so.[38]

Bin Taymiyah further considered the following two hadiths as authentic, asserting that *the divine will is not bound to any law*:

37. Fakhry, تاريخ الفلسفة الإسلامية: من القرن الثامن حتى يومنا هذا [The History of Islamic Philosophy: From the Eighth Century to the Present Day], 336–337.

38. Ahmad Bin Taymiyah, القضاء والقَدَر [Judgment and Decree], 97. My translation.

God holds firmly to two matters, and so he said, "This goes to paradise and I do not care, and this goes to the fire and I do not care." . . . God, when he created Adam, showed him his descendants to the right and left, and then said, "Those to the fire and I do not care, and those to paradise and I do not care."[39]

Thus, the Ash'arite school won, and Bin Taymiyah became the larger source of contemporary Salafism. This led to the adoption of the Tahawite Confession (after Abu Jaafar Al Tahawi, who died in AD 933), which capsulizes the belief about the attributes of God, and which "found acceptance by all schools of jurisprudence that included the Ash'arites, the Matrudites and Salafites, so that each of these considered it their confession."[40] The following are samples of this confession regarding the attributes of God:

- Article 27: "He guides who he wills, and protects and forgives as *favor*, and he leads astray whom he wills, and abandons and causes tragedy as *justice*."[41]

- Article 39: "The one who describes God with one meaning of the meanings of humanity, blasphemes. He who sees this is elevated, avoids the sayings of the blasphemers, and knows that *his attributes are not like of humanity*."[42]

- Article 47: "For our Lord, may he be exalted and elevated, is described by the attributes of oneness, and is attributed the attributes of uniqueness, the meaning of which is *not known by any of his creation*."[43]

- Articles 53–54: "And God knew the number of those still entering paradise and those entering hell, one sentence, and the number will not increase or decrease, as well as their works as to whether any of them knew to do."[44]

Thus, according to Absolute Oneness, to claim a promise from God would be to bind him to a course of action. Macdonald comments that this understanding of God reduces him to an unknowable and an indefinable force:

---

39. Ahmad Bin Taymiyah, 84.

40. The Tahawite Confession, العقيدة الطحاوية "مكان المتن بين أهل السنة", accessed 1 May 2014, http://ar.wikipedia.org/wiki/العقيدة_الطحاوية_(كتاب)

41. Abu Jaafar Al Tahawi, متن العقيدة الطحاوية: بيان عقيدة أهل السُّنّة والجماعة [The Essence of the Tahawite Confession: The Statement of the Faith of the People of the Sunnah], 11.

42. Abu Jaafar Al Tahawi, 13.

43. Abu Jaafar Al Tahawi, 15.

44. Abu Jaafar Al Tahawi, 16.

But in the God of the formal theology of Islam [*kalam*], removed from all kindly influences of love, sympathy, interest, we have an iron force, unaffectable, unchangeable, which has not even the one safeguard which goes with the forces of nature, that they are calculable and foretellable. He, rather, has in him an element which makes him incalculable; no one can reckon on him, for nobody has the right to say that he must, or will, do this or that. That is entirely an affair of his "irresponsible" will.[45]

Summary

God's attributes in Absolute Oneness may be summarized in several foundational concepts. First, all attributes of action stem from the attribute of power to fulfill the unbounded will of God. Second, the rest of the attributes of action are imperfect, while the attributes of power and will are perfect. Third, the attributes of action do not necessarily work in harmony with one another. Fourth, humankind cannot know *God* through the attributes of action. Figure 6.1 illustrates this.

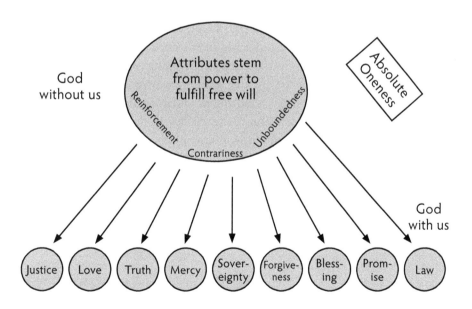

Figure 6.1: Attributes of Action in Absolute Oneness

45. Macdonald, "God: A Unit or a Unity?," 13.

3. The Prevention from Comparing the Attributes of Action

Since God's attributes in Absolute Oneness stem from God's power to fulfill his will, Absolute Oneness found great difficulty in comparing God's attributes to those of humankind, as demonstrated in its dealing with anthropomorphic expressions. In the qur'anic surahs God is described as seeing (Surah 52:48; 96:14), having hands (39:67; 48:10) and a face (55:27), writing (7:145), having a throne on which he sits (69:17; 57:4) and as the best of crafters (3:54), among other examples that are also found in the Hadith. There was an obstacle to Absolute Oneness's acceptance of these anthropomorphic terms because they were also viewed as bringing God down to the level of humankind or bringing humankind up to the level of God.[46]

The Mu'tazilites

To solve this problem, the Mu'tazilites emphasized the transcendence of God and refrained "from debate about the implications of passages [of the Qur'an] involving human comparisons."[47] They said that "to predicate qualities of God is to be in danger of *tashbih* (i.e. likening God to creatures). But the dilemma is that the Qur'an does apply epithets to God. The only solution therefore is to remove these from the essential nature of God and class them with other attributes, holding in mind that these have no effect on the immutable essence."[48]

The Mu'tazilites therefore conceived of God as removed and unassociated with his creatures, not just in essence but in presence as well.[49] They insisted that it is impossible to define God, and rejected likening God to human beings, calling for the distancing of the qur'anic anthropomorphic expressions from God's essence. They therefore called for an allegorical understanding of them. This is the logical conclusion that even Jewish theologians like Philo came to in spite of the fact that anthropomorphic expressions are used in the Old Testament. In this way, both Philo and the Mu'tazilites ended up with what Sweetman calls effectively "an anthropomorphic scripture with a philosophizing interpretation."[50]

---

46. Sweetman, *Islam and Christian Theology*, 2:33.
47. 'Abduh, *Theology of Unity*, 39.
48. Sweetman, *Islam and Christian Theology*, 2:24.
49. L. Gardet, "Allah," in Bearman et al., *Encyclopaedia of Islam*, 1:410.
50. Sweetman, *Islam and Christian Theology*, 2:25.

The Ash'arites

The Ash'arites, on the other hand, responded by asserting that the Mu'tazilites's concept of transcendence amounted to making what the qur'anic text says ineffective.[51] They accused the Mu'tazilites of putting the cart before the horse,[52] and maintained that the Mu'tazilites's danger was that the religion of Islam became "in their hands a philosophy inspired by a revelation instead of a revelation supported by dialectic."[53] The Ash'arites took the principle of *mukhalafah* (difference), that is, God's difference from all created things,[54] and came to the famous principle of: "without inquiring how and without making comparison."[55] Allah is different from any created being. This is also expressed by another common rhyme: "Everything that comes into your mind is perishing, and Allah is different from that." That is to say, "Allah is different from any thought we can possibly have, for our thoughts are of transitory things."[56]

Thus the Ash'arites deduced God's attributes partly dialectically and partly based on the Qur'an.[57] Macdonald comments,

> No terms applicable to a created being may be applied to him, or if they are – as so often in the Koran – it must be clearly understood that their meaning as applied to created things is no clue to their meaning when applied to Allah . . . So, in general, from the anthropomorphic terms in the Koran, we must not draw any conclusions as to Allah's nature. He may be called "Most Merciful" there, but that does not mean that he has a quality, Mercy, corresponding to anything in man. If he could be so described – that is, in similar terms with man – then he, too, would be a created being.[58]

---

51. Gardet, "Allah," in *Encyclopaedia of Islam*, ed. Bearman et al., 1:410; T. J. Boer, تاريخ الفلسفة في الإسلام [The History of Philosophy in Islam], trans. Muhammad 'Abd Al-Hadi 'Abu Ruwaydah, 55.

52. Thomson, "Al-Ash'ari and His Al-ibanah," 246.

53. Thomson, 247.

54. Thomson, 247.

55. Sweetman, *Islam and Christian Theology*, 2:29; Gardet, "Allah," in *Encyclopaedia of Islam*, ed. Bearman et al., 1:411; D. B. Macdonald, "Allah," in *Shorter Encyclopaedia of Islam*, ed. Gibb and Kramers, 37.

56. Macdonald, "Allah," 38.

57. Macdonald, "God: A Unit or a Unity?," 13.

58. Macdonald, 15–16.

In the final analysis, both the Ash'arites and the Mu'tazilites make it impossible for human beings to know how these anthropomorphisms are related to God.

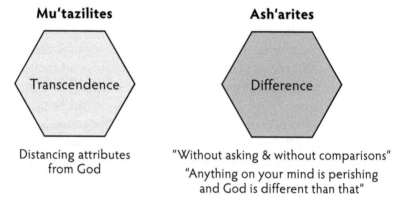

Figure 6.2: Anthropomorphisms with the Mu'tazilites and Ash'arites

4. The Resultant Inconsistency

Weakness in the logic of Absolute Oneness appeared in the many serious attempts to avoid the conclusion of the capriciousness of God. The thinkers of Absolute Oneness resorted to at least one moral attribute.

The Mu'tazilites

The Mu'tazilites appealed to God's reasonableness, their view being that God does not issue his decrees in a haphazard manner but for reasonable motives, which in turn is parallel to his justice and wisdom. Majid Fakhry summarizes this:

The principle that distinguished the Mu'tazilites from others, to begin with, was their revolutionary method of deciding what is called the reasonable aspect of God's ways and actions. So they tried to prove this with evidences from reason without denying the holiness of divine words. And one of the most important issues they raised in this regard was their claim that good and evil were not only by decree or the subjective with their legitimacy springing from divine command, as the Ash'arites maintained, but they were reasonable sayings, proven by ways of reason. And from this dangerous introduction, the Mu'tazilites launched their claim asserting that God does not command what contradicts reason, and does not act without care for his creatures, which necessarily is a violation of his, most high, justice and wisdom.[59]

The Ash'arites

In alignment with the Mu'tazilites, but with some differences, the Ash'arites resorted to wisdom, but then reintroduced limitations dictated by the divine will! To begin with, 'Abduh, who based his whole system of theology on God's special option of power, maintained that God is neither frivolous nor deceptive in his deeds because his actions are directed by his wisdom, which has as its aim the "preservation of order or restraining both particular and general corruption."[60] Based on this, "the deeds of an intelligent agent are never pointless or idle"[61] because "an intelligent agent is one who knows in his willing the intended consequence of his action."[62]

Thus, after falling short in defining the attributes of God, the philosophers of Absolute Oneness returned to depending on them. For, as expected, Absolute Oneness was forced early on to harmonize the divine will with the divine wisdom. Albare Nasri explains the rise of systematic theology by showing how it entered many untouched areas such as God's attributes, sovereignty and free will, and how it began to use logic to defend its positions.[63]

In attempting to harmonize the will and wisdom of God, the revered Bin Taymiyah of the thirteenth century AD stated that God's wisdom is above human understanding: "All things are created by Allah, managed by his will and enforced by his wisdom. What he wills happened even if it is not the will of man, and what he does not will, did not happen. There is no one that can challenge his wisdom or stop his command."[64]

The Arab historian and philosopher Majid Fakhry further shows that the final position of the Ash'arites is that the commitment of Absolute Oneness

---

59. Fakhry, تاريخ الفلسفة الإسلامية: من القرن الثامن حتى يومنا هذا [The History of Islamic Philosophy: From the Eighth Century to the Present Day], 96–97.

60. Fakhry, 58.

61. Fakhry, 59.

62. Fakhry, 59.

63. Albare Nasri, مدخل إلى الفرق الإسلامية السياسيّة والكلامية [Introduction to the Islamic Political and Theological Sects], 41.

64. Taymiyah, القضاء والقَدَر [Judgment and Decree], 84.

to the powerful will of God called it to redefine wisdom, so that wisdom itself became determined by fiat! He writes,

> The conclusions of Al Ash'ari constitute the essence of his conviction regarding God's absolute power and authority over the whole universe, and the inevitability of his moral and religious decrees. It is his right alone to enforce the affairs of men as he wills, and it is the duty of the "slave" to obey without questioning. And contrary to the Mu'tazilites, the human agent has no role whatsoever in the matter of choosing or doing, or any right in the moral or religious benefits that result from any action . . . And after the Ash'ari determined God's overall power and absolute authority, he hurried to deduce some moral implications. The denial of the moral role of man in choosing and doing, and deferring the responsibility of his actions and decision to God, imply implicitly the justice of God; nevertheless, to say that man's actions are by "God's judgment and decree" does not necessarily mean negating his justice. For injustice is either going against a higher will, or blaming for doing what is outside one's ability. In either case, injustice cannot be attributed to God, the undisputed Lord of the universe.[65]

Thus, it is clear that the contradiction between wisdom and will was not resolved. Wisdom remained vague and mere nomenclature that did not extend any benefit to human beings. Fadi Abu Deeb asserts that this wisdom is not connected to moral attributes and does not benefit human beings, but only justifies the absolute freedom of will.[66] Macdonald adds,

> But if it be said that for Allah to inflict pain without cause is vile on his part and unfitting his wisdom, it may be said, Is not the vile that which does not agree with an object? Then no action of Allah can be vile because he has no object which he desires to attain, and he need not consider the object desired by anyone else. And as for wisdom, his wisdom is to know the real nature of things and arrange their action according to his will.[67]

65. Fakhry, تاريخ الفلسفة الإسلامية: من القرن الثامن حتى يومنا هذا [The History of Islamic Philosophy: From the Eighth Century to the Present Day], 325–226.

66. Abu Deeb, "جذور الوحدانية الإسلامية" [The Roots of Islamic Oneness], 10.

67. Macdonald, "God: A Unit or a Unity?," 17.

All this affirms again the inconsistent outcome which resulted from viewing God's attributes as sourced in his will, centralized in his power and impossible to know. The recourse of the Ash'arites to the attribute of wisdom and then repositioning it in the will reveals the extent of this inconsistent outcome.

The Conflict Regarding the Attributes of Essence

While the attributes of action deal with God's activity in creation, i.e., "God with us," the attributes of essence deal with God's activity in himself apart from creation, i.e., "God without us." The conflict regarding the attributes of essence revolved around the separation of the attributes of action from the attributes of essence, the separation of the attributes of essence from the essence, and the resultant inconsistency.

1. Separation of Attributes of Action from Attributes of Essence

As expected, the Mu'tazilites and the Ash'arites agreed on the separation of the attributes of action from the attributes of essence. Accordingly the Ash'arites stressed that human beings must not make any attempt to know the attributes of the essence of God or to ask about their meaning. The Ash'arites also maintained that defining God means limiting him, and that any attempt to understand God is vain, dangerous, mythical and blasphemous, for it is an attempt to understand what cannot be understood and to define what cannot be defined. 'Abduh explains this by placing the qualities of life, power, will, knowledge and speech as philosophical attributes that are supported by reason and necessarily belong to God. However, he goes a step further in asserting that human beings are limited to studying God's actions in creation in accidents and their effects. Yet human beings cannot deduce from them the attributes of essence. 'Abduh claims that Muhammad declared the import of the entire Qur'an to be, "Ponder the creation of God, but do not take your meditations into the Divine essence, or you will perish."[68] 'Abduh uses this to divorce God's attributes of action from his attributes of essence. In other words, any activity of God in the history of humankind has no relationship to what God is like in himself. 'Abduh explains his position thus:

---

68. 'Abduh, *Theology of Unity*, 53.

Any right estimate of human reason will agree that the utmost extent of its competence is to bring us to the knowledge of the accidents of the existents [things that exist] that fall within the range of human conception, either by senses, or feeling or intellection, and then from that to the knowledge of their causation and to a classification of their varieties so as to understand some of the principles appertaining to them. But reason quite lacks the competence to penetrate to the essence of things. For the attempt to discern the nature of things, which necessarily belongs with their essential complexity, would have to lead to the pure essence and to this, necessarily, there is no rational access. So the utmost that our rationality can attain is a knowledge of accidents and effects.

. . . thought on the essence of the creator, or the demand to know the essence – these are *interdicted to human reason*. For there is, as we know, a *complete otherness* between the two existences, and the Divine Being is immune from all compositeness. To ask to know it is totally to over-extend the power man possesses and is a *vain and dangerous* enterprise. It is in fact a delusion because it essays the *inconceivable*, and a danger because it conduces to an offence against faith, involving a will to definition of the *indefinable* and the limitation of the *illimitable* [emphasis added].[69]

Thus, in Absolute Oneness there is a great chasm between what God does on earth and what he is in himself, and therefore between human beings and God. Again, the result is that there remains *no content for faith* in the attribute of essence.

Absolute Oneness

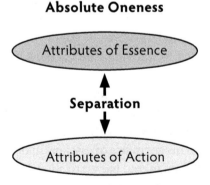

Figure 6.3: The Separation of Attributes of Action from Attributes of Essence

---

69. 'Abduh, 53–55.

2. Separation of the Attributes of Essence from the Essence

The question here revolved around whether God's attributes were his essence or in his essence, that is, separate from his essence.

The Mu'tazilites

The Mu'tazilites maintained that God's attributes are his essence and not in his essence.[70] They asserted that, "if they are separate from that essence, then there is multiplicity in Allah, and they may even be hypostatized into persons in Allah's essence."[71] The Mu'tazilites believed that "the division of attributes has often led to belief in a god for every power of nature."[72] On this basis, they rejected the use of the definite article in the names of God (e.g. *the* Knower, *the* Living One) and declared God to be "alive in his essence [or in himself] and not by [the attribute of] life, powerful in his essence and not by power, willful in his essence and not by will, knowledgeable in his essence and not by knowledge, speaking in his essence and not by speech."[73] Sweetman explains that, in Mu'tazilite theology, God's attributes of essence differ than those of human beings:

> God has no particular knowledge, power of life by which he knows and exercises power and lives. Whatever in us seems to result from the possession of some quality, is in God from and by his essence and has no real distinction from God himself. When we say that God is Omniscient or Omnipotent or that he is the Living God, though we were to multiply such predicates *ad infinitum* we should only assert that God *is*.[74]

The Ash'arites

In contrast to the Mu'tazilites, and in submission to the qur'anic text, the Ash'arites, maintained that the attributes of God subsist *in* his essence.[75] However, they maintained several guarding concepts. (1) The Ash'arites considered the attributes neither as defining the essence nor as independent

---

70. Boer, تاريخ الفلسفة في الإسلام [The History of Philosophy in Islam], 55.

71. Macdonald, "God: A Unit or a Unity?," 13.

72. Sweetman, *Islam and Christian Theology*, 2:19.

73. Al-Yaziji, معالم الفكر العربي في العصر الوسيط [Highlights of the Arab Thought in the Middle Ages], 1:161. My translation.

74. Sweetman, *Islam and Christian Theology*, 2:22.

75. Al-Yaziji, معالم الفكر العربي في العصر الوسيط [Highlights of the Arab Thought in the Middle Ages], 162.

of the essence.[76] Thus, to the Ash'arites, the attributes are "neither him nor other than him." (2) They maintained that God is "alive by life, powerful by power, willful by will, knowledgeable by knowledge, speaking by speech."[77] (3) As expected, the Ash'arites withdrew from any attempt at interpretation, and confessed ignorance regarding how the existence of the attributes was possible.[78]

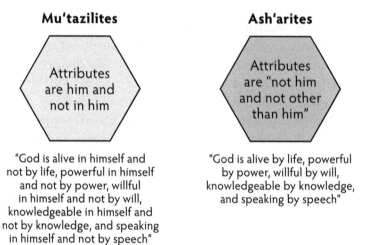

Mu'tazilites	Ash'arites
Attributes are him and not in him	Attributes are "not him and not other than him"
"God is alive in himself and not by life, powerful in himself and not by power, willful in himself and not by will, knowledgeable in himself and not by knowledge, and speaking in himself and not by speech"	"God is alive by life, powerful by power, willful by will, knowledgeable by knowledge, and speaking by speech"

Figure 6.4: Separation of the Attributes of Essence from the Essence

With this perception of the separation of the attributes of essence from the essence, there is a depriving of God from revealing truths about his essence if he so chooses. And even if he did, there is also a depriving of humanity from attempting to understand what God reveals of himself. Accordingly, there is no bridge across the chasm between God and humanity.[79]

3. The Resultant Inconsistency

The inconsistent outcome appeared in the question whether the Qur'an, which is related to the attribute of speech, was created or uncreated. This became a

---

76. Sweetman, *Islam and Christian Theology*, 2:105.

77. Al-Yaziji, معالم الفكر العربي في العصر الوسيط [Highlights of the Arab Thought in the Middle Ages], 1:162. My translation.

78. Al-Yaziji, 162; Sweetman, *Islam and Christian Theology*, 2:105.

79. See W. St Clair Tisdall, "Islamic Substitutes for the Incarnation," *Muslim World* 1 (1911): 255.

costly debate in the history of Islamic theological development. Regarding this debate, 'Abduh says that there was much unjustified bloodshed:

> Several of the 'Abbasid Caliphs adopted the dogma of the Qur'an's being created, while a considerable number of those who held to the plain sense of the Qur'an and the Sunnah either abstained from declaring themselves or took a stand for uncreatedness. The reticence arose from a reluctance to give expression to what might conduce to heresy. The dispute brought much humiliation to men of reason and piety and much blood was criminally shed. In the name of faith the community did violence to faith.[80]

The Mu'tazilites

The Mu'tazilites had no difficulty asserting that all the attributes of action occurred within time. Since speech was considered an attribute of action, the Qur'an, which is the speech of God, was considered by the Mu'tazilites to have been created. They further maintained that to hold to the eternality of the Qur'an would violate the divine unity.[81] They rather asserted that the Qur'an represented speech within the bounds of time, being given on certain historical occasions, and being evidenced by repeated abrogation.[82]

The Ash'arites

This became a real challenge to the Ash'arites.[83] It led Al-Ash'ari in his *Ibanah* to ask why, on the one hand, one should deny the eternal attributes of God and then, on the other hand, accept temporal attributes in him?[84] In the end, the Ash'arites took a middle position. They distinguished between meaning and utterance (i.e. the Qur'an) and spoke of a mediating realm which they called "self-speech."[85] They maintained that, "since utterance was created, then there is nothing to prevent self-speech which is expressed in utterance, to be

80. 'Abduh, *Theology of Unity*, 35–36.

81. Sweetman, *Islam and Christian Theology*, 2:21.

82. Al-Yaziji, معالم الفكر العربي في العصر الوسيط [Highlights of the Arab Thought in the Middle Ages], 163.

83. Cf. Sweetman, *Islam and Christian Theology*, 2:23.

84. See Thomson, "Al-Ash'ari and His Al-ibanah," 242–260; Sweetman, *Islam and Christian Theology*, 2:24; Olari, *Arab Thought and Its Role in History*, 182–184.

85. Olari, 163.

uncreated. The Qur'an in this sense is eternal no doubt."[86] Speech was thus defined as an eternal quality of God subsisting in his essence without words, sounds or language.[87]

> The inconsistency in the final position of Absolute Oneness on the Qur'an appeared as follows. On the one hand, it proclaimed that the inspiration in the earthly attribute of speech, of which the Qur'an is a part, is an expression of the eternal speech of God. On the other hand, it also *insisted on the* separation of the attributes of action, of which inspiration is a part, from the divine attributes of essence.

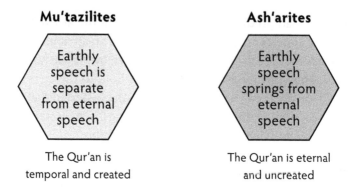

Mu'tazilites

Earthly speech is separate from eternal speech

The Qur'an is temporal and created

Ash'arites

Earthly speech springs from eternal speech

The Qur'an is eternal and uncreated

Figure 6.5: The Relationship between God's Speech in History and in Eternity

Summary and Conclusion

Absolute Oneness presents to the world the enormous conflict that results from rejecting the doctrine of the Trinity. This can be summarized in the following

---

86. Al-Yaziji, معالم الفكر العربي في العصر الوسيط [Highlights of the Arab Thought in the Middle Ages], 163. In spite of the wide divergence of the Christian λόγος concept from the qur'anic concept, Robert Haddad sees a theological convergence. In both religions their respective conceptions of λόγος led to the debate whether the λόγος was created or uncreated. Haddad states, "And those in the Christian and Muslim mainstreams produced, though not without intense internal strife, precisely the same resounding reply: the logos – the arguments of Arians and Mu'tazila notwithstanding – is *uncreated*, existing from all eternity with God" (Robert M. Haddad, "Eastern Orthodoxy and Islam: An Historical Overview," *Greek Orthodox Theological Review* 31 [1986]: 18).

87. Al-Yaziji, معالم الفكر العربي في العصر الوسيط [Highlights of the Arab Thought in the Middle Ages], 163.

beliefs of Absolute Oneness, some held in common by the Mu'tazilites and the Ash'arites, and some related to the Ash'arites alone, which became the orthodox position.

1.   Absolute Oneness rejects the presence of an active eternal relationship in God as in the Trinity. This presented Absolute Oneness with the challenge of answering the inevitable question of how the attributes of God could be active eternally apart from creation without God existing in a relationship. The conflict between the Mu'tazilites and the Ash'arites in answering this question exposed the conflict of Absolute Oneness.

2.   It is impossible to know the meaning of the attributes of action because they stem from the power of God to fulfill his will that is free from any law or promise, because anthropomorphisms are outside the realm of inquiry regarding their meaning or attempts at their explanation, and because even the wisdom that is supposed to regulate God's actions is subject to his free will.

3.   The attributes of action, drawn from God's immense power in fulfilling his free will, are lacking in perfection, as in the case of the power and will of God, and they also work independently of one another, leading to capriciousness.

4.   In spite of the contradiction in describing the attribute of earthly speech as springing from the attribute of eternal speech, there is also an insistence on the complete separation of attributes of action from attributes of essence. This means that, even if it was possible for human beings to have a picture of the attributes of God in his dealings with creation, these have no relation to God's own attributes as he is in himself.

5.   In addition to the impossibility of knowing the meaning of the attributes of action, it is also impossible to depend on the attributes of essence, for they are separate from God's essence so that they are not him nor other than him.

6.   The ninety-nine names of God became mere verbal expressions that only emphasize the unlimited power of God. For they are general or abstract vocalizations without real meaning.[88]

---

88. "The nominalists regard the usual attributions of God as having no objective basis in the divine nature, and hence as being simply names that are subjectively applied to the deity. This view greatly influenced a number of Arabic and Jewish philosophers, as well as certain

7.   There is no content for faith except in being confined to the existence and oneness of God, without any solid foundation.

Table 6.6 summarizes the differences and similarities between the Mu'tazilites and the Ash'arites, showing the conflict over the attributes of action and the attributes of essence.

God's attributes	Subject	Mu'tazilites	Ash'arites
Attributes of Action (with us)	The source	Unknown because the attributes are temporal, contingent & changing	Eternal in God's absolute free will
	The manifestation	In absolute justice according to human expectations	In absolute power to fulfill divine will
	The knowledge	Anthropomorphisms point to transcendence explained figuratively	Anthropomorphisms point to difference "Without asking how and without comparison"
	Resultant inconsistency	Resorted to reasonableness	Resorted to wisdom then re-established it in will
Attributes of Essence (without us)	Relationship to essence	No relationship	No relationship
	Relationship to attributes of action	Not separate from God's essence Him and not in him	Separate from essence "Not him and not other than him"
	Resultant inconsistency	The speech of God created in history is separate from his eternal speech	The speech of God created in history springs from his eternal speech

Table 6.6: Differences and Similarities between Mu'tazilites and Ash'arites

Christian theologians" (Henry, *God Who Stands and Stays*, 128).

7

The Answer of Oneness in Trinity

Introduction

This chapter presents the main differences of Oneness in Trinity which will be discussed through the rest of this book. This includes the answer to the inevitable question and its ramifications regarding God's attributes of action and attributes of essence. This chapter summarizes the main points of Absolute Oneness as they were explained in the previous chapter, and presents the opposite view of Oneness in Trinity for each point. What this study presents is the difference in the concept of God, not between the Bible and a specific religion, but between the Bible and the philosophy of Absolute Oneness!

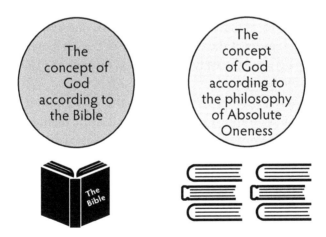

**Figure 7.1: The Difference in the Concept of God
between the Bible and Absolute Oneness**

The Answer to the Inevitable Question

Oneness in Trinity reveals that the reason for the eternal activity of God's attributes outside creation is that he *exists eternally in relationship within himself*. For every attribute requires a relationship, and *the presence of a relationship assures the protection of each attribute*. This revelation answers the inevitable question regarding how the attributes of God are eternally active.

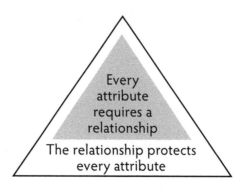

Figure 7.2: The Answer of Oneness in Trinity to the Inevitable Question

The foundational reason for the conflict of Absolute Oneness is its inability to provide a convincing alternative to the truth that *every attribute requires a relationship*, just as love requires the lover, the beloved and the activity of love itself. For the activity of God's temporal attributes of action in relationship with creation springs from the eternal activity of the attributes of essence in the relationship between the Father and the Son through the Holy Spirit, who joins all the attributes of God.

As is covered in detail in chapter 8, the existence of a person is philosophically not confined to existence, but must include existence in relationship. In other words, two elements are necessary for the existence of a person. The first is existence, and the second is existence in relationship.[1] Therefore, John Zizioulas asserts that these two elements are identical, so that the principle of "existence in relationship" is the only principle that gives a person meaning to his or her existence, otherwise there would be no person and no relationship:

---

1. See Zizioulas, *Being As Communion*, 83–84; Schelling, *Ages of the World*, 96–97; Athanasius, "Four Discourses against the Arians," in Schaff and Wace, *Nicene and Post-Nicene Fathers*, Second Series, Vol. 4, 20, 88.

To be and *to be in relation* becomes identical. For someone or something to be, two things are simultaneously needed: being itself (*hypostasis*) and *being in relation* (i.e. being a person). It is only in relationship that identity appears as having an ontological significance, and if any relationship did not imply such an ontologically meaningful identity, then it would be no relationship.[2]

The subject of relationship within the oneness of God occupies most of this book in order to demonstrate that God cannot be God without being in the beauty of the relationship as Trinity.

The Answer in Regard to the Attributes of Action

Oneness in Trinity deals with the conflict of Absolute Oneness in regard to the attributes of action which arose between the Mu'tazilites and the Ash'arites. This relates to the source, the manifestation, the comparison and the resultant coherence of the attributes of action.

1. The Source of the Attributes of Action

While the Mu'tazilites considered the source of the attributes of action to be unknown for being, in their view, temporal, contingent and changing, Absolute Oneness adopted the thinking of the Ash'arites that his attributes of action spring from God's free will eternally. This resulted in the impossibility for human beings to depend on God's attributes. In contrast, Oneness in Trinity declares that *the attributes of action spring, not from an unpredictable will of God, but from his revealed nature, which combines all his attributes as he is in himself.* This in turn leads to the possibility of depending upon and trusting the attributes of God. Because of the rejection by Absolute Oneness of the presence of a relationship within the nature of God, his attributes are believed to stem from his will, resulting in a wavering content of faith. Contrary to this, Oneness in Trinity depends on the active presence of a relationship in God so that his attributes stem from his nature, resulting in a sure content of faith. Figure 7.3 illustrates this.

---

2. Zizioulas, 83–84.

Attributes of Action

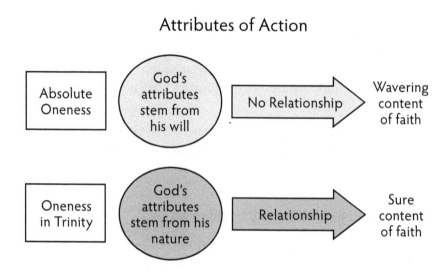

Figure 7.3: The Source of God's Attributes of Action: His Will or His Nature

2. The Manifestation of the Attributes of Action

In Absolute Oneness, the manifestation of the attributes of action is accomplished through the consolidation of God's unlimited power to fulfill his free will. The consolidation of God's power is done through the reinforcement of the attributes, the contrariness of the attributes and the unboundedness of the attributes as reflected in the ninety-nine names. The consolidation of God's power was done by stressing the unboundedness of the attributes such that there is independence of God's power from any other attribute. So, while the Mu'tazilites proclaimed that the manifestation of the attributes of action is in the work of God in ultimate justice according to human expectations, Absolute Oneness adopted the position of the Ash'arites who proclaimed that the manifestation of the attributes of action is in the work of God in ultimate power to fulfill his will. On this basis, God is not bound to any law or promise, not even those coming from himself. However, Oneness in Trinity presents a completely different concept.

In Regard to Consolidation of Power

The attributes of God in Oneness in Trinity are distinct in the manifestation of the attributes of action, and this can be noted in several areas.

1. Every attribute of God is perfect, lacking in nothing. There is no attribute, such as will or power, that is more active or more dominant than any other attribute, and there is no attribute that is secondary to any other attribute.

2. Each attribute of God works in full coordination with all his other attributes. All the attributes are active in full harmony.

3. There is no attribute that works independently from any other attribute. All the attributes work in full harmony and interdependently with one another.

4. On this basis, God is committed to every law and promise that comes from himself. This commitment is not a reflection of his weakness, but rather a reflection of his commitment to the harmony of all his attributes with one another.

5. The above portrait requires a greater power than that confined to fulfilling a random will. This guarantees a secure foundation for faith.

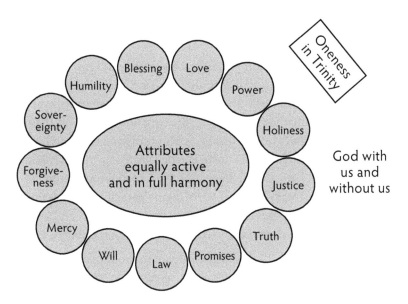

Figure 7.4: The Attributes of Action in Oneness in Trinity

6. The above description of the attributes of God in Oneness in Trinity is an expression of what is called in theology "the simplicity of God."

What is meant by "simplicity" is that God is not compound, for he is not the sum of his attributes, but is his attributes. R. C. Sproul states,

> Simplicity is not contrasted with difficulty but with composition . . . God, as a simple being, is not made up of parts as we are . . . He is not constructed of various segments of being that are assembled together to compose His whole being. It is not so much that God has attributes but that He is His attributes.[3]

Simplicity thus means that every attribute is described by the other attributes. Sproul adds,

> All of God's attributes help define all of His other attributes. For example, when we say God is immutable, we are also saying that His immutability is an eternal immutability, an omnipotent immutability, a holy immutability, a loving immutability, and so on. By the same token, His love is an immutable love, an eternal love, an omnipotent love, a holy love, and so forth.[4]

Conversely, simplicity also means that every attribute describes the other attributes. Carl Henry states,

> If God is non-composite, and his essence and existence are identical, then all divine attributes are mutually inclusive. Each attribute in the nature of God interpenetrates every other attribute and no conflict or contrast among them is possible. God's wisdom is his omnipotence, and God's omnipotence is his justice, God's justice is his love, and so on. God and holiness, and God and love are mutually exhaustive synonyms . . . No divine perfection is therefore inferior or subordinate to another; all God's perfections are equally ultimate in the simplicity of his being.[5]

Sproul adds that simplicity prevents from pitting one attribute against another. He also warns against adopting some of God's attributes while ignoring others, because this forms a basis for

---

3. Sproul, *God's Love*, 107.
4. Sproul, 107.
5. Henry, *God Who Stands and Stays*, 132.

idolatry. By doing so, a person would worship a god of his or her own making as a replacement for the real God. Sproul writes,

> By remembering that God is a simple being and that He is His attributes, we can resist the temptation of pitting one of God's attributes against another . . . We cannot take our plates and help ourselves to only those attributes of God we find tasteful and pass by those attributes we find unpalatable. In practice, this is done every day. It is the basis of idolatry; we first deconstruct God by stripping Him of some of His attributes and then refashion Him into a different God more to our liking. An idol is a false god that serves as a substitute for the real God. In antiquity and in contemporary primitive societies, we see idolatry practiced in crude forms. The idol maker who fashions a deity out of a block of stone or wood, then addresses it as if it is alive or has the power to do anything may seem somewhat foolish or stupid to us, for we live in more sophisticated times and are not quite as prone to worship the works of our hands in such a crass manner. But we have not yet escaped the propensity to worship idols created by our minds. We must guard against a facile dismissal of the threat of idolatry. We must remember that the proclivity for idolatry is one of the strongest inclinations of our fallen natures.[6]

7.   Oneness in Trinity, which depends on the Bible, warns of punishment, it adds a declaration missing in the teaching of Absolute Oneness, and that is the revelation of the grace and mercy of God given freely to those who believe in spite of their undeservedness:

> And you were dead in your trespasses and sins, in which you formerly walked according to the course of this world, according to the prince of the power of the air, of the spirit that is now working in the sons of disobedience. Among them we too all formerly lived in the lusts of our flesh, indulging the desires of the flesh and of the mind, and were by nature children of wrath, even as the rest. *But God, being rich in mercy, because of His great*

---

6. Sproul, *God's Love*, 107–108.

love with which He loved us, even when we were dead in our transgressions, made us alive together with Christ (by grace you have been saved), and raised us up with Him, and seated us with Him in the heavenly places in Christ Jesus, *so that in the ages to come He might show the surpassing riches of His grace in kindness toward us* in Christ Jesus. For by grace you have been saved through faith; and that *not of yourselves, it is the gift of God;* not as a result of works, so that no one may boast. (Eph 2:1–9)

But to the one who does not work, but *believes in Him who justifies the ungodly,* his faith is credited as righteousness, just as David also speaks of the blessing on the man to whom God credits righteousness apart from works: "Blessed are those whose lawless deeds have been forgiven, and whose sins have been covered. Blessed is the man whose sin the Lord will not take into account." (Rom 4:5–8)

8.   These distinctives of the Christian faith form part of a necessary *foundation for the doctrine of the Trinity.*

3. The Comparison of the Attributes of Action

Since God's attributes in Absolute Oneness stem from God's power to fulfill his will, Absolute Oneness found great difficulty in comparing God's attributes to those of human beings, as expressed in its dealing with anthropomorphic expressions. The Mu'tazilites emphasized the transcendence of God, calling for the distancing of the qur'anic anthropomorphic expressions from God by interpreting them allegorically. But Absolute Oneness adopted the Ash'arite position in calling on the difference of God from anything human beings can conceive of him. It therefore insisted on not asking how this could be, and on not comparing God to anything.

In contrast to Absolute Oneness – and as will be covered in Volume 2 in the chapter entitled "The Activity of the Attributes of God Outside Creation" – anthropomorphisms have a special meaning in Oneness in Trinity. First, anthropomorphisms are an expression of the fact that human beings were *created in the image of God.* Second, anthropomorphisms are, in the end, theomorphisms; that is, it is *human beings who are likened to God* and not God who is likened to human beings. Third, the anthropomorphisms mean that human beings can understand the attributes of God, though to a limited extent, yet to a sufficient level to have faith in them and to rely upon them.

Based on humanity being in the image of God	An invitation to understand the attributes of God	A privilege and a responsibility to represent God

It is not that he is like us, but that we are like him!

Figure 7.5: Anthropomorphisms in Oneness in Trinity

Kevin Giles, quoting Thomas Aquinas, asserts that it is possible to understand the attributes ascribed to God in three ways. (1) The univocal meaning sees a human being's attributes as exactly equal to God's. But this is impossible because the infinite Creator must be greater than the finite creature. (2) The equivocal meaning sees a human being's attributes as completely different from anything in God. This is what Absolute Oneness proclaims. (3) The analogical meaning sees a human being's attributes as similar to God's but with a difference in perfection. Giles states,

> Speech used of God could be one of three things. (1) It could be univocal. Saying that God loves me means the same as saying that my wife or my parents love me. If our language of God were univocal, it would mean that God is just like human beings. (2) It could be equivocal. Saying that God loves me means something altogether different from saying that my parents or wife love me. If our language used of God were equivocal, we could not say anything factual about God. (3) It could be analogical. Saying that God loves me tells me something true about God but only captures part of the reality. If our language used of God is analogical, as Aquinas argued, it means we can speak of and understand God in the categories of human thought but never fully comprehend him . . . There can be an overlap of meaning between how we use a word in reference to creatures and how we use it in reference to God. Theology, then, is the discipline of finding where that overlap lies and also where the meanings diverge. But at every point we must make a distinction between a word's application to

God and to creaturely realities. That is the very task of theology. Without this discipline we fall into idolatry and mythology, speaking of God as if God were a creature or projecting upon God creaturely understandings. The Fourth Lateran Council made this point forcefully when it ruled, "Between the Creator and the creature no similarity can be expressed without including greater dissimilarity."[7]

4. The Resultant Coherence

Absolute Oneness attempted to avoid the conclusion of the capriciousness of God. This led it to a great contradiction and to go against what it had proclaimed, namely, to resort to at least one moral attribute. The Mu'tazilites appealed to God's reason, and the Ash'arites appealed to God's wisdom! But more than this, Absolute Oneness, which adopted the Ash'arite position, defined wisdom as springing from the will of God! So its journey was from will to wisdom and back to will. This resulted in great inconsistency.

In contrast, complete consistency and coherence are found in Oneness in Trinity. For each of God's attributes is perfect, which is the meaning of the holiness of God. And each attribute works in full harmony with all other attributes, which is the meaning of the righteousness of God. The subject of the activity of the attributes of God outside and inside creation will be dealt with in two chapters in Volume 2.

The Answer in Regard to the Attributes of Essence

The beauty of Oneness in Trinity appears in the relationship of the attributes of action to the attributes of essence, the relationship of the attributes of essence to the essence, and the resultant coherence.

1. The Relationship of the Attributes of Action to the Attributes of Essence

The Mu'tazilites and the Ash'arites agreed on the separation of the attributes of action from the attributes of essence. In other words, any work of God in history, in their view, had no relationship to what God is like in himself. Thus, in Absolute Oneness again there remains *no content for faith.*

---

7. Giles, *Eternal Generation of the Son,* 22–23, quoting Thomas Aquinas, *Summa Theologica* 1, q.13, a.3.1, 57, and Tanner, *Decrees of the Ecumenical Councils,* vol. 1, 232.

Contrary to this, Oneness in Trinity declares that the attributes of action stem from the attributes of essence. So God's temporal activity *inside* creation with humanity (God with us) springs from God's eternal activity *outside* creation in himself (God without us). Karl Rahner expresses this by stating that "The 'economic' Trinity is the 'immanent' Trinity and the 'immanent' Trinity is the 'economic' Trinity."[8] In other words, who God is forms the basis for how he acts. If his attributes are active in history, it is because they are active outside of history. His *ad extra* attributes are the expression of his *ad intra* attributes.

So God's dealings with humanity in the attributes of action, such as power, love, mercy, forgiveness, fulfilling promises and applying the law, spring from the work of the Father, Son and Holy Spirit in God in the attributes of essence, such as power, will, holiness, love, truth, sovereignty, humility and blessing. The outpouring of the attributes of action (God with us) from the attributes of essence (God without us) is illustrated in Figure 7.6.

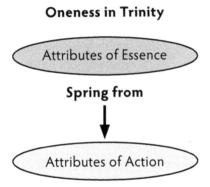

Figure 7.6: The Attributes of Action Spring from the Attributes of Essence

Naturally, what Christ exhibited while he was on earth about his relationships with the Father and with the Holy Spirit was only a partial expression of what these relationships are like in their eternal activity. For the eternal relationship between the persons of the Trinity is far greater than was revealed through the works of Christ in his incarnate state.

---

8. Rahner, *The Trinity*, 22.

2. The Relationship of the Attributes of Essence to the Essence

The Mu'tazilites maintained that God's attributes are his essence and not in his essence, otherwise God, in their view, becomes compound, leading to belief in a god for every attribute. For, in their view, God exists in himself and not in attributes. Absolute Oneness adopted the thinking of the Ash'arites, which asserted that God exists in his attributes, but which prevented any attempt to define his attributes because defining him meant limiting him. Therefore, it maintained that defining him was blasphemy! It then declared that the only recourse was to accept that God's attributes do not define the essence, nor are they independent of the essence. This led adherents of Absolute Oneness to proclaim that God's attributes are "neither him nor other than him."

But these words are full of negation, with no positive expression! Macdonald comments that these words provide no defensible concept:

> But the final orthodox position, based apparently on human psychology, seems to have been that, while they [the attributes] are "necessary to his essence," they are, "in addition to his essence," so that we cannot say either that they are He, or that they are other than He. There they are in some way, but either statement would carry us into an indefensible position.[9]

But Oneness in Trinity says exactly the opposite. For though the rejection of the idea of a god for every attribute led Absolute Oneness to consider God's attributes of essence to be without any meaning that could be known, *Oneness in Trinity preserves the rich meanings of God's attributes which are possible for human beings to know*. To begin with – and as will be covered in depth in Volume 2 in the chapter entitled "The Significance of the Name 'Holy Spirit'" – the idea of a god for every attribute is impossible. The reason for this is that the Holy Spirit, in one sense, includes all the attributes of God, but being a person, he joins all the attributes of God in his person, guaranteeing the oneness of God. In addition, God in Oneness in Trinity calls people to know his attributes, to be sure of them and to experience them. Defining his attributes does not limit God, but gives human beings the privilege to experience a taste of his infinite attributes. This is the beauty of faith and not the ugliness of blasphemy. It is the rejection of knowing God or the prevention of any definition of his attributes that is the opposite of faith. Oneness in Trinity makes it possible for people to have a personal relationship with God.

---

9. Macdonald, "God: A Unit or a Unity?," 14.

Carl Henry adds that evangelical theology, which adopts Oneness in Trinity, insists on the simplicity of God. "Simplicity" here guarantees, on the one hand, that God is not composed of attributes, and, on the other hand, that the diversity of his attributes speaks of divine life characterized by perfection:

> Evangelical theology insists on the simplicity of God. By this it means that God is not compounded of parts; he is not a collection of perfections, but rather a living center of activity pervasively characterized by all his distinctive perfections. The divine attributes are neither additions to the divine essence nor qualities pieced together to make a compound . . . God's variety of attributes does not conflict with God's simplicity because his simplicity is what comprises the fullness of divine life. Augustine wrote of God's "simple multiplicity" or "multifold simplicity."[10]

3. The Resultant Coherence

The inconsistency in Absolute Oneness is that it proclaims that the inspiration in the earthly attribute of speech is an expression of the eternal speech of God, while also insisting on the separation of the attributes of action from the attributes of essence.

But the concept is entirely different in Oneness in Trinity. Harmony clearly reigns, and in several respects, as will be elaborated on more fully, especially in the chapters of Volume 2 of this study. First, according to Oneness in Trinity, the attribute of speech expresses God's desire to communicate with humanity in order to reveal his nature. Second, the speech of God historically in his relationship to humanity springs from his speech eternally in the relationship within himself. Third, the relationship of the Word of God to God is not the relationship of power to will, but the relationship of the Son to the Father which includes the activity of all the attributes of perfection in full harmony. Fourth, the Word of God was incarnated in a person in history. So the true meaning of life comes not in human philosophy, but in knowing this unique person.

Two Parallel Lines

The difference is summarized in the two columns representing Absolute Oneness and Oneness in Trinity in Figure 7.7. Absolute Oneness rejects

---

10. Henry, *God Who Stands and Stays*, 131.

the presence of a relationship within the person of God. Accordingly, God's attributes of action stem from his will and are manifested in power. Also, describing God with human attributes is seen as unrelated to God. In addition, attributes of action are seen as separate from attributes of essence, and attributes of essence nevertheless cannot be known or understood. As a result, there is a wavering content of faith, and no basis for a personal relationship with God.

In contrast, Oneness in Trinity proclaims an eternal relationship within God. Accordingly, attributes of action stem from his nature and are manifested in being equal and in harmony. Also, describing God with human attributes comes from humanity's being made in the image of God. In addition, attributes of action stem from attributes of essence, and attributes of essence can be known and understood. As a result, there is a steadfast content of faith, and an abiding basis for a personal relationship with God.

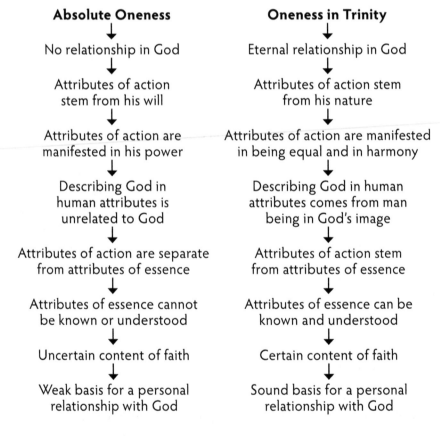

Figure 7.7: Absolute Oneness in Contrast to Oneness in Trinity

In the end, the strong message of Oneness in Trinity is that the relationship of the one true God with us stems from the relationship of the Father, Son and Holy Spirit without us.

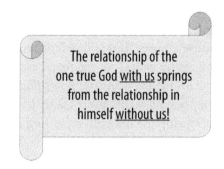

The relationship of the one true God <u>with us</u> springs from the relationship in himself <u>without us!</u>

Appeal to Believers and Non-Believers

The appeal of this book to believers in Oneness in Trinity is to cease viewing the Trinity as a problem to be solved. It is a call to see the Trinity as a beauty to be continually discovered and enjoyed. Likewise, believers in Oneness in Trinity must beware of doubting the perfection of God's attributes and their trustworthiness, and must not place one attribute above another. They in turn must be wary of becoming unsure about the stability of the promises and laws of God. For *it is possible for believers in Oneness in Trinity to move toward Absolute Oneness* knowingly or unknowingly. This results in a wavering faith without consistent content. Thus, believers in Oneness in Trinity must thank God that he has revealed his relational nature, and that this nature is the fountain of attributes which work in full equality and harmony. They must be thankful that they can be sure of these attributes and can grow in faith through knowing and understanding them and trusting them. Thus, believers in Oneness in Trinity have access to an unshakable foundation for a personal relationship with God.

As to non-believers in Oneness in Trinity, the appeal of this book is, in the first place, for them to examine themselves to find any obstacles that are preventing them from receiving what God has revealed about himself. For adherents of Absolute Oneness cannot speak of God's attributes and actions in history and at the same time reject a part of God's revelation of his inner nature.

> If God did not exist eternally in an active relationship within himself, human beings could have no knowledge of him. This in turn would mean they could not give God true worship or gratitude. In addition, if God could not be known, he could not enter into a relationship with human beings. In short, the lack of relationship within God would result in humanity's lack of worship of him and humanity's lack of relationship with him.

The appeal of this book to adherents of Absolute Oneness is that they begin the journey of trust in the perfection, equality and harmony of all God's attributes. This will make their faith grow so that they enter a personal relationship with God, and then become receptive to any revelation from God about his nature, no matter how difficult it is for them to change their thinking. If they remain at this level of faith, they will find that the discovery of the inner relationship of God within his unity is the greatest discovery of all, because of its rich meanings.

8

Consistency of the Trinity with Logic

Introduction

The doctrine of the Trinity is a theological conclusion based on what God has revealed about himself. This doctrine is not man-made, but rather it came by divine revelation in the word of God, the Bible. However, the doctrine of the Trinity is consistent with logic because revelation is the higher logic. Moreover, human beings were created in the image of God, so human logic derives from divine logic.

However, what follows here is written in reverence, honor and worship to God. As the New Testament declares,

> Oh, the depth of the riches both of the wisdom and knowledge of God! How unsearchable are His judgments and unfathomable His ways! For who has known the mind of the Lord, or who became His counselor? Or who has first given to Him that it might be paid back to Him again? For from Him and through Him and to Him are all things. To Him be the glory forever. Amen. (Rom 11:33–36)

Therefore, the purpose of this study is not to arrive at the doctrine of the Trinity through logic, it is not to prove the doctrine of the Trinity through logic, but it is rather *to demonstrate the consistency of the doctrine of the Trinity with logic*. As shared in chapter 1, the use of logic is in the spirit of the well-known principle of "faith seeking understanding" of Augustine (AD 354–430) followed by Anselm (AD 1030–1109). The use of logic is not because of a lack in revelation, but for the sake of a deeper understanding, protecting, supporting, explaining and applying revelation to all of life. In this there is enrichment of faith, growth in knowledge and a coming nearer to God.

This chapter seeks to demonstrate four affirmations:

- The eternal existence of God is in harmony with the eternal *activity* of his attributes.
- The eternal activity of his attributes presupposes a *relationship* between persons.
- The relationship is protected by *threeness* of persons.
- The threeness of persons is guaranteed perfection through *oneness*.

The Eternal Existence of God Is in Harmony with the Eternal Activity of His Attributes

Logically, it is impossible for God to exist without all his attributes being eternally active. This applies not only to his non-relational attributes, but also to the relational attributes.[1] All of this is in the presence or lack of presence of creation. So the eternal existence of God harmonizes with the eternal activity of his attributes. There are several evidences for this.

1. The Existence of God Means the Existence of His Attributes

It is necessary for God's attributes to exist with his existence, for several reasons:

1. Anything that exists has attributes, otherwise it would not exist.[2] God has attributes because he exists.

2. Since God exists from eternity past, his attributes must also exist from eternity past. The Arab Christian philosopher Awad Samaan asserts that "the oneness of God cannot be devoid of positive attributes, nor, as Absolute Oneness, without any possibility of the eternal and real existence of attributes."[3]

3. There is no attribute that is derived from another; otherwise God would become dependent on what or who is outside of himself, and that is impossible.

---

1. In the chapter in Volume 2 entitled "The Activity of the Attributes of God Outside Creation," the classification adopted is of relational and non-relational attributes.

2. Awad Samaan, الله، ذاته ونوع وحدانيته [God, His Essence and His Kind of Unity], 54.

3. Samaan, 46.

4. There is no attribute that came to be possessed, because that would mean that God was in a state of existence for a time without a certain attribute. The attributes of God exist with his existence. His immutability, power, knowledge, goodness, love and holiness, to name a few examples, are all his attributes from eternity past to eternity future, without beginning or end.

2. The Existence of God's Attributes Requires Positive Description

It is possible to describe God in negative terms. This can be appealing, as in saying that he does not forget, does not sleep or does not get tired. However, the difficulty is in confining descriptions of God to negative terms only (as in "not impotent" instead of "powerful"; "not ignorant" instead of "all-knowing"; "not coercive" instead of "drawing"). This is not fitting, for several reasons:

1. Confinement to negative descriptions presupposes the knowledge of what is positive. Geisler and Feinberg assert, "All negations imply some positive knowledge. One cannot say God is 'not-that' unless he has some knowledge of the 'that.' Further, how would one know what does not apply to God unless he knows what does apply? In short, negations imply prior affirmations."[4]

2. Restricting the description of God to negative terms without any positive characterization may point to a deficiency in God. Samaan says that ascribing only negative descriptions to God "means ascribing defect to him when he is perfect in all perfection."[5]

3. Confinement to negative descriptions does not inspire hope or bring joy to human beings. For example, to say that God is not impotent may imply that he does not wish to help those in need. So it is best to describe God in negative terms only when a positive meaning can be assured.

4. Confinement to negative descriptions makes it difficult to show the supremacy of God over his creatures. In turn, it actually becomes impossible to prove his uniqueness.

5. As was covered in chapter 7, positive descriptions of God indicate similarities between God and human beings, though to a limited

---

4. Geisler and Feinberg, *Introduction to Philosophy*, 306.
5. Samaan, الله، ذاته ونوع وحدانيته [God, His Essence and His Kind of Unity], 56.

extent, yet to a sufficient level to have faith in them and to rely upon them. Kevin Giles states that it is possible to understand attributes ascribed to God in three ways. The first is the univocal meaning, which sees human attributes as exactly equal to God's. The second meaning is the equivocal meaning, which sees human attributes as completely different from anything in God. The third meaning is the analogical meaning, which sees human attributes as similar to God's but with a difference in perfection.[6] Naturally, the univocal meaning is not acceptable because of God's supremacy over humanity. The equivocal meaning, which is adopted by Absolute Oneness, is also unacceptable because it is unreasonable that God should have revealed his attributes without intending that they would be understood by human beings. It is the analogical meaning that is the most natural and logical.

6.   Positive descriptions do not necessarily indicate limitation, but rather they are a miniature picture of the same attributes but to an infinite degree in God.

3. The Positivity of God's Attributes Requires Their Activity

It is necessary not only for the attributes of God to exist eternally, but also for them to be active eternally. This means that it is the nature of God to be active apart from creation. However, *some think that the activity of God's attributes is not an essential condition*, based on the reasoning that such activity is only linked to his activity in creation. Accordingly, the attributes of God are potentially and not actually active from eternity past, and they only became active after creation.[7] So it is said that, though God can be described with attributes acting in time, it would be ridiculous to believe in the activity of attributes in eternity past. For example, in this thinking, God can be the keeper, the giver, and the hearer without the actions of keeping, giving and hearing to be active eternally. Those who think along these lines insist that the ability to do these acts is eternal but the acts themselves do not need to be eternal. Thus, according to them, God did not see, hear, know, give life or exercise

---

6. Giles, *Eternal Generation of the Son*, 22–23, quoting Thomas Aquinas, *Summa Theologica* 1, q.13, a.3.1, 57, and Tanner, *Decrees of the Ecumenical Councils*, vol. 1, 232. See chapter 7 for a fuller discussion.

7. See Sweetman, *Islam and Christian Theology*, 4:23–25.

power to fulfill his will until he created life for himself and what needs to be seen, heard, known, and so on.

However, there are a number of difficulties with confining God's activity to after the act of creation:

1. Ascribing an attribute to God then denying its activity means negating what was originally ascribed. This means lying about the attribute proclaimed. This is what the Arab philosopher Ammar Al Basri from the ninth century AD says:

    > If you say "so and so is one who sees," we say, "does he have sight?" If you say "no," it means that you have lied about him in calling him "one who sees." For naming him as "one who sees" must pertain to what he possesses of sight. Then, when you say "I did not mean in my affirmation that he is 'one who sees' that he has sight, but only to negate that he has blindness," this shows that you wanted to negate his blindness by ascribing sight to him, but then you negate his sight, which in turn affirms the blindness you negated.[8]

2. Limiting the work of God's attributes to after creation means that his eternal activity is dependent on the existence of creation. This means that his eternal attributes are limited to being within what is contingent. But this is impossible because the Creator does not depend on creation, and the necessary being does not depend on what is contingent – rather the opposite. Furthermore, the act of creation was by divine decree.

3. The confining of the work of God's attributes to after creation implies change in him. For if God's attributes were potential and not active before creation, their becoming active after creation implies a certain change in his nature. This goes against his immutability. Awad Samaan clarifies,

    > There is no doubt that these attributes were not idle in God from eternity past, and then became active when he created angels, humans and other creatures. But they were active in themselves (without any influence outside of himself), and before the existence of anyone else.

---

8. Ammar Al Basri, كتاب البرهان [The Book of Evidence], 47–48.

For, if the situation was different than this, God would have undergone change by becoming active after he was inactive. But his state does not change at all. And if the situation was different, creatures would be necessary for God to resort to in order to manifest his attributes in them and reveal himself through them. But the truth is that, because of his complete perfection, his attributes are manifested plainly and revealed in him fully, regardless of the existence or lack of existence of creatures.[9]

4. Limiting the activity of the attributes of God to after creation implies his imperfection. For if, for example, the attribute of knowledge did not become active until after creation, this would mean that God was ignorant of something before creation. But this is impossible and contrary to the nature of God, who is all-knowing. There was no time when God did not practice his knowledge, holiness, justice, goodness, and so on. Awad Samaan expresses the same thoughts:

> Truly a person may have sight without something to see. But if we realize that God is completely perfect in himself, and that he does not change or develop or gain anything for himself at all, it will become clear that it is impossible for his attributes to be inactive in eternity past and then become active because of the presence of creatures he created in time. Rather, it is certain that his attributes were active in themselves from eternity past to the degree of perfection, before the existence of any being other than him.[10]

5. If, as adherents of Absolute Oneness believe, the attributes of God spring from his will and not from his nature (as was covered in detail earlier), this would mean that the law of God sprang from his will and not from his nature. Accordingly, his laws, like his attributes, would have no relationship to him as he is in himself, and in turn could not be specified or defined. And if the attributes of God were potential and not active outside creation, his law must also be inactive apart from creation. But his law is connected to his life, for

---

9. Awad Samaan, الله، ذاته ونوع وحدانيته [God, His Essence and His Kind of Unity], 8. See also Awad Samaan, الله بين الفلسفة والمسيحيّة [God, Between Philosophy and Christianity], 56.

10. Samaan, الله بين الفلسفة والمسيحيّة [God, Between Philosophy and Christianity], 58.

it is "the law of the Spirit of life" (Rom 8:2). So if the attributes of God were not active before creation, God would have been without life. This is impossible.

6. The restriction of the activity of God's attributes to after creation means having no experience of them and no knowledge of the meaning of any of them. This is a problem because to perform an action in creation requires prior knowledge and prior experience of it outside creation. Atfield says that the prior inactivity of a person's attributes amounts to their original non-existence:

> These properties (omniscience, omnipotence, etc.) . . . of their very nature are only to be ascribed to a person on the basis of their conscious employment. They are personal powers the existence of which is verified by trying. One cannot know or be able personally to do *x* without being aware of having this knowledge and ability. In a role where this awareness is absent and these qualities are not displayed, it will be as though they do not exist.[11]

7. The Bible declares that, in the incarnation, Christ emptied himself through the partial and temporary manifestation of all of his attributes, because of the fallen condition of humanity. But in his eternal state in glory, there is no need for him to limit any of his attributes. For a deeper study of this, see the chapter in Volume 2 entitled "The Manifestation of the Trinity in the Self-Emptying of Christ."

8. The confinement of the activity of God's attributes to after creation results in unlimited dangers, an example of which appeared in the conflict that was covered in chapter 6.

4. The Activity of God's Attributes Requires His Self-Sufficiency

The eternal self-sufficiency of God is evident on several grounds:

1. God's self-sufficiency is a requirement of his perfection. For God is perfect and complete without the existence of creation. "All attempts to discover an adequate divine object outside of God must fail."[12]

---

11. Atfield, "Can God Be Crucified?," 54.
12. Chafer, *Chafer Systematic Theology*, 1:293.

2. If God was dependent on another, *he would no longer be God*, and this other would be God!

3. It is impossible for finite creation to satisfy the infinite Creator. His resources in himself are full and complete and satisfy all his desires. And in his relationship with creation, he is the giver and not the receiver. There is nothing that satisfies his nature except his own infinite and eternal nature. He finds in himself the source of perfect fulfillment and gratification, from eternity past to eternity future. Samaan adds that God's *self-sufficiency makes it possible for him to be active as subject and object in total independence from creation and without being composite:* "Thereby he is from eternity past without beginning, knower and known, demonstrating reason and accepting reason, owning his will and recognizing the will of another, seeing and being seen, hearing and being heard, loving and being loved, without being composite in himself or having a partner with him, all in full harmony with his perfection and independence in himself of anything in existence."[13]

The Eternal Activity of God's Attributes Presupposes a Relationship between Persons

If the activity of God's attributes is eternal, this presupposes the existence of a relationship between real persons. This is supported by several factors.

1. The Activity of God's Attributes Depends on a Relationship

It is self-evident that the activity of any attribute depends on the existence of a relationship. There are several points to make in this regard.

1. As was covered in chapter 7, the existence of a person is philosophically not confined to existence, but to existence in relationship. This means that there are two necessary elements required for the existence of a person. The first is existence, and the second is existence in relationship.[14] Therefore, John Zizioulas asserts that these two elements are identical, so that the principle of "existence in relationship" is the only principle that gives a person meaning to his

---

13. Awad Samaan, الله، ذاته ونوع وحدانيته [God, His Essence and His Kind of Unity], 9.

14. See Zizioulas, *Being As Communion*, 83–84; Schelling, *Ages of the World*, 96–97; Athanasius, "Four Discourses Against the Arians," 20, 88.

or her existence, otherwise there would be no person. For "*to be* and *to be in relation* becomes identical . . . It is only in relationship that identity appears as having an ontological significance."[15] *Personhood becomes evident in relationship.*

2. God loves, not because he can love as a decision of his will, but because *he is love in his nature*, and he is love in his nature because he loves from eternity, and he does so because he is in relationship.[16] This is fair and sound reason. There is really no other option.

3. The relationship would be deficient and lacking if it was restricted to a relationship with the self, as in saying that a man loves himself or God loves himself. For a relationship requires an activity between a subject and an object that are distinct from one another. This applies to people as well as to God, but without God being composite. There are several reasons why a relationship cannot be with self:

   • The insistence on confining a relationship to the self is possible in word and in theory, but is impossible existentially or in reality.

   • The subject and object cannot be one and the same in number and identity. For it is impossible in a reciprocal relationship for the subject to be the object at the same time.

   • Confining relationship to self lacks the expression outside of self, and restricts it to caring for self only, which would pollute the purity of moral attributes. Using the example of love, the theologian Schelling asserts that love does not seek what is its own, and that its presence alone without a relationship between distinct persons deprives from the principle of personality, and is rather the opposite of the meaning of personality:

   > All agree that the deity is a being of all beings, the purest love, infinite communicativeness and emanation . . . By itself, however, love does not come to be . . . it does not seek what is its own, and therefore also by itself cannot have being. Hence a being of all beings is by itself without support . . . is by itself the antithesis of personality. Thus another power making for personality must give it a ground . . . There are thus two principles even in what is necessary in God:

---

15. Zizioulas, 83–84.
16. See Glaser, "Concept of Relationship as a Key," 58.

the outflowing, outspreading, self-giving essence, and an equally eternal power of selfhood, of return unto self, of being-in-self. Without his further deed, God is in himself both of these, that essence and this power.[17]

Richard of St Victor asserts similarly that if God were one person, he would not experience sharing the richness of what he owns, and this would deprive him of pleasure forever:

Certainly if there were only one person in Divinity, He would not have anyone with whom He might share the riches of His greatness. But conversely that abundance of delights and sweetness, which would have been able to increase for him on account of intimate love, would be lacking in eternity . . . And for the magnificence of His honor, He rejoices over sharing the riches as much as He glories over enjoying the abundance of delights and sweetness. On the basis of these things, consider how impossible it is for some one person in Divinity to lack the fellowship of association . . . Nothing can be discovered that gives more pleasure than the sweetness of loving; there is nothing by which the soul is more delighted.[18]

- The attribute of humility is one of the attributes of God that requires order in submission. But how can self submit to itself? The subject of submission will be treated at length in Volume 2 in the chapters entitled "The Manifestation of the Trinity in Christ's Submission to God" and "The Manifestation of the Trinity in the Self-Emptying of Christ."
- It is impossible to know a person by knowing only that he or she exists. Knowing a person comes through knowing the relationships of the person. The more that is known about the nature of these relationships, the more the attributes of the person become known.
- The more intimate the relationships of a particular person are, the greater the possibility of knowing the person deeply through knowledge of these relationships. The most intimate of

---

17. Schelling, Ages of the World, 96–97.

18. Richard of St Victor, Book Three of the Trinity, 387–388.

relationships is that of fatherhood. In human terms, fatherhood is superior to the marriage relationship because the father has the same nature as his son or daughter. In divine terms, fatherhood and sonship would be eternal, without beginning or end. The history of Israel in the Old Testament and the revelation of the Son in the New Testament show that the relationship of sonship to God is superior and prior to messiahship, prophethood, priesthood and kingship.

2. The Relationship Depends on Equal Persons

The existence of God in relationship means that his oneness is unique, made up of distinct persons in the following fashion:

1. The Existence of God in Relationship within His Oneness Means That *His Oneness Is of a Unique Kind*

1. It is impossible for the subject and the object to be the eternal God and the temporal creation because creation is contingent, that is, its existence is dependent on him, and there was a time when it did not exist.

2. It is impossible for the subject and object to be *two gods*, because there is only one God.

3. It is impossible for the subject and the object to be *parts in God,* because this would mean that he is composite. But as mentioned in chapter 7, God is simple, meaning that he is not the sum of his attributes; rather he is his attributes:

    > Simplicity is not contrasted with difficulty but with composition . . . God, as a simple being, is not made up of parts as we are . . . He is not constructed of various segments of being that are assembled together to compose His whole being. It is not so much that God has attributes but that He is His attributes.[19]

4. Since God is not composite, a relationship between at least two rational beings within himself is inevitable, and this is an expression of his unique oneness. Samaan expresses this:

---

19. Sproul, *God's Love*, 107.

The exercise of these attributes cannot take place except between two rational beings at least, or between one rational being and himself if he was composite. But since God in his oneness and unique eternality and non-composite being would have been practicing these attributes between himself and his essence eternally . . . it is certain that his oneness . . . is not a oneness devoid of positive attributes, nor Absolute Oneness, but oneness of a different kind, so that there is none like him.[20]

2. The Relationship Must Be *Between Distinct Persons* in God

1. The presence of a relationship within God's oneness naturally requires that the relationship is between equal persons. There must be a reciprocal and equal interaction in thought, will, purpose, emotions and holiness. So, if the subject is a person, the object is a person also. Chafer writes,

> Since the divine nature includes plurality, it must be a plurality of Persons. Such a plurality cannot be predicated of the divine Essence, for the Scriptures distinctly testify to the truth there is but *one God*. Similarly, this plurality cannot be that of mere offices or modes of manifestations, for such could not serve in the relation to each other as agent and object. Nothing short of Persons can serve the reciprocity. In the case of the exercise of the attributes which are moral, both the agent and the object must exhibit intelligence, consciousness, and moral agency. In the experience of communion, the necessity is as much on the object as it is on the agent, that there shall be similarity of thought, disposition, will, purpose, and affection. If the agent be a person, the object must be a person also; whatever pertains to Deity is of necessity eternal.[21]

In the case of human beings, interaction is between distinct but separate persons. However, in the case of God, interaction is between *distinct persons who are not separate from one another.* This is what distinguishes God, who is multi-personal, from human beings,

20. Awad Samaan, الله، ذاته ونوع وحدانيته [God, His Essence and His Kind of Unity], 8–9.
21. Chafer, *Chafer Systematic Theology*, 1:293. Cf. Berkhof, *Systematic Theology*, 84–85.

who are unipersonal. Awad Samaan calls the persons "designates," stressing that it is necessary for God to have a plurality of designates so that each of them is God. Accordingly, the natural requisite is for all of God's attributes to be active in eternal perfection. Samaan states,

> Since God, with his unique eternality and being non-composite, has been practicing these attributes from eternity in himself, it is certain that his oneness of essence itself joins a multiplicity. In other words, he is not one designate but designates . . . Therefore, all his attributes do actually exist before the existence of any other being, or from eternity past. And if God is designates, it is self-evident that each of these designates is not a part of God, but is God himself, because he is not compound from elements or parts . . . Therefore, each of the designates is the eternal God, the knower, who wills, powerful, seeing, hearing, speaking, completely perfect, and independent completely. So he is knower and known, willing and being willed, seeing and being seen, hearing and being heard, loving and being loved, and so on to the point of perfection with no perfection beyond it, without being composite in himself or having a partner with him.[22]

2.   If the attributes of God are eternal, the persons must also be eternal. For the perfection of the relationship requires that every person equally loves and accepts love eternally. Each equally understands and enjoys the other person eternally. The will of one person agrees equally with the will of the other person eternally.

3.   The existence of God in relationship between persons is the best explanation for the existence of creation. It is an outflow of the relationship he already has, and not a fulfillment of the need for a relationship he does not have, for he eternally enjoys the full pleasure of a perfect relationship of equal persons in himself. So, out of the fecundity of the eternal activity of his attributes, he created in order to share them with his creation. In other words, he created not to receive but to give. He entered into a relationship with people

---

22. Samaan, الله بين الفلسفة والمسيحيّة [God, Between Philosophy and Christianity], 104–105. Cf. Edwards, *Jesus the Wisdom of God*, 96.

because he is in relationship in himself. Therefore, God is relational with people because he is relational in himself.

4.   Human beings are relational because they were created in the image of God. Human beings are relational because God is relational. In other words, a person finds greater joy in a relationship with another person equal to him or her because God also has the greatest joy in a relationship in himself between equal persons.

The Relationship Is Protected by Threeness of Persons

The reality is that many have difficulty finding evidence to limit the number of persons in God to three, that is, at the least three and at the most three. For example, Samaan exposes the weakness of his argument by his over-dependence on mathematics:

> As to the number of persons, of course the least number needed to assure exclusive and inclusive oneness [i.e. Oneness in Trinity] is the number 3. Many philosophers agree with us . . . And there is a belief among people in general that the number 3 is the first full number . . . and in Mathematics, the first shape is the one that has three sides, and the first volume is three-dimensional.[23]

Others do not see any difficulty with the persons being more than three. For example, Hodgson says that there has not been any convincing argument for the number 3 and one should be open to the possibility that God may reveal more persons in himself. He writes,

> Why should there be three Persons and only three? Various attempts have been made to demonstrate this as a matter of logical necessity, but none of them is really convincing. God has actually made himself known to us in three Persons. Why should we not cherish the hope that someday he may further reveal himself to us in a fourth, fifth, or more? It would indeed be more reasonable to expect this than to think of him as going back on what he has already done.[24]

However, although God is greater than what he has revealed of himself in the Bible, Hodgson does not explain why a revelation one day of a larger number

---

23. Samaan, الله، ذاته ونوع وحدانيته [God, His Essence and His Kind of Unity], 16–17.

24. Hodgson, *How Can God Be Both One and Three?*, 13.

of persons in God would be a hope to cherish and a reasonable expectation. Is not the Bible, whose canon is closed, sufficient in what it has revealed, especially about the nature of God as Triune?

Contrary to what Samaan, Hodgson and like-minded thinkers suppose, there is good evidence for three persons, that is, *at least three and at most three*. This also finds support in Scripture.

1. Three Persons at Least

There are indications that support the notion of three persons at least.

1. The existence of a third person ensures multiple shared activities in addition to dual exchanged activity. In other words, it is necessary for the activity exchanged between two persons to include shared activity with a third person. This guarantees all forms of relationship between persons.[25] Therefore, it is logical that there are not fewer than three. For example, the love exchanged between two extends beyond the two to become a shared love between three, thereby becoming completed love. So there is a necessity for two together to share the role of subject or object with a third who functions as object or subject respectively.

    Without threeness, therefore, the relationship is deprived of shared activity, which is a foundational attribute for an eternal and complete relationship. Richard of St Victor adds that the absence of threeness strips love of sharing, exchange, assurance, harmony and passion:

    > When one person gives love to another and he alone loves only the other, there certainly is love, but it is not a shared love. When two love each other mutually and give to each other the affection of supreme longing; when the affection of the first goes out to the second and the affection of the second goes out to the first and tends as it were in diverse ways – in this case there certainly is love on both sides, but it is not shared love. Shared love is properly said to exist when a third person is loved by two persons harmoniously and in community, and the affection of the two persons is fused into one affection by the flame

---

25. See Chafer, *Chafer Systematic Theology*, 1:294.

of love for the third. From these things it is evident that shared love would have no place in Divinity itself if a third person were lacking to the other two persons. Here we are not speaking of just any shared love but of supreme shared love – a shared love of a sort such that a creature would never merit from the Creator and for which it would never be found worthy.[26]

2. The third person protects from separation and exclusion. Leonardo Boff maintains that three persons avoids the solitude of confinement to oneness, the separation of confinement to duality and the narcissism of both. Instead, it ensures openness and communion:

> If God were one alone, there would be solitude and concentration in unity and oneness. If God were two, a duality, Father and Son only, there would be separation (one being distinct from the other) and exclusion (one not being the other). But God is *three*, a Trinity, and being three avoids solitude, overcomes separation and surpasses exclusion. The Trinity allows identity (the Father), difference of identity (the Son) and difference of difference (the Holy Spirit). Trinity prevents face-to-face confrontation between Father and Son in a "narcissistic" contemplation. The third figure is the difference, the openness, communion. Trinity is inclusive because it unites what separated and excluded (the Father–Son duality).[27]

3. The dual relationship guarantees interaction by choice and not out of compulsion. Using the example of love, S. Lewis Johnson says that, if God were a duality only instead of being a Trinity, the response of love would be imposed and not optional. But threeness guarantees the integrity of freedom in choosing the love and the beloved. So there must be a sufficient number for the response to come not out of coercion, but out of free will. And this relationship must be in God himself first, apart from his relationship with creation. Johnson asserts,

---

26. Richard of St Victor, *Book Three of the Trinity*, 392; cf. comments on St Victor by Edwards, *Jesus the Wisdom of God*, 97.

27. Boff, *Trinity and Society*, 3. His emphasis.

If God is perfect, he can only realize himself as love through relationships within his own being. Since he is eternal, his relationships must antedate the creation. He must have loved from eternity because he's an eternal being. And if he must have an object who does not have to return that love, then there must be at least three persons involved in this love triangle . . . If he loves the son [*sic*] and the son is the only other person, you might say he loves the son because the son returns his love. But if there is also a spirit, the three, then we may have the perfect expression of love of which there is no required return. And thus even logically we come to something like a Trinity because we must have love perfected. That may only be done within the divine.

We must have love that is eternal that rules out all of human participation in this love. And since we must have at least enough persons for there to be response without impelling or compulsion, then we must have at least three, so that the father theoretically may love the son who in turn may love the spirit who in turn may love the father. And thus each loves out of his own desire to express himself perfectly in love with no requirement or compulsion that that love be returned to that other person. So the idea of a trinity is a very logical thing, really.[28]

2. Three Persons at Most

There are indications from the Bible and from reason to support the notion of three persons at most.

1.   An argument for the maximum number of three arose by uniting the plurality of persons with the most essential attributes. This was expressed brilliantly by the Christian Arab philosopher of the ninth century AD, Ammar Al Basri, who states that the import of the doctrine of the Trinity is that God is alive by his Spirit and speaking

---

28. S. Lewis Johnson, "The Holy Trinity, or the Uniqueness of Christianity, Part II," sermon preached at Believers Chapel, Dallas, https://s3-us-west-2.amazonaws.com/sljinstitute-production/doctrine/systematic_theology/011_SLJ_Systematic_Theology.pdf. Copyright 2007.

by his word. He then compares God with human beings: just as created human beings have life and speech, so does their creator. However, while a human being is one person with his or her life and speech, God is three persons with his life and speech because of his infinite superiority over human beings. So his superior life is the Holy Spirit, and his superior Word is the Son, and thus he is three persons.[29]

2. The question that arises is: Why confine personhood to life and the Word? What about hypostatizing the other attributes, such as hearing, seeing, wisdom, power and knowledge? Ammar Al Basri answered by again comparing God with a human being, saying that what distinguishes God and a human being from earthly creatures is life and speech. All that has been created is of two kinds: that which has life and that which does not. Then of that which has life there are two kinds: that which has speech, expressing reason, and that which does not. So life and speech are essential to the essence of human beings. It is possible for them to keep their personhood without any of the other attributes, but not without life and speech. Likewise, life and speech are of the essence of God. But he is infinitely superior to human beings, such that his life and speech/word are persons in him.[30]

3. It is impossible for each attribute to be hypostatized as a person; otherwise the number of persons would equal the number of attributes. Furthermore, this would mean giving deity to each description in addition to the one described, namely, God, which would lead to idolatry. For example, God would become love and love would become God, and human beings would then worship love as they would worship God. This is impossible.

4. Rather than focusing on the number of persons, another argument for the maximum number of three arose by focusing on the number of relationships that spring from the attributes. To begin with, it is impossible to have a relationship for each attribute; otherwise the number of relationships would equal the number of attributes. For it is the nature of a perfect relationship, which is found only

29. Ammar Al Basri, كتاب البرهان [The Book of Evidence], 48–49.

30. Ammar Al Basri, 52–53.

in an eternal relationship, for all the attributes to be active in one relationship.

5. It is the nature of a perfect relationship for all the attributes to work without the absence of any attribute and without any deficiency in any attribute. So the attribute of love, for example, does not work without the attribute of holiness or with only a portion of the attribute of holiness. And the attribute of power does not work without the attribute of wisdom or with only a portion of the attribute of wisdom, and so on. All the attributes thus work fully and in full harmony in one relationship. The attributes of God will be studied more fully in Volume 2 in the chapters entitled "The Activity of the Attributes of God Outside Creation" and "The Activity of the Attributes of God Inside Creation."

6. It is in harmony with reason for all the attributes active between two persons to be joined by a third in order to avoid unlimited plurality.
    •   The third person preserves one relationship characterized by unending self-sufficiency so that the relationship between the first and second persons becomes through and with the third person.
    •   The third person prevents deifying any of the attributes. For example, God is love without love becoming God, and human beings worship God without worshipping love.
    •   The third person protects from any conflict such as occurred between the Muʿtazilites and the Ashʿarites, especially around the two extremes of either deifying the attributes or avoiding giving meaning to them. The third person, who is represented by the Holy Spirit, unites all the attributes in himself, preventing idolatry. At the same time, the third person gives meaning to all the attributes so that faith may be practiced in reliance upon them. This work of the Holy Spirit will be explained in more detail in Volume 2 in the chapter entitled "The Significance of the Name 'Holy Spirit.'"

7. The Bible also expresses harmony with the maximum number of three. For the Bible declares that the relationship of the Son to the Father is the only eternal relationship. It declares that the Son is "the one and only [or "only begotten"] to the Father" (John 1:14), "the one and only [or "only begotten"] who is in the bosom of the Father" (John 1:18) and "his one and only [or "only begotten"]" (John

3:17–18; 1 John 4:9). The expression "one and only" (used by NIV, ESV, NET, NLT and others), also rendered "only begotten" (NASB, KJV, ASV and others), points to a unique relationship, one like no other. No other person has this kind of relationship to the Father. The uniqueness of this relationship will be studied in Volume 2 in the chapter entitled "The Activity of the Attributes of God Outside Creation."[31]

8. This unique relationship between the Father and the Son is active through the Holy Spirit. As will be explained in Volume 2 in the chapter entitled "The Significance of the Name 'Holy Spirit,'" the Holy Spirit takes two roles. In addition to his role as a person equal to the Father and to the Son, the constant use of the name "Spirit" signifies that all the attributes of perfection which are exchanged between the Father and the Son are bound to the Holy Spirit. So the activity of the unique relationship between the Father and the Son is through the Holy Spirit, whom the Bible calls the Spirit of the Father and the Spirit of the Son.

9. Based on the above, safeguarding the number of persons to a maximum of three is an inevitable necessity that guarantees simplicity without complexity in God as well as unity with plurality. As referred to earlier, Ammar Al Basri asserts that threeness does not nullify oneness, and oneness does not nullify threeness.[32]

The Threeness of Persons Is Guaranteed Perfection through Oneness

The Trinity preserves the plurality of persons in God on the one hand and the oneness of God on the other. For it is a oneness that joins persons ensuring that all the requisites are present for the eternal activity of the attributes. It is also a oneness of a one and only God who excludes the presence of any other god. This oneness is necessary in order to guarantee the perfection and eternality of the attributes.

---

31. The two main translations are of the adjective μονογενής (*monogenase*) and will be studied in depth in the chapter in Volume 2 entitled "The Activity of the Attributes of God Outside Creation."

32. Ammar Al Basri, كتاب البرهان [The Book of Evidence], 48–49.

1. The Triune Relationship Requires the Perfection of Attributes

The presence of an eternal relationship requires the attributes to be perfect, without any deficiency or impurity. For the presence of any deficiency or impurity in any of the attributes destroys the relationship and in turn nullifies the eternality. Therefore, the attributes of God must stem from his unchanging nature and not from a capricious will. So the relationship in God becomes eternal because his attributes are eternal by virtue of their perfection.

2. The Perfection of Attributes Requires Oneness

The perfection of the attributes of God means that their activity is eternal, without beginning or end. And what guarantees their perfection and eternality is their oneness because oneness means the absence of any deficiency or impurity. The presence of any deficiency or impurity would destroy the oneness. An eternal oneness guarantees the perfection of the attributes that is parallel to their eternality.

3. Oneness Depends on the Perfection of Attributes

Just as the perfection of attributes requires oneness, so oneness requires the perfection of attributes, that is, that the activity of the attributes between the persons is fully operational and in harmony, with independence from each other. Anything other than that not only destroys the relationship, it also destroys the oneness. The oneness of God means the infinite perfection of all his attributes.

Summary and Conclusion

The eternal existence of God means the eternal activity of his attributes, which means a relationship between persons, which is protected through the perfection of threeness of persons, which in turn is guaranteed perfection through oneness. And all of this is an eternal inevitability. This is congruent with the revelation of the Bible about the Trinity.

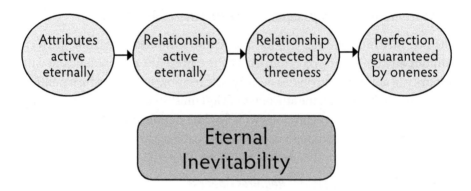

Figure 8.1: The Logic of the Trinity

Many who believe in God defend his oneness, but without realizing the richness of the meaning of Oneness in Trinity. With great insight, Awad Samaan explains this notion by stating that it is here that the quarrel between adherents of different religions takes place. Some neglect reflecting upon God, either because they are busy with the affairs of life or because they think it is not warranted for them to do so. They settle by adopting titles of God without deep conviction. However, others study and ponder the nature of God and reach a deeper knowledge of him that makes them realize that his oneness is of a wondrous kind.[33]

It is this oneness that the current study endeavors to show. The journey of discovery continues in Volume 2.

---

33. Awad Samaan, الله بين الفلسفة والمسيحيّة [God, Between Philosophy and Christianity], 93–94.

Appendix 1

The Repeated Mention of the Persons of the Trinity

There is repeated mention of the persons of the Trinity, the Father, Son and Holy Spirit, in about 120 New Testament passages *with simplicity, without defense, without explanation and without apology*! This occurs in two ways: either without mention of oneness; or with the mention of oneness. Each person is referred to by name or by other titles or attributes as indicated by *the emphasis* in the passages below.

Occurrences of the Three Persons without Mention of Oneness

Mention of the three persons of the Trinity is repeated in the New Testament presupposing the oneness of God. This *draws the reader to seek a deeper understanding*. The following are a few examples:

> Now the birth of *Jesus Christ* was as follows: when *His* mother Mary had been betrothed to Joseph, before they came together she was found to be with *child* by the *Holy Spirit*. And Joseph her husband, being a righteous man and not wanting to disgrace her, planned to send her away secretly. But when he had considered this, behold, an angel of *the Lord* appeared to him in a dream, saying, "Joseph, son of David, do not be afraid to take Mary as your wife; for *the Child* who has been conceived in her is of the *Holy Spirit*." (Matt 1:18–20)

> The angel answered and said to her, "The *Holy Spirit* will come upon you, and the power of *the Most High* will overshadow you; and for that reason *the holy Child* shall be called the *Son of God*." (Luke 1:35)

And *the Holy Spirit* descended upon *Him* in bodily form like a dove, and a voice came out of heaven, "*You* are *My beloved Son*, in You *I am* well-pleased." (Luke 3:22)

John testified saying, "I have seen *the Spirit* descending as a dove out of heaven, and *He* remained upon *Him*. I did not recognize *Him*, but *He* who sent me to baptize in water *said* to me, 'He upon *whom* you see *the Spirit* descending and remaining upon *Him*, this is *the One* who baptizes in *the Holy Spirit*.'" (John 1:32–33)

I will ask the *Father*, and He will give you *another Helper*, that He may be with you forever; that is *the Spirit of truth*, whom the world cannot receive, because it does not see *Him* or know *Him*, but you know *Him* because *He* abides with you and will be in you. I will not leave you as orphans; I will come to you. (John 14:16–18)

But *the Helper, the Holy Spirit*, whom *the Father* will send in *My name*, *He* will teach you all things, and bring to your remembrance all that *I* said to you. (John 14:26)

But *I* tell you the truth, it is to your advantage that *I* go away; for if *I* do not go away, *the Helper* will not come to you; but if *I* go, *I* will send *Him* to you . . . But when *He, the Spirit of truth*, comes, *He* will guide you into all the truth; for *He* will not speak on *His* own initiative, but whatever *He* hears, *He will* speak; and *He* will disclose to you what is to come. *He* will glorify *Me*, for *He* will take of *Mine* and will disclose it to you. All things that *the Father* has are *Mine*; therefore *I* said that *He* takes of *Mine* and will disclose it to you. A little while, and you will no longer see *Me*; and again a little while, and you will see *Me*. (John 16:7, 13–16)

. . . until the day when *He* was taken up to heaven, after *He* had by *the Holy Spirit* given orders to the apostles whom *He* had chosen . . . Gathering them together, *He* commanded them not to leave Jerusalem, but to wait for what *the Father* had promised, "Which," *He said*, "you heard of from *Me*; for John baptized with water, but you will be baptized with *the Holy Spirit* not many days from now." (Acts 1:2, 4–5)

Therefore having been exalted to the right hand of *God*, and having received from *the Father* the promise of *the Holy Spirit*, *He* has poured forth this which you both see and hear. (Acts 2:33)

Paul, a bond-servant of *Christ Jesus*, called as an apostle, set apart for the gospel of *God*, which *He* promised beforehand through *His* prophets in the holy Scriptures, concerning *His Son*, who was born of a descendant of David according to the flesh, who was declared *the Son of God* with power by the resurrection from the dead, according to the *Spirit of holiness, Jesus Christ our Lord.* (Rom 1:1–4)

However, you are not in the flesh but in *the Spirit*, if indeed *the Spirit of God* dwells in you. But if anyone does not have *the Spirit of Christ*, he does not belong to *Him* . . . But if *the Spirit of Him* who raised *Jesus* from the dead dwells in you, *He* who raised *Christ Jesus* from the dead will also give life to your mortal bodies through *His Spirit* who dwells in you. (Rom 8:9, 11)

Therefore I make known to you that no one speaking by the *Spirit of God* says, "*Jesus* is accursed"; and no one can say, "*Jesus* is *Lord*," except by the *Holy Spirit*. Now there are varieties of gifts, but the same *Spirit*. And there are varieties of ministries, and the same *Lord*. There are varieties of effects, but the same *God* who works all things in all persons. (1 Cor 12:3–6)

The grace of *the Lord Jesus Christ*, and the love of *God*, and the fellowship of *the Holy Spirit*, be with you all. (2 Cor 13:14)

But when the fullness of the time came, *God* sent forth *His Son*, born of a woman, born under the Law, so that *He* might redeem those who were under the Law, that we might receive the adoption as sons. Because you are sons, *God* has sent forth *the Spirit of His Son* into our hearts, crying, "Abba! *Father!*" Therefore you are no longer a slave, but a son; and if a son, then an heir through *God*. (Gal 4:4–7)

There is one body and one *Spirit*, just as also you were called in one hope of your calling; one *Lord*, one faith, one baptism, one *God and Father* of all who is over all and through all and in all. (Eph 4:4–6)

. . . who, although *He* existed in the *form of God*, did not regard *equality with God* a thing to be grasped, but emptied *Himself*, taking the form of a bond-servant, *and* being made in the likeness of men. Being found in appearance as a man, *He* humbled *Himself* by becoming obedient to the point of death, even death on a cross.

For this reason also, *God* highly exalted *Him*, and bestowed on *Him* the name which is above every name, so that at the name of *Jesus* every knee will bow, of those who are in heaven and on earth and under the earth, and that every tongue will confess that *Jesus Christ is Lord*, to the glory of *God the Father.* (Phil 2:6–11)

But in case I am delayed, I write so that you will know how one ought to conduct himself in the household of *God*, which is the church of the living *God*, the pillar and support of the truth. By common confession, great is the mystery of godliness: *He* who was revealed in the flesh, was vindicated in *the Spirit, seen* by angels, *proclaimed* among the nations, *believed* on in the world, *taken up* in glory. (1 Tim 3:15–16)

But when the kindness of *God our Savior* and His love for mankind appeared, He saved us, not on the basis of deeds which we have done in righteousness, but according to His mercy, by the washing of regeneration and renewing by *the Holy Spirit*, whom He poured out upon us richly through *Jesus Christ our Savior.* (Titus 3:4–6)

. . . how much more will the blood of *Christ*, who through the *eternal Spirit* offered Himself without blemish to *God*, cleanse your conscience from dead works to serve the living *God*? (Heb 9:14)

. . . according to the foreknowledge of *God the Father*, by the sanctifying work of *the Spirit*, to obey *Jesus Christ* and be sprinkled with His blood: May grace and peace be yours in the fullest measure. (1 Pet 1:2)

For *Christ* also died for sins once for all, the just for the unjust, so that *He* might bring us to *God*, having been put to death in the flesh, but made alive in the *spirit.* (1 Pet 3:18)

But you, beloved, building yourselves up on your most holy faith, praying in the *Holy Spirit*, keep yourselves in the love of *God*, waiting anxiously for the mercy of our *Lord Jesus Christ* to eternal life. (Jude 20–21)

Occurrences of the Three Persons with Mention of Oneness

Mention of the three persons of the Trinity has been seen in the above verses without direct mention of God's oneness. This is because oneness is always presupposed as an essential biblical teaching. However, there are other New

Testament passages that combine the mention of both the three persons and the oneness of God. The following are some examples:

> Go therefore and make disciples of all the nations, baptizing them in the *name of the Father and the Son and the Holy Spirit.* (Matt 28:19)

> My Father, who has given them to Me, is greater than all; and no one is able to snatch them out of the Father's hand. *I and the Father are one.* (John 10:29–30)

> And Jesus cried out and said, "He who believes in Me, does not believe in Me but *in Him who sent Me. He who sees Me sees the One who sent Me* . . . For I did not speak on My own initiative, but *the Father Himself who sent Me* has given Me a commandment as to what to say and what to speak." (John 12:44–45, 49)

> Jesus said to him, "I am the way, and the truth, and the life; no one comes to the Father but through Me. If you had *known Me, you would have known My Father* also; from now on *you know Him, and have seen Him.*" Philip said to Him, "Lord, show us the Father, and it is enough for us." Jesus said to him, "Have I been so long with you, and yet you have not come to know Me, Philip? *He who has seen Me has seen the Father;* how can you say, 'Show us the Father'? Do you not believe that *I am in the Father, and the Father is in Me?* The words that I say to you I do not speak on My own initiative, but *the Father abiding in Me* does His works." (John 14:6–10)

> Yet for us there is but *one* God, the Father, from whom are all things and we exist for Him; and *one* Lord, *Jesus Christ,* by whom are all things, and we *exist* through Him. (1 Cor 8:6)

> Grace to you and peace, *from* Him [the Father] who is and who was and who is to come, and *from* [the Holy Spirit] the seven spirits [attributes] who are before His throne, and *from Jesus Christ,* the faithful witness, the firstborn of the dead, and the ruler of the kings of the earth. To Him who loves us and released us from our sins by His blood – and He has made us to be a kingdom, priests *to His God and Father* – to Him be the glory and the dominion forever and ever . . . "I am the Alpha and the Omega," says the *Lord God,* "who is and who was and who is to come, the Almighty." (Rev 1:4–8)

Appendix 2

The Deity of Christ

The following is an outline of the most important New Testament witness to the deity of Christ.[1]

1. Divine Works and Attributes of Christ in His Relationship to Creation

1. Creator (John 1:3; Col 1:16; Heb 1:2)
2. Sustainer of creation (1 Cor 8:6; Col 1:17; Heb 1:3)
3. Author of life (John 1:4; Acts 3:15)

2. Divine Works and Attributes of Christ in His Relationship to People

1. Total sovereignty (Matt 18:18; Rom 14:9; Rev 1:5)
2. Healer of the sick (Mark 1:32–34; Acts 3:6; 10:38)
3. Authoritative teacher (Mark 1:21–33; 13:31)
4. Forgiver of sin (Mark 2:1–12; Luke 24:47; Acts 4:12; 5:31; Col 3:13)
5. Grantor of salvation and eternal life (Acts 4:12; Rom 10:12–13)
6. Nearly stoned for claiming deity (John 8:56–59; 10:31–33)
7. Sender of the Holy Spirit (John 14:16–17; 15:26; Acts 2:17, 33)
8. Baptizer in the Holy Spirit (Matt 3:11; John 1:33; Titus 3:5)
9. Raiser of the dead (Luke 7:11–17; John 5:21; 6:40)
10. Judge (Matt 25:31, 46; John 5:22–23, 26–27; Acts 17:31; 1 Cor 4:4–5)
11. All-knowing (Luke 6:8; John 2:24; 16:30; 21:17; Col 2:3; Rev 2:23)
12. The object of praise (Matt 21:15–16; Eph 5:19; Rev 5:8–14)

---

1. Arrangement of the information here came with the aid of Harris's plan (Harris, *Jesus as God*, 315–117).

13. The recipient of prayer (Acts 1:24; 7:59–60; 9:10–16; 22:16, 19; 1 Cor 1:2; 16:22; 2 Cor 12:8)
14. The object of worship (Matt 8:2; 14:33; 21:15–16; 28:9, 17; John 20:27–29; Acts 7:59; 1 Cor 1:2; Phil 2:9–11; Rev 5:8–14)
15. The object of faith (John 14:1; Acts 10:34; 16:31; Rom 10:8–13)
16. Joint source of blessing in the Trinity (1 Cor 1:3; 2 Cor 1:2; Gal 1:3; 1 Thess 3:11; 2 Thess 2:16)
17. Object of doxologies (2 Tim 4:18; 2 Pet 3:18; Rev 1:5–6; 5:13)

3. Divine Works and Attributes of Christ in His Relationship to the Father

1. Pre-existence and eternal existence (John 1:1; 8:56–58; 12:41; 17:5; 1 Cor 10:4; Heb 13:8; Jude 5)
2. Equality with the Father (John 10:30–33; 14:9; 5:17–18)
3. Equality of his works to those of the Father (Mark 2:5; John 5:17–18)
4. Equality of worth and honor to that of the Father (Matt 28:19; John 5:23)
5. The full revelation of the Father (John 1:18; 14:9; Col 1:15; Heb 1:1–3)
6. The embodiment of truth (John 1:9, 14; 6:32; 14:6; Rev 3:7, 14)
7. Superior to angels (Heb 1:4–14)
8. Sharing ownership with the Father of the kingdom (Eph 5:5; Rev 1:6; Rev 11:15)
9. Sharing ownership with the Father of the churches (Acts 20:28; Rom 16:16; Rev 1:4–20)
10. Partnering with the Father in the work of the Holy Spirit in believers (Rom 8:9; Phil 1:19)
11. Partnering with the Father in the heavenly city (Rev 14:1; 21:22; 22:1, 3)
12. Sharing the throne with the Father (Rev 3:21; 22:1, 3)

4. Use of Yahweh's Description in the OT to Refer to Jesus in the NT

1. The character of Yahweh is the character of Jesus (Exod 3:14 is used in John 8:58 and Rev 1:4, 8; Ps 102:25–27 [MT & LXX 101:26–28] is used in Heb 1:11–12; Isa 44:6 is used in Rev 1:17)
2. The holiness of Yahweh is the holiness of Christ (Isa 8:12–13 is used in 1 Pet 3:14–15)

3. The worship of Yahweh is the worship of Christ (Isa 45:23 is used in Phil 2:10–11; LXX Deut 32:43 and LXX Ps 96:7 [MT 97:7] is used in Heb 1:6; Isa 6:1 is used in John 12:41)
4. The work of Yahweh in creation is the work of Christ (Ps 102:25 [LXX 101:26] is used in Heb 1:10–11)
5. The salvation of Yahweh is the salvation of Christ (Joel 2:32 [LXX 3:5] is used in Rom 10:13 and in Acts 2:21; Isa 40:3 is used in Matt 3:3)
6. The judgment of Yahweh is the judgment of Christ (Isa 6:10 is used in John 12:40–41)
7. The trustworthiness of Yahweh is the trustworthiness of Christ (Isa 28:16 is used in Rom 9:33; 10:11; 1 Pet 2:6)
8. The victory of Yahweh is the victory of Christ (Ps 68:18 [LXX Ps 68:19] is used in Eph 4:8)

5. Divine Titles and Attributes Declared by Christ and Ascribed to Him

1. Son of Man (Matt 9:6; 12:8; 16:27–28; 24:30; 26:63–64; John 1:51; Acts 7:56)
2. Son of God (Matt 11:27; 16:16; Mark 14:61–62; 15:39; John 10:29–33; 19:7; 20:31; Rom 1:4; Gal 4:4; Heb 1:2)
3. Lord (Mark 12:35–37; John 20:28; Rom 10:9; 1 Cor 8:5–6; 12:3; 16:22; Phil 2:11; 1 Pet 2:3; 3:15)
4. Messiah (Matt 16:16; Mark 14:61; John 20:31)
5. Alpha and Omega (Rev 1:8; 21:6; 22:13)
6. The image of God [the Father] (2 Cor 4:4; Col 1:15)
7. The form of God [the Father] (Phil 1:6)
8. God (John 1:1, 18; 20:28; Rom 9:5; Titus 2:13; Heb 1:8; 2 Pet 1:1)
9. The character of God's being (Heb 1:3)
10. Firstborn (a title of eminence because he is Creator, not created; Col 1:16)
11. Fullness of deity (Col 1:19; 2:9)
12. The full revelation (John 1:18; Heb 1:1–3)

Appendix 3

The Personhood and Deity of the Holy Spirit

The Bible declares that the Holy Spirit is a person who has a divine nature equal to the Father and the Son.

The Personhood of the Holy Spirit

There is usually a question regarding the deity of Christ and not his personhood, but the opposite is the case in regard to the Holy Spirit. For there is usually a question about the personhood of the Holy Spirit and not his deity. It is therefore necessary to affirm that the Holy Spirit is not confined to being a power or an influence, but is a person equal to the Father and the Son.

Gender does not always determine the personhood of the Holy Spirit. There are other factors that do so (see below). The word "spirit" occurs 378 times in the Old Testament and 379 times in the New Testament (about four times as dense as the Old Testament). Though the word "spirit" is feminine in the Hebrew language, it occurs in the Old Testament with verbs, pronouns or adjectives in both the feminine and the masculine (there is no neuter gender in the Hebrew language). Where the word "spirit" is in the role of subject, the verbs used with it can be in the feminine (30% of the time) and the masculine (12% of the time). But when the word "spirit" is not in the role of subject, no verb is used with it (58% of the time). So the word "spirit" occurs in the Old Testament with feminine verbs (e.g. Gen 1:2; Num 11:25–26; 24:2; Judg 6:34; Job 33:4; Isa 11:2; 63:14; Ezek 2:2; 11:5; Hag 2:5), and occurs with pronouns and adjectives in the feminine (e.g. Job 32:8; Ps 143:10; Neh 9:20). It also occurs with masculine verbs (e.g. Gen 6:3; 2 Sam 23:2; 1 Kgs 18:12; 2 Kgs 2:16; Isa 32:15; 59:21; Mic 2:7).

As to the New Testament, the word "spirit" is in the neuter. But it is used with adjectives and participles to point to both the Spirit of God and other than the Spirit of God. This occurs with the feminine (35% of the time; e.g. John 14:17; Rom 1:4; 8:2, 15; 1 John 4:6), the masculine (24% of the time; e.g. Matt 5:3; Eph 1:13; Gal 5:22; 1 Cor 2:12; 1 John 4:2) and the neuter (41% of the time; e.g. Matt 12:43; Luke 4:33; Acts 19:15–16; 1 Cor 6:17; 15:45; Phil 1:27; 1 Pet 3:4).

The personhood of the Holy Spirit is evident for the following reasons:

1. *Use is made of pronouns and demonstratives that belong to rational beings* to point to the Holy Spirit. The masculine demonstrative ἐκεῖνος (*ekeinos*), meaning "he" or "this one," is used to refer to the Holy Spirit (John 14:26; 16:8, 13, 14). Likewise, the masculine third person pronoun αὐτός (*autos*), meaning "him," is used to refer to the Holy Spirit (John 16:7).

2. *The Holy Spirit has a will of his own* that points to his personhood (John 3:5–8; 1 Cor 2:10; 6:19; 12:11).

3. *The Holy Spirit has emotions that are characteristic of persons.* He has love (Rom 5:5; 15:30), and it is possible to grieve him (Isa 63:10; Eph 4:30) and to quench him (1 Thess 5:19).

4. *Relationship is possible with the Holy Spirit as a real person.* The New Testament declares that it is possible to blaspheme the Holy Spirit (Matt 12:31–32), lie to him (Acts 5:3), test him (Acts 5:9) and resist him (Acts 7:51).

5. *The works that the Holy Spirit performs belong to rational beings.* The Bible says that the Holy Spirit creates (Ps 104:30), gives wisdom (Isa 11:2), teaches and guides (Luke 12:12; John 14:26; 1 Cor 2:13; 1 Pet 1:11), comforts (John 14:16, 26), testifies (John 15:26; Acts 5:32), commands and sends missionaries (Acts 13:2–4), involves believers in making decisions with him (Acts 15:28), prevents certain ministries (Acts 16:6), appoints bishops (Acts 20:28), is concerned with specific matters (Rom 8:6, 27), intercedes (Rom 8:27), sanctifies (Rom 15:16), examines the things of God (1 Cor 2:10–11), distributes gifts (1 Cor 12:11; Heb 2:4), gives life (John 3:8; 2 Cor 3:6), warns (1 Tim 4:1; Heb 3:7) and inspires (2 Tim 3:16 [literally "God breathed"; 2 Pet 1:21).

6. *The Holy Spirit is the other comforter alongside the Son* (John 14:16, 26; 15:26; 16:7). The Holy Spirit is "another," ἄλλος (*allos*), of the

same kind, and not ἕτερος (*heteros*), of a different kind. Some prefer using the transliteration *paraclatos* for the Greek original παράκλητος because of the rich meanings of the word. The common translations of it include "counselor," "comforter," "guide," "helper" and "intercessor." The translations "counselor" and "comforter" stress the emotional aspect. The translation "guide" stresses the wisdom aspect. The translation "helper" stresses the obedience and application aspect. The translation "intercessor" stresses the judicial aspect.

The Deity of the Holy Spirit

The deity of the Holy Spirit is strongly evident in his attributes, titles and works that he shares equally with the Father and the Son and which are expressed in the worship due to him.

1. *The Holy Spirit belongs to the Father and the Son.* God refers to the Holy Spirit as "my Spirit" (Gen 6:3; Isa 42:1; 44:3; 59:21; Ezek 37:14; 39:29; Joel 2:28; Matt 12:18; Acts 2:17–18). The Holy Spirit is called "the Spirit of God" (Matt 3:16; 12:28; Rom 8:9, 14; 15:19; 1 Cor 2:11, 14; 3:16; 6:11; 7:40; 12:3; 2 Cor 3:3; Eph 4:30; Phil 3:3), "the Spirit of the Father" (Matt 10:20; Luke 11:13; John 14:26; 15:26; Acts 2:33), "the Spirit of the Lord" (Luke 4:18; 2 Cor 3:17–18), "the Spirit of Jesus" (Acts 16:7), "the Spirit of Christ" (Rom 8:9; 1 Pet 1:11), "the Spirit of His Son" (Gal 4:6) and "the Spirit of Jesus Christ" (Phil 1:19).

2. *The Holy Spirit has divine attributes.* The Holy Spirit is an "eternal Spirit" (Heb 9:14), a "Spirit of Truth" (John 4:24; 14:17; 15:26; 16:13; 1 John 4:6), "Spirit of glory" (1 Pet 4:14) and "Spirit of life" (Rom 8:2).

3. *What the Lord said in the Old Testament, the Holy Spirit said in the New Testament* (compare Isa 6:8–9 with Acts 28:25–26; Jer 31:33 with Heb 10:15–16; Ps 95:8–11 with Acts 7:51).

4. *What was ascribed to God is ascribed to the Holy Spirit.* This includes possession of the temple (compare 1 Cor 3:16; 6:19 with 2 Cor 6:16; Eph 2:22), inspiration (compare 2 Tim 3:16 with Luke 1:70; Eph 3:5; Heb 1:1; 1 Pet 1:11; 2 Pet 1:20–21), the new birth (compare John 3:6 with 1 John 3:9), giving of spiritual gifts (compare 1 Cor 12:9–11 with 1 Cor 12:28) and being lied to (Acts 5:3–4).

5. *The works of the Holy Spirit are the works of God.* This includes creating (Gen 1:1–2; Ps 104:30), speaking through the prophets (Ezek 11:5; 1 Pet 1:11; 2 Pet 1:21), raising to life (John 6:63; Rom 8:11; Rev 11:11), regenerating (John 3:5–8), administering the church by appointing leaders (Acts 13:2; 20:28), guiding ethical conduct (Acts 15:28), guiding believers (Luke 12:12; John 14:26), sanctifying believers (2 Thess 2:13) and convicting unbelievers (John 16:8–11).

6. *What the Holy Spirit does, Christ does.* This includes coming (compare John 14:16; 16:7 with John 5:43; 16:28; 18:37), being sent (compare John 14:26 with John 5:43), being the truth (compare John 14:17; 15:26; 16:13 with John 14:6), being holy (compare John 14:26 with Luke 1:35), personal knowledge of him (compare John 14:17 with John 14:7, 9), presence with the disciples (compare John 14:17 with John 14:20, 23; 15:4, 5; 17:23, 26), in teaching (compare John 14:26; 16:13–15 with John 6:45, 59; 7:14, 28; 8:20), in being rejected (compare John 14:17 with John 5:43; 12:48), in not knowing him (compare John 14:17 with John 8:14, 19; 14:7; 16:3), in testifying against the evil world (compare John 16:8–11 with John 7:7), in guiding in regard to what is to come (compare John 16:13 with John 4:25–26), and in glorifying (compare John 16:14 with John 8:28–29; 12:28; 14:13; 17:4–5).

7. *Christ baptizes people in the Holy Spirit* in order to unite them to his redemptive work in dying and being raised with him, and to unite them to his body, the church (Matt 3:11; Mark 1:8; Luke 3:16; John 1:33; Acts 1:4–5; Rom 6:3–10; 1 Cor 12:13; Eph 4:5; Col 2:12).

8. *The Holy Spirit receives the same honor given to the Father and the Son.* This is evident in the giving of the Great Commission (Matt 28:19), in the apostolic benediction (2 Cor 13:14), in the title "Lord" (compare Exod 34:34 with 2 Cor 3:17–18), in prayer (Eph 2:18) and in punishing blasphemers and those who insult him (Matt 12:31–32; Heb 10:29).

9. *The Holy Spirit continues to work in the hearts* of people as an extension and application of the work of the Father and the Son (John 7:39; 14:16–25; 16:7).

10. *Worship of and prayer to the Holy Spirit is requested and expected.*
    - Though the pattern of prayer in the Bible is that it is addressed to the Father in the name of the Son and intercession of the Holy

Spirit, it can, however, be addressed to the Holy Spirit who is equal in divinity to the Father and Son.

- The Lord asks Ezekiel to make a special request of the Holy Spirit (Ezek 37:9–10).

- Paul said, "We worship the Spirit of God" (Phil 3:3; my translation). The most common translation is, however, "worship God in the Spirit" because πνεύματι (*neuma*) appears in the dative case. However, the object of the verb λατρεύω (*latreuw*) and its derivatives are always in the dative case, without exception. So the translation "we worship the Spirit of God" is the literal rendering.[1]

11. *The Holy Spirit is in the presence of the Father and the Son in heaven.* The book of Revelation declares that the Holy Spirit is present with the Father and the Son by speaking about the seven spirits – that is, the seven attributes that represent all of the attributes of God, which are joined by the Holy Spirit – being before the Father's throne (Rev 4:5) and in the presence of Christ who owns them (Rev 3:1; 5:6).

---

1. The object of the verb λατρεύω (*latreuw*), translated "worship" or "serve" in the following verses, is always in the dative case in the Greek: "serve him," i.e. αὐτῷ (*auto* in Matt 4:10; Luke 4:8; Rev 7:15); "serve me," i.e. μοι (*moi* in Acts 7:7); "serve the host of heaven," i.e. στρατιᾷ (*stratia* in Acts 7:42); "God whom I serve," i.e. ᾧ (*ho* in Rom 1:9; 2 Tim 1:3); "worshipped the creature," i.e. τῇ κτίσει (*teh ktiseh* in Rom 1:25); "serve a copy and shadow of the heavenly things," i.e. ὑποδείγματι καὶ σκιᾷ (*hupodagmati kai skia* in Heb 8:5); "serve God," i.e. θεῷ (*theo* in Heb 9:14); "serve the tabernacle," i.e. τῇ σκηνῇ (*teh skaneh* in Heb 13:10). If Paul's intention was that the Spirit be only a medium for worship or service, he would have used the preposition ἐν (*en*), as indeed he did when the Spirit was functioning in this way: "for through Him we both have our access in one Spirit [ἐν ἑνὶ πνεύματι; *en heni neumati*] to the Father" (Eph 2:18).

Bibliography

المراجع العربية **Arabic Sources**

البصري، عمار. كتاب البرهان. تحقيق ميشال الحايك. بيروت، لبنان: دار المشرق، دون تاريخ.

_____. كتاب المسائل والأجوبة. تحقيق ميشال الحايك. بيروت، لبنان: دار المشرق، دون تاريخ.

ابن تيميّة، تقي الدين أبو العبّاس أحمد. القضاء والقَدَر. طبعة ثانية. دار الكتاب العربّي، 1997.

ابن كثير. تفسير القرآن العظيم. الجزء الثاني. بيروت: دار الجليل، 1988.

ابن المهالي، جلال الدين محمد؛ والسيوطي، جلال الدين أبي بكر. تفسير الجلالين. بيروت: در الوفاق، دون تاريخ.

البخاري. صحيح البخاري. أربعة أجزاء. اسطنبول: المكتبة الاسماعيلية. دون تاريخ.

أبو ديب، فادي. "جذور الوحدانية الإسلامية." ورقة غير منشورة لمادة علم الثالوث، مؤسسة الدراسات اللاهوتية، JETS، الهيئة الإنجيلية الثقافية الأردنية، 2012.

أبو قرّة، ذيوذورس. التّراث العربي المسيحي، في سلسلة التّراث العربي المسيحي، تنقيح أغناطيوس ديك. جونة، لبنان: المكتبة البولوسيّة، 1982.

باكر، تجي. آي. معرفة الله. ترجمة بهيج خوري. بيروت: كنيسة الاتحاد المسيحي، دون تاريخ.

البغدادي، عبد القاهر بن طاهر. الفَرْق بين الفِرَق. بيروت: دار الفقه الجديدة، 1973.

بولاد، هنري. منطق الثالوث. بيروت: دار المشرق، 1993.

البيضاوي. أنوار التنزيل وأسرار التأويل. بيروت: دار الجليل. دون تاريخ.

أنس، جيمس. علم اللاهوت النظامي. نتقيح منيس عبد النور. القاهرة: الكنيسة الإنجيلية بقصر الدوبارة، 1999.

تسدل، سنت كلير. مصادر الإسلام. ترجمة وليم ميور. إدنبراه: ت. و ت. كلارك، 1901.

توزر، أ. و. معرفة القدوس. ترجمة عدلي فام. بيروت: منشورات النفير، 1987.

ثيسن، هنري. محاضرات في علم اللاهوت النظامي. ترجمة دكتور فريد فؤاد عبد الملك. القاهرة: دار الثقافة، 1987.

الحايك، ميشيل. عمار البصري، كتاب البرهان وكتاب المسائل والأجوبة. باريس، 1975.

_____. العرب. بيروت: دار العلم للملايين، 1946.

حتّي، فيليب. تاريخ العرب. بيروت: دار الكشاف للنشر والطباعة والتوزيع، 1965.

الحريري. قس ونبي. 1979. دون معلومات نشر.

الخضري، حنا جرجس. تاريخ الفكر المسيحي: يسوع المسيح عبر الأجيال. القاهرة: دار الثقافة، 1981.

الرازي، الفخر. تفسير الفخر الرازي. ستة عشر جزء. دار الفكر، 1981.

الزوزوني. شرح المعلقات السبع. بيروت: دار الصدر، دون تاريخ.

السبزواري، محمد. الجديد في تفسير القرآن المجيد. سبعة أجزاء. بيروت: دار التعارف للمطبوعات، دون تاريخ.

سفر الحوالي، "توحيد الأسماء والصفات." [enilno] موقع فضيلة الشيخ الدكتور سفر الحوالي. مذكورة 21 نيسان، 2014. متوفرة من:
http://www.alhawali.com/indExodcfm?method=home.SubContent&ContentID
=2207#Ayat6004282

سعيد، عبد المغني. الجديد حول أسماء الله الحسنى. بيروت والقاهرة: دار الشوق، 1980.

سمعان، عوض. الله بين الفلسفة والمسيحية. شتوتغارت: نداء الرجاء. دون تاريخ.

_____. الله: ذاته ونوع وحدانيته. شتوتغارت: نداء الرجاء. دون تاريخ.

189

شحاده، عماد. الآب والابن والروح القدس، إله واحد آمين: ضرورة التعددية في الوحدانية الإلهية. بيروت: دار المنهل للحياة، 2009.

ـــــــــ. الله معنا وبدوننا. الجزء الأول: الوحدانية بثالوث مقابل الوحدانية المُطلقة. بيروت: دار المنهل للحياة، 2018.

الطحاوي، أبو جعفر. متن العقيدة الطحاوية: بيان عقيدة أهل السُّنة والجماعة. بيروت: دار ابن حزم للطباعة والنشر والتوزيع، 1995.

عبده، محمد. رسالة التوحيد. بيروت: دار الكتب العلمية, 1986.

علم اللاهوت النظامي. القاهرة: دار الثقافة 1971.

موقع ويكيبيديا، الموسوعة الحرة. مذكورة 1[online]العقيدة الطحاوية. "مكان المتن بين أهل السنة." أيار، 2014. متوفرة من:
http://ar.wikipedia.org/wiki/(كتاب)_العقيدة_الطحاوية

عطية، عزيز سوريال، الفهارس التَّحليليّة لمخطوطات طور سينا العربيّة. ترجمة جوزيف نسيم يوسف. الإسكندريّة، دار المعارف بالتعاون مع Johns Hopkins Press.1954

العقاد، عباس محمود. الله: كتاب في نشأة العقيدة الإلهية. القاهرة: دار الثقافة، 1998.

علم اللاهوت النظامي. القاهرة: دار الثقافة، دون تاريخ.

العيد، فرحان. "عندما اعتنق إله الجزيرة العربية الإسلام." ورقة غير منشورة لمادة علم الثالوث، مؤسسة الدراسات اللاهوتية JETS.2005،

غطاس، يزن. "عدم معرفة الابن." ورقة غير منشورة لمادة علم الثالوث، مؤسسة الدراسات اللاهوتية، JETS، الهيئة الإنجيلية الثقافية الأردنية، 2017.

فتياتي، خالد إبراهيم الفتياتي. محاضرات في علوم القرآن. دار عمار. دون تاريخ.

فخري، ماجد. تاريخ الفلسفة الإسلامية: من القرن الثامن حتى يومنا هذا. ترجمة: كمال اليازجي. طبعة ثانية. بيروت: دار المشرق، 2000.

القرآن الكريم. ترجمة عبدالله يوسف علي. ماري لاند: شركة الأمانة، 1989.

قسطة، يوسف. هل الله واحد أم ثلاثة؟ بيروت: دار النشر المعمدانية، 1986.

قطب، سيد. في ظلال القرآن. 6 مجلدات. جدة: دار العلم للطباعة والنشر، 1986.

مشرقي، صموئيل. الإلهيات. شبرا، مصر: الكنيسة المركزية للمجمع، 1964.

ـــــــــ. الذات الإلهية. شبرا، مصر: الكنيسة المركزية للمجمع، 1989.

مسلم. صحيح مسلم. خمسة أجزاء. اسطنبول: المكتبة الاسماعيلية. دون تاريخ.

مرجان، محمد مجدي، الله واحد أم ثالوث. القاهرة: دار النهضة العربية. دون تاريخ.

نادر، ألبير نصري. مدخل إلى الفرق الإسلامية السياسية والكلامية. بيروت: دار المشرق، 1989.

والفورد، جون ف. يسوع المسيح ربنا. القاهرة: دار الثقافة، 1969.

اليازجي، كمال. معالم الفكر العربي في العصر الوسيط. بيروت: دار العلم للملايين، 1966.

خليل، سمير. مقالة في التوحيد للشيخ يحي بن عدي. جونية، لبنان: المكتبة البولوسية، 1980.

Sources in English, French and German

Note: Arabic names of individuals and publishing houses that are not transliterated are given as such by the publishers. Furthermore, the Arabic article "Al" (or "El") is ignored in the alphabetization.

Abba, R. "The Divine Name Yahweh." *Journal of Biblical Literature* 80, no. 4 (1961): 320–328.

Abd-el-Jalil, Jean Muhammad. *Brève histoire de la littérature Arabe*. Edited by G. P. Maisonneuve. Paris: Librairie Orientale et Américaine, 1946.

'Abduh, Muhammad. *Risalat al Tawhid* [The Theology of Unity]. Translated from Arabic by Ishaq Musa'ad and Kenneth Cragg. London: George Allen and Unwin, 1966.

Albright, W. *Yahweh and the Gods of Canaan*. University of London: Athlone Press, 1968.

Aquinas, Thomas. *Catena Aurea. A Commentary on the Four Gospels*. Christian Classics Ethereal Library. OakTree Software, Inc. Version 1.1.

———. *Summa Theologica*. Translated by Fathers of the English Dominican Province. Benziger Bros. edition, 1947. Electronic text hypertexted and prepared by OakTree Software, Inc.

Atfield, D. G. "Can God Be Crucified? A Discussion of J. Moltmann." *Scottish Journal of Theology* 30 (1977): 47–57.

Atiya, Aziz S. "The Arabic Palimpsests of Mount Sinai," in *The World of Islam: Studies in Honor of Philip K. Hitti*, edited by James Kritzeck and R. Bayly Winder. London: Macmillan, 1959.

Ayoub, Mahmoud M. *Islam: Faith and History*. Oxford: One World, 2004.

Badawi, Jamal. *Bridgebuilding Between Christian and Muslim*. Halifax, NS: Islamic Information Foundation, n.d.

———. "Jesus: Beloved Messenger of God." In *The Light of Truth*. Dalhousie and Saint Mary's Universities: The Maritime Muslim Students' Association, n.d.

Balthasar, Hans Ur von. *Credo: Meditations on the Apostles' Creed*. Translated by David Kipp. New York: Crossroad, 1990.

———. *Life Out of Death: Meditations on the Easter Mystery*. Translated by Davis Perkins. Philadelphia: Fortress, 1985.

———. *Mysterium Paschale*. Translated by Aidan Nichols. Edinburgh: T&T Clark, 1990.

———. *Prayer*. Translated by Graham Harrison. San Francisco: Ignatius, 1986.

———. *Theodramatik*. Vol. 2. San Francisco: Ignatius, 1990.

———. *Theodramatik*. Vol. 3. San Francisco: Ignatius, 1992.

Barth, Karl. *Church Dogmatics*. Edinburgh: T&T Clark, 1975.

Bauckham, Richard. *God Crucified*. Grand Rapids: Eerdmans, 1998.

Bauer, W., F. W. Danker, W. F. Arndt and F. W. Gingrich (BDAG). *A Greek–English Lexicon of the New Testament and other Early Christian Literature*. Chicago: University of Chicago Press, 2000.

Bearman, P., T. Bianquis, C. E. Bosworth, E. van Donzel and W. P. Heinrichs, eds. *The Encyclopaedia of Islam*. New ed. Leiden: Brill, 1986.

Beasley-Murray, George R. *John*. Word Biblical Commentary. Dallas: Word Books, 1999.

Berkhof, L. *Systematic Theology*. Grand Rapids: Eerdmans, 1982.

Bernard, J. H. *A Critical and Exegetical Commentary on the Gospel According to St John*. 2 vols. Edinburgh: T&T Clark, 1928.

Blum, Edwin A. "John." In *The Bible Knowledge Commentary: New Testament*, edited by J. F. Walvoord and R. B. Zuck. Wheaton: Victor Books, 1985.

Boff, Leonardo. *Trinity and Society*. Translated by Paul Burns. Maryknoll, NY: Orbis, 1988.

Bok, Nico Den. *Communicating the Most High: A Systematic Study of Person and Trinity in the Theology of Richard of St Victor*. Paris/Turnhout: Brepols, 1996.

Botterweck, G. Johannes, and Helmer Ringgren, eds. *Theological Dictionary of the Old Testament (TDOT)*. Translated by John T. Willis. Grand Rapids: Eerdmans, 1986.

Boyd, Gregory A. *Oneness Pentecostals and the Trinity*. Grand Rapids: Baker, 2000.

Bray, Gerald. "The Double Procession of the Holy Spirit in Evangelical Theology Today: Do We Still Need It?" *Journal of the Evangelical Theological Society* 41, no. 3 (Sep 1998): 415–426.

Brown, David. *The Divine Trinity*. London: Sheldon, 1969.

Brown, Francis, S. R. Driver and Charles A. Briggs, eds. *Enhanced Brown–Driver–Briggs Hebrew and English Lexicon (BDB)*. Electronic ed. Oak Harbor, WA: Logos Research Systems, 2000.

Brown, Raymond E. *The Gospel According to John*. 2 vols. Anchor Bible. Garden City, NY: Doubleday & Co., 1966, 1970.

Bruce, F. F. *The Epistle to the Hebrews*. New International Commentary on the New Testament. Grand Rapids: Eerdmans, 1981.

Brunner, Frederick Dale. *A Theology of the Holy Spirit*. Grand Rapids: Eerdmans, 1970.

Calvin, John. *Commentaries*. Edited and translated by Joseph Haroutunian and Cyrus H. McCormick. Philadelphia: Westminster Press, 1958.

———. *Institutes of the Christian Religion*. Translated by Henry Beveridge. London: James Clarke & Co., 1953.

Carson, D. A. *The Gospel According to John*. Pillar New Testament Commentary. Edited by D. A. Carson. Grand Rapids: Zondervan, 1991.

———. *Jesus the Son of God: A Christological Title Often Overlooked, Sometimes Misunderstood, and Currently Disputed*. Wheaton: Crossway, 2012.

———. *Matthew*. Expositor's Bible Commentary. Edited by Frank E. Gaebelein. Grand Rapids: Zondervan, 1995.

Chafer, Lewis Sperry. *Chafer Systematic Theology*. Vol. 1. Dallas: Dallas Seminary Press, 1980.

Clarke, Adam. *Adam Clarke's Commentary on the Whole Bible*. Christian Classics Ethereal Library. http://www.ccel.org.

Cole, Allen. *Exodus*. Tyndale Old Testament Commentary. Downers Grove: InterVarsity Press, 1973.

Colwell, E. C. "A Definite Rule for the Use of the Article in the Greek New Testament." *Journal of Biblical Literature* 52 (1933): 12–21.

Cragg, Kenneth. *Muhammad and the Christian*. London: Oxford University Press, 1999.

Cranfield, C. E. B. *The Epistle to the Romans*, Vol. 1. International Critical Commentary. Edited by S. R. Driver, A. Plummer, C. A. Briggs. Edinburgh: T&T Clark, 1985.

Crawford, R. G. "The Relation of the Divinity and the Humanity in Christ." *Evangelical Quarterly* 53 (Oct–Dec 1981): 237–240.

Cross, F. L., and E. A. Livingstone, eds. *The Oxford Dictionary of the Christian Church*. 3rd rev. ed. Oxford: Oxford University Press, 2005.

Cunningham, David S. *These Three Are One: The Practice of Trinitarian Theology*. Oxford: Blackwell, 1998.

Dahms, John V. "The Subordination of the Son." *Journal of the Evangelical Society* 37, no. 3 (Sep 1994): 351–364.

Davis, John. "The Patriarchs' Knowledge of Jehovah: A Critical Monograph of Exodus 6:3." *Grace Theological Journal* 4, no. 1 (Winter 1963): 29–43.

Dean, Robert L., Jr. "The Problem of *En Pneumati* in 1 Cor 12:13." Paper presented in a doctoral seminar on Pneumatology, Dallas Theological Seminary, Spring 1987.

Duncan, Robert L. "The Logos: From Sophocles to the Gospel of John." *Christian Scholar Review* 9 (1979): 121–130.

Dunn, James D. G. *Baptism in the Holy Spirit*. London: SCM, 1970.

———. *Romans 1–8*. Word Biblical Commentary 38A. Electronic ed. Logos Library System; Dallas: Word, 1998.

Durham, John I. *Exodus*. Word Biblical Commentary 3. Electronic ed. Logos Library System; Dallas: Word, 2002.

Edgar, Thomas R. "The Cessation of the Sign Gifts." *Bibliotheca Sacra* 145 (Oct–Dec 1988): 371–386.

———. *Miraculous Gifts: Are They for Today?* Neptune, NJ: Loizeaux Brothers, 1983.

Edwards, Denis. *Jesus the Wisdom of God*. Maryknoll, NY: Orbis, 1995.

Elwell, W. A., and P. W. Comfort. *Tyndale Bible Dictionary*. Wheaton: Tyndale House, 2001.

Erickson, Millard. *God in Three Persons: A Contemporary Interpretation of the Trinity*. Grand Rapids: Baker, 1995.

———. *Making Sense of the Trinity: Three Crucial Questions*. Grand Rapids: Baker, 2000.

Fatula, Mary Ann. *The Triune God of Christian Faith*. Collegeville, MN: Liturgical, 1990.

Feinberg, John. *No One Like Him: The Doctrine of God*. Wheaton: Crossway, 2001.

Freedman, D. N. "The Name of the God of Moses." *Journal of Biblical Literature* 79: 151–156.

Freedman, D. N., ed. *The Anchor Bible Dictionary*. New York: Doubleday, 1992.

Gacek, Adam. *The Arabic Manuscript Tradition: A Glossary of Technical Terms and Bibliography*. Handbook of Oriental Studies 58. Leiden/Boston/Cologne: Brill, 2001.

Gavin, Frank. *Some Aspects of Contemporary Greek Orthodox Thought*. Milwaukee: Morehouse, 1923.

Geisler, Norman. *Christian Apologetics*. Grand Rapids: Baker, 1976.

———. "Colossians." In *The Bible Knowledge Commentary*, Vol. 2: *New Testament*, ed. J. F. Walvoord and R. B. Zuck. Wheaton: Victor Books, 1985.

Geisler, Norman L., and Paul D. Feinberg. *Introduction to Philosophy: A Christian Perspective*. Grand Rapids: Baker, 1999.

Geisler, Norman L., and William E. Nix. *A General Introduction to the Bible*. Chicago: Moody, 1986.

George, Timothy. *Is the Father of Jesus the God of Muhammad?* Grand Rapids: Zondervan, 2002.

Gianotti, Charles R. "The Meaning of the Divine Name YHWH." *Bibliotheca Sacra* 142 (Jan–Mar 1985): 38–51.

Gibb, H. A. R., and J. H. Kramers, eds. *Shorter Encyclopedia of Islam*. Ithaca, NY: Cornell University Press, 1974.

Giles, Kevin. *The Eternal Generation of the Son: Maintaining Orthodoxy in Trinitarian Theology*. Downers Grove: InterVarsity Press, 1990.

Glaser, Ida. "The Concept of Relationship as a Key to the Comparative Understanding of Christianity and Islam." *Themelios* 11 (1986): 57–60.

Godet, Fredric. *Commentary on the Gospel of John*. Translated by Timothy Dwight. New York: Funk & Wagnalls, 1886. Reprint ed., Grand Rapids: Kregel, 1980.

Goitein, S. D. "The Birth-Hour of Muslim Law?" *Muslim World* 50 (1960): 23–29.

Graham, Finlay Morrison. "The Unity of the Godhead as Reflected in the *Filioque* Controversy." ThD diss., Southwestern Baptist Theological Seminary, July 1965.

Grassmick, John D. "Mark." In *The Bible Knowledge Commentary: New Testament*, edited by J. F. Walvoord and R. B. Zuck. Wheaton: Victor Books, 1985.

Grudem, Wayne. *Systematic Theology: An Introduction to Biblical Doctrine*. Grand Rapids: Zondervan, 1995.

Guidi, Ignazio. "Le traduzioni degli Evangelii in Arabo e in Etiopien." Atti della Reale Accademia dei Lincei, anno cclxxv (1988), 5–37.

Gunton, Colin E. *Act and Being: Towards a Theology of the Divine Attributes*. Grand Rapids: Eerdmans, 2003.

———. *The Promise of Trinitarian Theology*. 2nd ed. Edinburgh: T&T Clark, 1997.

Hannah, John D. "Exodus." In *The Bible Knowledge Commentary: Old Testament*, edited by J. F. Walvoord and R. B. Zuck. Wheaton: Victor Books, 1985.

Hanson, R. P. C. *The Search for the Christian Doctrine of God*. Edinburgh: T&T Clark, 1988.

Harris, Murray J. *Jesus as God: The New Testament Use of Theos in Reference to Jesus*. Grand Rapids: Baker, 1992.

Harris, R. L. "The Pronunciation of the Tetragram." In *The Law and the Prophets*, edited by J. H. Skilton. Philadelphia: Presbyterian and Reformed, 1974.

Harrison, Everett F. "The Theology of the Epistle to the Hebrews." *Bibliotheca Sacra* 121 (Oct–Dec 1964): 484.

Hastings, James, J. A. Selbie and J. C. Lambert. *Dictionary of the Apostolic Church*. New York: Scribner's Sons, 1951–1954.

Hawthorne, Gerald F. *Philippians*. Word Biblical Commentary 43. Dallas: Word, 2002.

Heinze, E. Charles. *Trinity and Triunity: Salvation and the Nature of God.* Dale City, VA: Epaphras, 1995.

Henry, Carl F. H. *God Who Stands and Stays.* Vol. 5 of *God, Revelation and Authority.* Waco, TX: Word, 1982.

Hick, John. "Jesus and the World Religions." In *The Myth of God Incarnate*, ed. John Hick. Philadelphia: Westminster Press, 1977.

Hodge, Charles. *Systematic Theology.* Vol. 2. New York: Charles Scribner and Co., 1872.

Hodgson, Leonard. *The Doctrine of the Trinity.* Welwyn: James Nisbet & Co., 1944.

———. *How Can God Be Both One and Three?* London: National Society, 1963.

القرآن الكريم *The Holy Qur'an.* Translated by 'Abdullah Yusuf 'Ali. Brentwood, MD: Amana Corporation, 1989.

Humphreys, Fisher. *Thinking About God: An Introduction to Christian Theology.* New Orleans: Insight, 1994.

Hunt, Anne. *The Trinity and the Paschal Mystery.* Collegeville, MN: Liturgical, 1997.

———. *What Are They Saying about the Trinity?* New York/Mahwah, NJ: Paulist, 1998.

Hyatt, J. Philip. *Exodus.* New Century Bible Commentary. Grand Rapids: Eerdmans, 1983.

———. "Was Yahweh Originally a Creator Deity?" *Journal of Biblical Literature* 86 (1967): 369–377.

Jacob, Beno. *The First Book of the Bible: Genesis.* Abridged, edited and translated by Ernest I. Jacob and Walter Jacob. New York: KTAV, 1974.

Jacob, Edmond. *Theology of the Old Testament.* New York: Harper & Brothers, 1958.

Jeffery, Arthur. *Islam, Muhammad and His Religion.* New York: Liberal Arts Press, 1958.

Jennings, Theodore W., Jr. *Beyond Theism.* New York: Oxford University Press, 1985.

Jenson, Robert W. *The Triune Identity: God According to the Gospel.* Philadelphia: Fortress, 1982.

Johnson, Alan. "Revelation." In *The Expositor's Bible Commentary*, edited by Frank E. Gaebelein. Grand Rapids: Zondervan, 1990.

Johnson, Aubrey R. *The One and the Many in the Israelite Conception of God.* Cardiff: University Press, 1961.

Johnson, Elizabeth. *She Who Is: The Mystery of God in Feminist Theological Discourse.* New York: Crossroad, 1992.

Johnson, S. Lewis. "The Holy Trinity, or the Uniqueness of Christianity, Part II." Sermon preached at Believers Chapel, Dallas. https://s3-us-west-2.amazonaws.com/sljinstitute-production/doctrine/systematic_theology/011_SLJ_Systematic_Theology.pdf. Copyright 2007.

Kautzsch, E. *Gesenius' Hebrew Grammar.* Oxford: Oxford University Press, 1983.

Keil, Carl Friedrich, and Franz Delitzsch. *Commentary on the Old Testament.* Peabody, MA: Hendrickson, 2002.

Keller, Timothy. *The Reason for God: Belief in an Age of Skepticism.* New York: Penguin, 2008.

Kelly, Anthony. *The Trinity of Love: A Theology of the Christian God*. Wilmington, DE: Michael Glazier, 1989.

Kidner, Derek. *Genesis*. Tyndale Old Testament Commentary. Downers Grove: InterVarsity Press, 1973.

Kimel, Alvin F. *Speaking the Christian God*. Grand Rapids: Eerdmans, 1992.

Kittel, G., and G. Friedrich, eds. *Theological Dictionary of the New Testament (TDNT)*. 10 vols. Translated by Geoffrey W. Bromiley. Grand Rapids: Eerdmans, 1964–1976.

Klein, Ernest. *A Comprehensive Etymological Dictionary of the Hebrew Language for Readers of English*. [Haifa]: University of Haifa, 1987.

Knight, G. A. F. *A Biblical Approach to the Doctrine of the Trinity*. Edinburgh: Tweedale Court, 1953.

Koehler, Ludwig, Walter Baumgartner, M. E. J. Richardson and Johann Jakob Stamm. *The Hebrew and Aramaic Lexicon of the Old Testament*. New York: Brill, 1994–1996.

Kruse, Colin F. *John*. Tyndale New Testament Commentary. Downers Grove: InterVarsity Press, 2003.

LaCugna, Catherine Mowry. *God For Us: The Trinity and Christian Life*. New York: HarperCollins / Edinburgh: T&T Clark, 1991.

Lang, David, ed. *Creeds, Confessions and Catechisms*. Altamonte Springs, FL: OakTree Software, Inc., 2006.

Larson, Duane H. *Times of the Trinity*. New York: Peter Lang, 1995.

Lee, Jung Young. *The Trinity in Asian Perspective*. Nashville: Abingdon Press, 1996.

Lindars, Barnabas. *The Gospel of John*. New Century Bible Commentary. Edited by Ronald E. Clements and Matthew Black. Grand Rapids: Eerdmans, 1987.

Litfin, Duane. "The Real Theological Issue Between Christians and Muslims." *Christianity Today* online, 9 August 2016. http://www.christianitytoday.com/ct/2016/july-web-only/christianity-vs-islam-about-cross.html.

Louw, J. P., and E. A. Nida (Louw & Nida). *Greek–English Lexicon of the New Testament: Based on Semantic Domains*. New York: United Bible Societies, 1989.

Maalouf, Tony. *Arabs in the Shadow of Israel*. Grand Rapids: Kregel, 2003.

Macdonald, Duncan Black. "God: A Unit or a Unity?" *Muslim World* 3 (1913): 11–20.

———. *Shared Life: The Trinity and the Fellowship of God's People*. Fearn: Christian Focus, 1994.

Marsh, Thomas. *The Triune God: A Biblical, Historical, and Theological Study*. Mystic, CT: Twenty-Third Publications, 1994.

McCarthy, D. J. "Exod 3:14: History, Philology and Theology." *Christian Biblical Quarterly* 40 (1978): 311–322.

McDowell, Josh, and Sean McDowell. *Evidence That Demands a Verdict*. Nashville, TN: HarperCollins, 2017.

Meerson, Michael Aksionov. *The Trinity of Love in Modern Russian Theology*. Quincy, IL: Franciscan Press, 1998.

Metzger, Bruce M. *The Early Versions of the New Testament*. Oxford: Clarendon, 1977.

————. *The Text of the New Testament: Its Transmission, Corruption, and Restoration.* 2nd ed. New York: Oxford University Press, 1968.

————. *A Textual Commentary on the Greek New Testament.* 2nd ed. Stuttgart: Deutsche Bibelgesellschaft, 1994.

Metzger, John. *Discovering the Mystery of the Unity of God.* San Antonio, TX: Ariel Ministries, 2010.

————. *The Tri-unity of God Is Jewish.* St Louis, MO: Cenveo-Plus Communications, 2005.

Miller, Gary. "The Deification of Jesus." *The Light of Truth.* Dalhousie and Saint Mary's Universities: The Maritime Muslim Students' Association, n.d.

Moltmann, Jürgen. *History and the Triune God: Contributions to Trinitarian Theology.* New York: Crossroad, 1992.

————. *The Trinity and the Kingdom: The Doctrine of God.* San Francisco: Harper & Row, 1981.

Mombasa, W. G. "Islam Not a Stepping-Stone towards Christianity." *Muslim World* 1 (1911): 365–372.

Morey, Robert. *The Trinity: Evidence and Issues.* Grand Rapids: World Publishing, 1996.

Morris, Canon Leon. *The Book of Revelation.* Tyndale New Testament Commentary 20. Leicester: InterVarsity Press, 1988.

————. *The Gospel According to John.* New International Commentary on the New Testament. Grand Rapids: Eerdmans, 1971.

————. *Studies in the Fourth Gospel.* Grand Rapids: Eerdmans, 1969.

Motyer, J. A. *The Revelation of the Divine Name.* London: Tyndale, 1959.

Mounce, Robert H. *The Book of Revelation.* New International Commentary on the New Testament. Grand Rapids: Eerdmans, 1988.

Mounce, William D., and Rick D. Bennett, eds. *Mounce Concise Greek–English Dictionary of the New Testament.* Tulsa, OK: OakTree Software, Inc., 2011.

O'Collins, Gerald. *The Tripersonal God: Understanding and Interpreting the Trinity.* New York/Mahwah, NJ: Paulist Press, 1999.

O'Donnell, John J. *The Mystery of the Triune God.* New York/Mahwah, NJ: Paulist Press, 1989.

Olari, Dilasi. *Arab Thought and Its Role in History.* Beirut: Dar Al-Kitab Al-Lubnani, 1972.

Packer, J. I. *Keep in Step with the Spirit.* Old Tappan, NJ: Fleming H. Revell, 1984.

Payne, J. B. *Theology of the Older Testament.* Grand Rapids: Zondervan, 1962.

Peters, Ted. *God As Trinity: Relationality and Temporality in Divine Life.* Louisville, KY: Westminster/John Knox Press, 1993.

Pierce, Larry. *Tense Voice Mood.* Ontario: Woodside Bible Fellowship, 1994.

Prestige. G. L. *God in Patristic Thought.* London: SPCK, 1952.

Qureshi, Nabeel. *No God But One: A Former Muslim Investigates the Evidence for Islam and Christianity.* Grand Rapids: Zondervan, 2016.

Rahner, Karl. *Foundations of Christian Faith: An Introduction to the Idea of Christianity.* Translated by William V. Dych. New York: Seabury, 1978.

———. *The Trinity*. Translated by Joseph Donceel. New York: Seabury, 1974.

Räisänen, Heikki. "The Portrait of Jesus in the Qur'an." *Muslim World* 70 (1980): 122–133.

Reeves, Michael. *Delighting in the Trinity: An Introduction to the Christian Faith*. Downers Grove: InterVarsity Press, 2012.

Rendtorff, Rolf. "The Paradigm Is Changing: Hopes – and Fears." *Biblical Interpretation* 1 (1993): 34–53.

Richard of St Victor. *Book Three of the Trinity*. Translated by Grover A. Zinn. New York: Paulist Press, 1979.

Robertson, A. T. *A Grammar of the Greek New Testament in the Light of Historical Research*. Nashville: Broadman, 1934.

Ross, Allen P. "Genesis." In *The Bible Knowledge Commentary: Old Testament*, edited by J. F. Walvoord and R. B. Zuck. Wheaton: Victor Books, 1985.

Ryrie, Charles C. *Basic Theology*. Wheaton: Victor Books, 1986.

———. *The Holy Spirit*. Chicago: Moody, 1985.

Sanders, Fred. *The Deep Things of God*. Wheaton: Crossway, 2010.

Sanders, Fred, and Klaus Issler. *Jesus in Trinitarian Perspective*. Nashville: B&H, 2007.

Schaff, Philip, *The Creeds of Christendom*. Vol. 1. New York: Harper & Brothers, 1919.

Schaff, Philip, and Henry Wace, eds. *The Nicene and Post-Nicene Fathers*. Second Series, Vol. 4: *Athanasius: Selected Works and Letters*. New York: Christian Literature Company, 1892.

———. *The Nicene and Post-Nicene Fathers*. Second Series, Vol. 7: *Cyril of Jerusalem, Gregory Nazianzen*. Oak Harbor/New York: Christian Literature Company, 1894.

Schelling, Friedrich. *The Ages of the World*. Translated by Fredrick de Wolfe Bolman, Jr. New York: Columbia University Press, 1942.

Schnackenburg, Rudolf. *The Gospel According to St John*. 3 vols. Vol. 1. Translated by Kevin Smyth. New York: Herder and Herder, 1968.

Scholer, David M. "Response to Stanley J. Grenz's 'What Does It Mean to Be Trinitarians?'" In *Commission on Doctrine and Interchurch Cooperation*, Baptist World Alliance, 5 July 2001.

Schwöbel, Christoph. *Trinitarian Theology Today: Essays on Divine Being and Act*. Edinburgh: T&T Clark, 1995.

Shehadeh, Imad. "A Comparison and a Contrast between the Prologue of John's Gospel and Quranic Surah 5." ThD diss., Dallas Theological Seminary, 1990.

———. "Ishmael in Relation to the Promises to Abraham." ThM thesis, Dallas Theological Seminary, 1986.

Sheppard, P. *The Greek East and the Latin West: A Study in the Christian Tradition*. London: Oxford University Press, 1959.

Smeaton, George. *The Doctrine of the Holy Spirit*. Edinburgh: T&T Clark, 1882.

Solomon, Sam, and Atif Debs. *Not the Same God: Is the Qur'anic Allah the Lord God of the Bible?* Charlottesville, VA: ANM, 2015.

Speiser, E. A. *Genesis*. The Anchor Bible 1. Edited by William Foxwell Albright and David Noel Freedman. New York: Doubleday & Co. Inc., 1962.

Sproul, R. C. *God's Love: How the Infinite God Cares for His Children*. Colorado Springs, CO: David C. Cook, n.d.

Staal, Harvey. *MT Sinai Arabic Codex 151*. Louvain: Corpus Scriptorum Christianorum Orientalium, 1984.

Stratoydaki-White, Despina. "Saint Photios and the Filioque Controversy." *The Patristic and Byzantine Review* 2, nos. 2–3 (1983): 246–250.

Sweetman, J. Windrow. *Islam and Christian Theology: A Study of the Interpretation of Theological Ideas in the Two Religions*. 4 vols. London: Lutterworth, 1967.

———. "Speaking in Tongues." Unpublished paper presented to Dallas Theological Seminary, 11 December 1984.

Tanner, Norman P. *Decrees of the Ecumenical Councils*. Vol. 1: *Nicaea I to Lateran V*. Washington: Georgetown University Press, 1990.

Tenny, Merrill C. "The Gospel of John." In *The Expositor's Bible Commentary*, edited by Frank E. Gaebelein. Grand Rapids: Zondervan, 1990.

Thayer, Joseph Henry. *Thayer's Greek–English Lexicon of the New Testament*. Tulsa, OK: OakTree Software, Inc., 1889.

Thomas, Robert L. *Revelation 1–7: An Exegetical Commentary*. Edited by Kenneth Barker. Chicago: Moody, 1992.

Thompson, John. *Modern Trinitarian Perspectives*. New York: Oxford University Press, 1994.

Thomson, William. "Al-Ash'ari and His Al-ibanah." *Muslim World* 32 (1942): 242–260.

Toon, Peter. *Our Triune God: A Biblical Portrayal of the Trinity*. Wheaton: Victor Books, 1996.

Torrey, R. A. *What the Bible Teaches*. New York: Fleming H. Revell, n.d.

VanGemeren, William A., ed. *New International Dictionary of Old Testament Theology*. Grand Rapids: Zondervan, 1997.

Vat. Arabo 13. Biblioteca Apostolical Vaticana, n.d.

Wainwright, Arthur W. *The Trinity in the New Testament*. London: SPCK, 1962.

Wallace, D. B. *Greek Grammar Beyond the Basics: Exegetical Syntax of the New Testament*. Grand Rapids: Zondervan, 1996.

Waltke, Bruce K., and M. O'Conner. *An Introduction to Biblical Hebrew Syntax*. Winona Lake, IN: Eisenbrauns, 1990.

Walvoord, John F. *The Holy Spirit*. Grand Rapids: Zondervan, 1985.

———. *Jesus Christ Our Lord*. Chicago: Moody, 1969.

Ware, Bruce A. "An Evangelical Reformulation of the Doctrine of the Immutability of God," *Journal of the Evangelical Theological Society* 29, no. 4 (Dec 1986): 432–446.

———. *Father, Son, and Holy Spirit: Relationships, Role, and Relevance*. Wheaton: Crossway, 2005.

Warfield, Benjamin B. *Biblical Doctrines*. New York: Oxford University Press, 1929.

Watt, W. Montgomery. "The Use of the Word 'Allah' in English." *Muslim World* 43 (1953): 245–247.

Weinandy, Thomas G. *Does God Change?* Still River, MA: St Bede's Publications, 1985.

———. *Does God Suffer?* Notre Dame, IN: University of Notre Dame Press, 2000.

———. *The Father's Spirit of Sonship: Reconceiving the Trinity.* Edinburgh: T&T Clark, 1995.

Westcott, B. F. *The Gospel According to St John.* London: John Murray, 1908.

Williams, Ernest Swing. *The Baptism with the Holy Spirit, in Pneumatology, Ecclesiology, Eschatology.* Springfield, MO: Gospel Publishing House, 1953.

Wood, Leon J. *The Holy Spirit in the Old Testament.* Contemporary Evangelical Perspectives. Grand Rapids: Zondervan, 1976.

Wouk, H. *This Is My God.* Garden City, NY: Doubleday & Co., 1959.

Wright, G. E. *God Who Acts.* London: SCM, 1952.

Youngblood, Ron. *The Genesis Debate.* New York: Thomas Nelson, 1986.

———. "A New Occurrence of the Divine Name 'I Am.'" *Journal of the Evangelical Theological Society* 15, no. 3 (Summer 1972): 144–152.

Zizioulas, John D. *Being As Communion.* Crestwood, NY: St Vladimir's Seminary Press, 1997.

Zwemer, Samuel M. *The Moslem Doctrine of God.* New York: American Tract Society, 1905.

Complete Scripture Index

New Testament

Langham Literature, with its publishing work, is a ministry of Langham Partnership.

Langham Partnership is a global fellowship working in pursuit of the vision God entrusted to its founder John Stott –

> *to facilitate the growth of the church in maturity and Christ-likeness through raising the standards of biblical preaching and teaching.*

Our vision is to see churches in the majority world equipped for mission and growing to maturity in Christ through the ministry of pastors and leaders who believe, teach and live by the Word of God.

Our mission is to strengthen the ministry of the Word of God through:
- nurturing national movements for biblical preaching
- fostering the creation and distribution of evangelical literature
- enhancing evangelical theological education

especially in countries where churches are under-resourced.

Our ministry

Langham Preaching partners with national leaders to nurture indigenous biblical preaching movements for pastors and lay preachers all around the world. With the support of a team of trainers from many countries, a multi-level programme of seminars provides practical training, and is followed by a programme for training local facilitators. Local preachers' groups and national and regional networks ensure continuity and ongoing development, seeking to build vigorous movements committed to Bible exposition.

Langham Literature provides majority world preachers, scholars and seminary libraries with evangelical books and electronic resources through publishing and distribution, grants and discounts. The programme also fosters the creation of indigenous evangelical books in many languages, through writer's grants, strengthening local evangelical publishing houses, and investment in major regional literature projects, such as one volume Bible commentaries like *The Africa Bible Commentary* and *The South Asia Bible Commentary*.

Langham Scholars provides financial support for evangelical doctoral students from the majority world so that, when they return home, they may train pastors and other Christian leaders with sound, biblical and theological teaching. This programme equips those who equip others. Langham Scholars also works in partnership with majority world seminaries in strengthening evangelical theological education. A growing number of Langham Scholars study in high quality doctoral programmes in the majority world itself. As well as teaching the next generation of pastors, graduated Langham Scholars exercise significant influence through their writing and leadership.

To learn more about Langham Partnership and the work we do visit **langham.org**

ightning Source UK Ltd.
'lton Keynes UK
HW02f2356121018
0460UK00013B/1121/P